WHAT ARE

SPIRITUAL GIFTS?

WHAT ARE

SPIRITUAL GIFTS?

RETHINKING THE
CONVENTIONAL VIEW

KENNETH BERDING

Kregel
Publications

To Trudi

What Are Spiritual Gifts?: Rethinking the Conventional View

© 2006 by Kenneth Berding

Published by Kregel Publications, a division of Kregel, Inc., P.O. Box 2607, Grand Rapids, MI 49501.

Library of Congress Cataloging-in-Publication Data
Berding, Kenneth.
What are spiritual gifts? : rethinking the conventional view / by Kenneth Berding.
    p. cm.
    Includes bibliographical references and index.
    1. Gifts, Spiritual. I. Title.
BT767.3.B385 2007
234'.13-dc22   2006029010

ISBN 0-8254-2124-1

Printed in the United States of America

06 07 08 09 10 / 5 4 3 2 1

Contents

Preface

ANOTHER BOOK ON spiritual gifts? What can be said that hasn't already been said many times?

The book you're holding *isn't* another book on spiritual gifts. No one should write a book on this topic until he or she has wrestled with the central issue addressed here: What is a spiritual gift?

Spiritual gifts have commonly been referred to as being the items that Paul lists in Ephesians 4:11; Romans 12:6–8; 1 Corinthians 12:8–10; and 1 Corinthians 12:28–30.[1] But what are the items in those lists? This book addresses a crucial question about these items: Does the Holy Spirit give special abilities that we must discover—as many suppose when they look at Paul's lists—or does the Holy Spirit call and place us into various ministries that build up the community that he has formed? What is, after all, Paul's central concern in these passages? Is it that believers try to unearth their hidden spiritual abilities, or that they be guided by the Holy Spirit into activities and positions of ministry that build up the community of faith?

The approach espoused in this book—an approach I occasionally refer to as a biblical alternative—likely will be liberating for many readers. It's doubtful that Paul ever imagined that the community of those who are in Christ would one day be trying to discover whether or not they have particular spiritual abilities. That's because Paul lived and breathed *ministry*. His vision for the church was a Spirit-filled corporate body that, despite the diversity of functions and assignments, was constantly being strengthened and unified through the ministries exercised in it.

The central motivation in my writing this book, however, is not related to practical implications for the church, although I'm convinced that these are significant. Rather, my main goal is a biblical one—to understand what Paul always intended to communicate, or not to communicate—about spiritual ministries (and/or abilities). My study of this issue began almost twenty years ago. I was reading through one of these passages in my Greek New Testament when I was struck with the realization that the Greek word *charisma* does not carry the theological weight of what I refer to in this book as the conventional view. This realization aroused in me a desire to study Paul's teaching in these passages on Paul's own terms. The genesis of the project was thus exegetical rather than practical. Still, the practical implications will quickly become evident and will emerge often as the book delves into the topic.

A word about the format of this book is in order. Part 1 (the first three chapters) is dialogical and personal. It is designed to clarify the issues related to spiritual gifts and introduce a few points of relevance for church life. Understanding is the central concern of part 1—understanding the premise itself and understanding its relevance. A hypothetical seminar with questions and answers is the setting for the first two chapters; a follow-up discussion over lunch is the context for the third chapter.[2] Part 2 (chaps. 4–14) contains the heart of the book, with chapters 9–12 as the heart of the heart. There, arguments for the position defended in this book are systematically presented. The book is designed in such a way that readers could skip part 1 and begin directly with part 2 and the arguments presented there. But part 1 is designed to help readers understand the position presented, as well as its relevance. Thus, directly moving to part 2 is probably not advisable in most cases.

Part 3 (chaps. 15–18) describes how the spiritual-ministries approach fits with four larger related (biblical-theological) themes in Paul's letters. Finally, part 4 (chaps. 19–22) explains the implications of my premise and offers recommendations for how to work it out practically.

This book is for all thinking Christians. The issues discussed affect everyone in the church, not just New Testament scholars, so it is written in a way that makes the material accessible to both the layperson and the advanced exegete. Occasionally, points in the discussion require more probing than many people will want to pursue; these areas have been relegated to notes at the end of the book.

As I began to study, I was keenly aware that a book of this kind must reflect my own wrestling with the text. For this reason, during the period of textual study and of writing the first draft of the book, I very rarely took side glances at secondary literature. I wanted to be certain that any arguments I set forth emerged from a fresh analysis of the central texts and that I was personally persuaded by those arguments. Scouring the secondary literature after finishing the first draft, I was heartened to find that some of the discoveries I had made for the first time while studying individual passages had been made by people who had studied those same passages before me. But whether or not my conclusions are well represented in the secondary literature, my commitment throughout has been to seek diligently Paul's intended meaning when he was writing these passages.

All English renderings of the Greek text are my own, and reflect a literal translation of the Greek text. To do so seemed necessary, at least in part, because some versions translate the sections under discussion in ways that influence readers to accept the conventional approach to these passages. (See appendix C for further discussion.) I have tried to provide a literal and accurate rendering of the Greek text in each passage with the aim of allowing interpretive decisions to emerge from a study of the verses in their contexts. Furthermore, for ease of reference as the discussion progresses, full translations of the list passages—Ephesians 4:1–16; Romans 12:1–8; 1 Corinthians 12:1–31—have been included just before chapter 1.

My deepest desire as I've worked through this study has been to honor God by treating his holy Word with care and reverence. I've labored to represent accurately what God has revealed about the ministry of the church through the hands of his servant, the apostle

Paul. You, the reader, must judge through your own study of the Scriptures whether I have been successful in this endeavor. I pray that God will use this book in your life to release you into the ministries that God has assigned to you as an expression of his grace.

Acknowledgments

THE SEEDS OF this book were planted long ago and I am indebted to various people with whom I have interacted over the years. Included are Rex Koivisto, Vern Poythress, Alan Hultberg, Josue Perez, Jonathan Lunde, Brian Wilson, Mike Gunderson, Ismail Kulakcioglu, Jeff Bruce, Andrew Faris, Mike Phay, the students of various semesters of my Pauline Literature elective at Biola University, and members of the Firm Foundations and Vantage Point classes at Whittier Hills Baptist Church.

I am, moreover, deeply grateful for those who have read portions or all of the manuscript at some stage in its composition and have edited, corrected, and offered many invaluable insights. These include Matthew Williams, Michelle Lee, Robert Bishop, David Huttar, Chris Coleman, Stephen Payne, John and Lisa Todd, Dale Schneeberger, Trudi Berding (my wife of twenty years), and Drew Berding (my father).

I especially want to thank Brian Asbill for his labor of love. He not only coauthored appendix C in this book (the beautiful charts are all his doing), but also performed secondary literature searches, prepared the indexes, and proofread various sections of the book. Of course, any and all mistakes are my own responsibility.

Also deserving my thanks are my department head, David Talley, and deans Dennis Dirks and Michael Wilkins, of Talbot School of Theology, for granting me a one-semester research leave to complete this book. Financial assistance for the leave was provided by Biola University's Vice Provost Faculty Research and Development Fund, administered by vice provost Chris Grace, from Talbot School of Theology, and Andrew Faris.

Finally, I would like to thank all the staff at Kregel, and in particular Jim Weaver, for recognizing the value of this book and for helping me to make it accessible to all thinking Christians, whether or not they have had the opportunity to pursue formal training in the language and literature of the New Testament.

I greatly appreciate all of these people for partnering with me in this ministry.

Abbreviations

Reference Work

BDAG   Bauer, W., F. W. Danker, W. F. Arndt, and F. W. Gingrich. *Greek-English Lexicon of the New Testament and Other Early Christian Literature.* 3d ed. Chicago, 2000.

Versions

MT   Masoretic Text
LXX   Septuagint

Bible Translations

AMP	The Amplified Bible
CEV	Contemporary English Version
ESV	English Standard Version
GNB/TEV	Good News Bible/Today's English Version
HCSB	Holman Christian Standard Bible
JB	The Jerusalem Bible
KJV	King James Version
LB	The Living Bible
MSG	The Message
NAB	New American Bible
NASB	New American Standard Bible
NCV	New Century Version
NEB	The New English Bible
NET	New English Translation
NIrV	New International Reader's Version
NIV	New International Version
NJB	The New Jerusalem Bible
NKJV	New King James Version

NLT	New Living Translation
NRSV	New Revised Standard Version
PHILLIPS	The New Testament in Modern English
RSV	Revised Standard Version
TNIV	Today's New International Version

Paul's Four Lists

Ephesians 4:11 • apostles • prophets • evangelists • pastor-teachers (or pastors and teachers)	**Romans 12:6–8** • prophecy • service/serving • one who teaches/teaching • one who encourages/ encouragement • one who gives • one who leads • one who shows mercy
1 Corinthians 12:8–10 • a word of wisdom • a word of knowledge • faith • healings • workings of miracles • prophecy • distinguishing of spirits • kinds of tongues • interpretation of tongues	**1 Corinthians 12:28–30** • apostles • prophets • teachers • miracles • healings • helps • administrations • kinds of tongues/speak in tongues • interpret [tongues][1]

The List Passages Translated

EPHESIANS 4:1–16

¹I, therefore, the prisoner in the Lord, urge you to walk worthy of the calling to which you have been called, ²with all humility and gentleness, with patience, showing tolerance toward one another in love, ³being diligent to maintain the unity of the Spirit in the bond of peace. ⁴There is one body and one Spirit—just as also you were called in one hope of your calling—⁵one Lord, one faith, one baptism, ⁶one God and Father of all, who is over all and through all and in all.

⁷But to each one of us grace was given according to the measure of the gift of Christ. ⁸Therefore it says,

> "When he ascended to the heights,
> he took captives captive;
> he gave gifts to men."

⁹(In saying, "He ascended," what does it mean but that he had also descended into the lower parts of the earth? ¹⁰The one who descended is himself also the one who ascended far above all the heavens, so that he might fill all things.) ¹¹*And he gave the apostles, the prophets, the evangelists, the pastor-teachers* ¹²*for the equipping of the saints for the work of ministry leading to the building up of the body of Christ,* ¹³until we all attain to the unity of faith and of the knowledge of the Son of God, to a mature man, to the measure of

the stature of the fullness of Christ, [14]that we might no longer be infants, tossed here and there by every wind of doctrine, by the trickery of men, by craftiness in deceitful scheming, [15]but speaking the truth in love, we must grow up in every way into him who is the head, even Christ, [16]from whom the whole body, joined and held together by every supporting ligament, according to the working of each individual part, causes the growth of the body, leading to the building up of itself in love.

ROMANS 12:1–8

[1]Therefore I urge you, brothers, by the mercies of God, to present your bodies as a living sacrifice, holy, acceptable to God, which is your spiritual worship. [2]And do not be conformed to this world, but be transformed by the renewing of your mind, so that you may prove what is the good, acceptable, and perfect will of God.

[3]For through the grace that has been given to me, I say to every one among you not to think more highly of yourself than you ought to think, but to think with sober judgment, to each as the Lord has measured a measure of faith. [4]For just as we have many members in one body, and all the members do not have the same function, [5]so we, the many, are one body in Christ, and individually members one of another, [6]and having *charismata*[1] according to the grace that has been given to us that differ: *whether prophecy, according to the proportion of faith, [7]whether service, in serving, whether the one who teaches, in teaching, [8]whether the one who encourages, in encouragement, the one who gives, in generosity, the one who leads, in diligence, the one who shows mercy, in cheerfulness.*

1 CORINTHIANS 12:1–31

[1]Now concerning the "spiritual things," brothers, I do not want you to be uninformed. [2]You know that when you were pagans, you were led astray to mute idols, however you were led. [3]Therefore, I make known to you that no one speaking by the Spirit of God says, "Jesus is cursed," and no one is able to say, "Jesus is Lord" except by the Holy Spirit.

[4]Now there are distributions of *charismata,* but the same Spirit. [5]And there are distributions of areas of service, but the same Lord. [6]And there are distributions of workings, but the same God who works all things in all persons. [7]But to each one is given the manifestation of the Spirit for the common good. [8]*For to one is given through the Spirit a word of wisdom, and to another a word of knowledge according to the same Spirit,* [9]*to another faith by the same Spirit, and to another* charismata *of healings by the one Spirit,* [10]*and to another workings of powers, and to another prophecy, and to another discernment of spirits, to another kinds of tongues, and to another interpretation of tongues.* [11]But one and the same Spirit works all these, distributing to each individually just as he wills.

[12]For just as the body is one and has many members, and all the members of the body, though many, are one body, so also is Christ. [13]For by one Spirit we were all baptized into one body—whether Jews or Greeks, whether slaves or free—we were all made to drink of one Spirit. [14]For even the body is not one member but many. [15]If the foot should say, "Because I am not a hand, I am not a part of the body," is it thereby not a part of the body? [16]And if the eye should say, "Because I am not an eye, I am not a part of the body," is it thereby not a part of the body? [17]If the whole body were an eye, where would the hearing be? If the whole were hearing, where would the smelling be?

[18]But now God has placed/appointed the members, each one of them, in the body just as he wanted. [19]If all were one member, where would the body be? [20]So now there are many members, but one body. [21]The eye cannot say to the hand, "I have no need of you," or again, the head to the feet, "I have no need of you." [22]On the contrary, the parts of the body that seem weaker are necessary, [23]and those parts of the body which we think less honorable we clothe with the greater honor, and our less respectable parts get greater respect, [24]whereas our more respectable members have no need of it. But God has so arranged the body, giving greater honor to the parts that lack it [25]that there may be no division in the body, but that the members may have the same care for one another. [26]And if one member suffers, all the members suffer together with it; if one member is honored, all the members rejoice together with it.

[27]Now you are the body of Christ and individually members of it, [28]whom also, on the one hand, God has placed/appointed in the church . . . *first apostles, second prophets, third teachers, then miracles, then* charismata *of healings, helps, administrations, kinds of tongues.* [29]*All are not apostles, are they? All are not prophets, are they? All are not teachers, are they? All do not do miracles, do they?* [30]*All do not have* charismata *of healings, do they? All do not speak in tongues, do they? All do not interpret, do they?* [31]But earnestly desire the greater *charismata.* And still I show you a more excellent way.

PART ONE

UNDERSTANDING
THE ISSUE

Interlude

IMAGINE A YOUNG married couple walking from a parking lot toward a church.

JASON.   I'm looking forward to this seminar. I've been interested in spiritual gifts for a long time and want to understand what they're all about. Maybe I'll have a better idea of what my own gifts are by the end of the day.

KRISTEN.   That's what I'm hoping for, too.

JASON.   Do you think they'll have some sort of questionnaire that will help us figure out what gifts we have?

KRISTEN.   I don't know. I only know that the pastor said that this seminar could revolutionize the way we understand spiritual gifts. I wonder what he meant by that . . .

JASON.   I'm not sure. We better hurry . . . it looks like we're a little late. Pastor Cole is just finishing up the introduction.

PASTOR COLE.   . . . let's welcome our speaker as he comes to guide us in a study of what the Bible teaches about the so-called spiritual gifts.

JASON (*whispering*).   Why did he call them the "so-called spiritual gifts"?

KRISTEN (*whispering back*).

I don't know . . . just listen . . . maybe we'll find out.

DR. MICHAELS.

Good morning. This morning, we'll begin our discussion of ministry in the Christian community with two sessions. In the first session, we'll look at the most common understanding of the so-called spiritual gifts—what I'll sometimes call the conventional approach. This may come as a surprise to you, but I don't believe the conventional approach is the biblical view. So in the second session, I'll offer a biblical alternative to the conventional approach and begin to introduce some practical implications for our lives and our churches.

Later this afternoon when we return from lunch, we'll open up our Bibles and I'll walk you through the biblical case for this alternative approach. I believe, however, that the single greatest difficulty in approaching this topic will be one of understanding. I want to be sure that you understand the main differences between the conventional approach and the biblical alternative before I build a case for the latter. So this morning we'll concentrate on understanding. Shall we begin?

ONE

Understanding the Conventional View

Spiritual Gifts as Special Abilities

DR. MICHAELS (*beginning his lecture*).

Let's begin by looking at the conventional approach to the so-called spiritual gifts. I refer to it as the conventional approach because it seems that most Christians—at least at this point in history—work within this paradigm when they think about the subject often referred to as "spiritual gifts." This approach says that the spiritual gifts are abilities, or enablements, given by the Holy Spirit to individual believers to help them serve others.[1] There are three main components in any conventional definition of a spiritual gift: (1) the entity itself is an ability or an enablement; (2) it is given by the Holy Spirit; (3) it is to be used in building up the community of believers. It could be diagrammed like this:

THE CONVENTIONAL APPROACH
Holy Spirit-given

All are abilities

THEY ARE TO BE USED IN MINISTRY

In this approach, every believer who has a relationship with God through Jesus Christ has been given at least one special ability that he or she is to discover and use in building the community of faith. Within the conventional approach, there's disagreement about whether believers have only one gift or whether they have more than one. Probably the majority position is that every believer has more than one of these special abilities, but each has at least one special spiritual ability that he or she can use in ministry.

But how can we know if we have special abilities or what they are? This is also a point at which opinions are divided among those taking the conventional approach. Some assert that first you need to discover your special abilities, say, by taking a spiritual gifts test, and then begin using the gifts you uncover.[2] Others say that you should begin serving, and through the process of serving you'll discover which special Spirit-given abilities you have.[3]

However it's done, most people working within this paradigm agree that you have to discover the special abilities you already have.[4] So these special God-given abilities need to be identified and activated as a means of helping you serve effectively and as a way to guide you into the types of ministries you'll be eventually involved in. It's often suggested by those teaching the conventional view that a person could have gifts and not be using them; such gifts lie dormant until the person discovers them and activates them.[5]

Let me give you some examples of how the conventional approach might work out in practice. Let's say Ashley is interested in knowing which spiritual gifts she has. One of her church leaders encourages her to take a test that will show her which gifts she has. After answering 150 or so questions, she's told that the test shows she has the gift of mercy and the gift of encouragement. The church leader encourages her to get involved in a ministry in an elderly community near the church and use her gifts there.

In another church, Ryan is occasionally asked to teach an adult Bible class. Each time he teaches, his teaching is well received. He enjoys the preparation and people seem to be growing through his teaching of the Bible. He becomes convinced that he has a special enablement from the Holy Spirit in teaching and decides to continue to teach as opportunities arise.

Many pastors and church leaders believe that an important part of growing a healthy church is helping believers like Ashley and Ryan discover their Spirit-given abilities so they can serve the community of faith.[6] Nevertheless, the conventional approach doesn't always work in practice. This is illustrated by the following quote from pollster George Barna, who apparently accepts the conventional approach himself:

> There has been a substantial deterioration regarding people's understanding of spiritual gifts, with a fivefold increase in born again adults who are aware of gifts saying God did not give them one, and half of all born again adults listing gifts they possess which are not among the spiritual gifts listed in the Bible. Even one-quarter of all Protestant pastors listed one or more gifts that they possess which are not identified in the Bible.[7]

Though Barna's conclusion as a result of the poll was to encourage people to become more aware of the so-called spiritual gifts, his comments also suggest that there's confusion and ambivalence among believers in general on the issue of spiritual gifts.[8] I believe that the primary reason for this confusion is that we've misunderstood at a fundamental level Paul's teaching about ministry in the church.

But before I begin laying out a biblical alternative, let me take some time for questions. Yes, you over there.

QUESTIONER.

Are there any differences between charismatics and non-charismatics on this issue?

DR. MICHAELS.

Actually, the foundational issue that we're discussing is neither a charismatic nor a non-charismatic issue. True— there's been a lot of discussion focused on whether the so-called miraculous gifts—like healings, prophecies, and tongues—are still available in our own day and age. But we need to be clear that, at a basic level, most charismatics[9] and non-charismatics[10] share the conventional view; they both agree that spiritual gifts are special abilities given by the Holy Spirit to individual believers that should be used to build the church. And both agree that somehow these special abilities must be discovered by each individual believer.

JASON (*raising his hand*).

Why do you keep using the word *so-called* before you say spiritual gifts? Pastor Cole did it, too, when he was introducing you.

DR. MICHAELS.

I do that because using the term *spiritual gift* often leads to a breakdown in understanding. It may even be wise to do away with the term *spiritual gift* altogether. Here's the reason: If what we've always called a spiritual gift— like prophecy, teaching, and so forth—is fundamentally an ability, then the term *gift* will always adversely affect the conversation. Those who translate the Bible into English use the word *gift* simply to mean "something that is freely given."[11] But in English the word *gift* has another meaning not found in the Greek language of the New Testament, that of "special ability."[12] Think of the following statements:

> He has such a *gift* for the piano.
> She is an intellectually *gifted* child.[13]

In the English language there are only two meanings of the word *gift*. In a discussion of "spiritual gifts," many people automatically interpret *gift* as special ability rather than to mean "something that is given." If we're going to understand this subject without our preconceptions interfering with our understanding, we'll have to use other terms.[14]

(*pausing*) Why don't we stand up and stretch our legs for a few minutes? I'll start again in five minutes.

Interlude

JASON.	Well, that was an interesting beginning. I wonder what his alternative is.
KRISTEN.	What he called the "conventional approach" is what I've always thought the spiritual gifts were.
JASON.	Or maybe we should be calling them the "so-called" spiritual gifts.
KRISTEN.	Whatever.
JASON.	But what he described—a gift as a special ability—that's what I've always thought, too. Isn't that what we've been taught? I thought the Greek word *charisma* meant "spiritual gifts," I mean, Spirit-given abilities.
KRISTEN (*wryly*).	I wouldn't know. I forgot Greek about the same time I forgot Arabic and Chinese.
JASON.	Heads up. Looks like we're about to start again.

TWO

A Biblical Alternative
Spiritual Ministries

DR. MICHAELS (*continuing his lecture*).

In our first session, I laid out the conventional approach to the subject usually called the spiritual gifts. In this session, I want to look at a biblical alternative. For now, my main concern is that you understand the alternative approach; later we'll carefully work through various passages that contain biblical arguments supporting this alternative approach.

Let me begin with a summary. In this alternative approach, the so-called spiritual gifts are not special abilities; they're Spirit-given ministries. According to the contextual evidence in the letters of Paul, the so-called spiritual gifts should not be viewed as special abilities to do ministry; rather, they should be viewed as the ministries themselves. Every believer has been assigned by the Holy Spirit to specific positions and activities of service, small and large, short-term and long-term. These ministry assignments have been given by the Holy Spirit to individual believers and, in turn, these individuals in their ministries have been given as gifts to the church.

God deeply desires that his glory be declared to the world through the community he has brought together by his grace, a community that Paul often refers to as the body of Christ.[1] Individual believers serve in their God-given roles to strengthen the collective body of believers so they can all grow in Christ. As a result, the glory of God and his salvation will be declared to the world.

Now if you wanted to describe the special-abilities view, you'd have to use words such as *abilities, enablements,* and *powers.* The spiritual-ministries approach, however, uses an entirely different set of words: *roles, functions, assignments,* and *ministries.*

THE CONVENTIONAL APPROACH   A BIBLICAL ALTERNATIVE

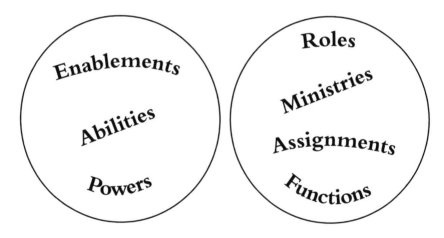

All the items in Paul's lists, without exception, can be described as Spirit-given ministries or as persons in their ministries. Still, there's a category of these spiritual ministries that are both ministries and special enablements.[2] These are the miraculous[3] ministries such as healings, prophecy, tongues, and miracles, which can't be done without a special—not simply general—enablement from the Holy Spirit.

In other words, the conventional approach describes
these all as abilities. The biblical alternative offered here
says that they're all ministries, but that some of them, that
is, the miraculous ministries, require special enablement.[4]
You can see the difference in this diagram:

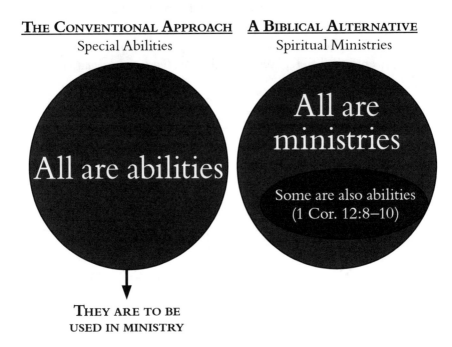

THE CONVENTIONAL APPROACH   **A BIBLICAL ALTERNATIVE**

Special Abilities   Spiritual Ministries

All are abilities

All are ministries

Some are also abilities
(1 Cor. 12:8–10)

**THEY ARE TO BE
USED IN MINISTRY**

Obviously, for any of these spiritual ministries to be
effective, whether those ministries are among the openly
miraculous or not, will require a work of the Holy Spirit to
make them effective. And how do we know that the Holy
Spirit makes our ministries effective? It's not because the
items in Paul's lists are themselves fundamentally abilities;
it's because Paul teaches throughout his letters that God
generally strengthens those he puts into ministry.[5] But
such strengthening is a general empowering for ministry,

whereas the conventional approach says that the ability itself is a special power that goes beyond such general empowering.

So, in the alternative approach, when Ashley thinks about how to serve the Lord, her question will not be, "God, how can I discover the special abilities that you have given me?" It will be simply, "God, where do you want me to serve?"

And in the alternative approach, rather than trying to find out what special abilities he's been given—a search that he'll never find any of the people in the Bible doing—Ryan should ask the Holy Spirit to guide him into specific areas of ministry that would most please God and build up the church.

Ashley and Ryan can use all the traditional means of guidance—searching the Scriptures, godly wisdom, good counselors, attention to the prodding of the Holy Spirit—in the process of deciding where to serve.[6] They can ask God to give them specific opportunities and open their hearts to minister in particular areas. The spiritual activities that God opens up to them and moves them to participate in will be their Spirit-given ministries.

It's actually not unusual to hear this theme taught by Bible teachers and preachers; some do emphasize that we need to ask God to guide us into specific assignments for effective ministry,[7] though insights from the spiritual-gifts passages are rarely brought into these discussions. That's probably because teachers and preachers, like most Christians, have become immersed in the conventional view that these passages are about special abilities. Still, I'm intrigued that there are people teaching—apparently from other passages—what I'm suggesting, and they often teach it without drawing on a theme that's rich in Paul's writings.[8]

Let's pause for a few questions right now. Yes, over on the right side.

QUESTIONER.

Why do people think that the special-abilities view is right? Certainly there are good arguments for the idea that these actually are abilities, aren't there?

DR. MICHAELS.

Actually, you'd probably be surprised to find out how little has been written on this fundamental issue. Almost every book by preachers and scholars alike about the so-called spiritual gifts begins with a conventional definition of the spiritual gifts and moves from there to discuss whatever particular area the author wants to discuss. These books rarely—in fact, almost never—include a defense of the definition, even though it's foundational to everything else they plan to discuss. I challenge you to pick up almost any book with the title Spiritual Gifts in it—you will see that what I'm claiming is true.[9]

Apart from the confusion created by the two meanings of the English word *gift* that I mentioned in the first segment, there's probably only one other main reason that people continue to accept the conventional approach: they know that miraculous activities like healing or prophecy require a special enablement from God, or the healing couldn't take place and the prophecy wouldn't be accurate. Plus, they spend a lot of time thinking about the God-given ability to do such miracles and forget that Paul explicitly tells us that these activities are intended for the edification of the body—which is another way of saying that they're all ministries.[10] The most basic reason the conventional view seems acceptable to so many is that the ability concept probably gets exported from the miraculous ministries of 1 Corinthians 12:8–10 into Paul's other discussions of ministry in the body.[11] We'll look at 1 Corinthians 12:8–10 and Paul's other lists in more detail after lunch. But, for now, please remember that the particular list found in 1 Corinthians 12:8–10— the list of miraculous activities—can be viewed both as ministries and enablements from the Holy Spirit. This does not, however, mean that we can force the other items in Paul's lists—items that are evidently ministry assignments—into a mold labeled "ability."

QUESTIONER.

I understand how you could call many of these activities "ministries," but how can you call something as spontaneous as speaking in tongues a "ministry"?

DR. MICHAELS.

When I use the word ministry, I'm simply referring to any activity that builds up the community of faith. It could be a special appointment to an ongoing ministry role, such as that of pastor-teacher,[12] or an activity that only lasts twenty seconds—like speaking in tongues. Paul is emphatic that speaking in tongues is a community-building activity—and thus a ministry—if, and only if, the tongue is interpreted. That's why he's so emphatic that tongues in a Christian meeting must be interpreted so that the activity will strengthen the overall ministry of the church.[13]

I think the church has been harmed by our using the word *ministry* primarily in reference to people who are "in the ministry," that is, members of the clergy. Instead, ministry can refer to any activity that builds up the body of Christ. Every Christian has been given specific ministries—both long-term and short-term—whether or not that Christian is a member of the clergy.[14] In some churches, it's already a common occurrence to talk about members "having ministries"; in such churches it wouldn't be strange to hear one person asking another on a Sunday morning, "So, what's your ministry in this church?" When I talk about a spiritual ministry, I'm talking about this sort of activity—any activity that builds up the Christian community.

Questioner.

How can a ministry be a gift that is given? Isn't a gift normally something that you have?[15]

Dr. Michaels.

Both Greek and English are similar in that they can use the words *give* and *gift* not just for things that someone possesses. One of my daughters, for example, had been assigned a large part in our church's Christmas musical, and she was very thankful that God had allowed her such a significant role. One night before bed, she said to me, "Daddy, God has given me such a gift by allowing me to play this part in the Christmas musical." On another occasion, when my daughters were in middle school, they decided to clean the house as a surprise while my wife and I were gone. They taped a note to the front door that we'd see as we walked into the house. The note said, "Dear Mom and Dad: Even with all the various ways to say 'I love you,' we sometimes have a hard time communicating what we actually feel. So we hope we can show it to you by giving you this gift. Thank you. We love you."[16] We were delighted—and certainly surprised—to find that the gift they had given to us was cleaning the house. As you can see from these comments by my children, there's nothing unusual in English about roles, functions, and tasks as being something freely given . . . like a gift. The Greek side of this discussion will be taken up this afternoon.[17]

QUESTIONER.

Why do you think that this alternate approach is correct?

DR. MICHAELS.

That question is without a doubt the most important one of the day. All of our afternoon sessions will in one way or another be dedicated to answering that question. Let me give you a quick preview of this afternoon's session, though I won't give any details now. Here are some of the reasons to view the so-called spiritual gifts as ministry assignments:

- First, many people assume that the Greek word *charisma* means special ability. It doesn't.
- Second, Paul's central concern in Romans 12; 1 Corinthians 12–14; and Ephesians 4 is that every believer fulfills his or her role in building up the community of faith. That's what he's writing about; that's what he cares about. The Corinthians, not Paul, were the ones who were interested in special abilities.
- Third, Paul doesn't use any concept of ability in his extended metaphor of the body in 1 Corinthians 12:12–27. His illustration is all about the roles— or the ministries—of the various members of the body.
- Fourth, the actual activities that Paul lists in Ephesians 4; Romans 12; and 1 Corinthians 12 can

all be described as ministries, but they cannot all be described as abilities.

- Next, the idea of ministry assignments is a common thread that weaves its way through Paul's letters. The theme of special abilities is not an important theme in his writings.

- Another reason, in approximately 80 percent of Paul's one hundred or so lists, he places a word or phrase that indicates the nature of the list in the immediate context. There are such indicators in all four of the lists we're studying today. This is significant because indicators like the words *appointed, functions,* and *equipping* help us read these lists as ministries.

- A further reason, when Paul uses the words *grace* and *given* together, he's discussing ministry assignments— either his own or those of others—in the immediate context. This combination appears in two of the three chapters that include ministry lists.

- Next, Paul talks in detail about his own ministry assignments and suggests that, just as he had received a ministry, all believers have also received ministry assignments.

- Further, the spiritual-abilities view suggests that service should flow out of our strengths; Paul says that sometimes—though not always—we're called to minister out of weakness.

- And most important, there are many indicators in the texts of Ephesians 4; Romans 12; and 1 Corinthians 12 that show that the items in the lists in those chapters belong better in the category of ministry assignments than in the category of abilities. We'll open our Bibles and look at those together this afternoon.

(*pausing*) Okay, let's take our lunch break now. Perhaps during your lunch you can spend some time discussing the implications of viewing the items that Paul talks about as *spiritual ministries* rather than as special abilities.

Interlude

JASON.

Now, that was interesting. I sure would like some time to talk further with our speaker.

KRISTEN.

Do you want to see if he has any plans for lunch? Maybe we could ask him our questions and talk to him directly about the implications while we eat.

JASON.

That's a good idea. I'll ask Pastor Cole if he's available. (*Walks to the front of the room.*) Hey, Pastor, do you know if Dr. Michaels has any plans for lunch?

PASTOR COLE.

We were thinking about getting some Chinese food.

JASON.

Is there any chance Kristen and I could join you? What we heard in the morning sessions already has us thinking about a lot of issues. We'd love to have a few minutes to talk through some of them with our speaker.

PASTOR COLE.

Great. I'm sure Dr. Michaels would be happy to have you join us.

THREE

So What?

Exploring Some Implications of the Spiritual-Ministries View

(*Over Lunch*)

PASTOR COLE.

I think we should start by talking through some of the practical implications of what you've been teaching since that's how you encouraged us to spend our lunch time.

DR. MICHAELS.

Yes, let's do that.

PASTOR COLE.

Jason and Kristen, what do you think of all this? Do you think that this new perspective makes any practical difference?

KRISTEN.

Sure it does. While Jason and I were walking in from the parking lot this morning, we were speculating about whether we might be given some sort of spiritual-gifts questionnaire to help us learn what our gifts—I mean, special abilities—were. The approach we've heard this morning pretty much eliminates the need to take tests like that.

JASON.

... or to try to discover our untapped spiritual abilities in whatever way.

DR. MICHAELS.

Right.

PASTOR COLE.

It also resolves the ongoing problem in the conventional approach of whether a spiritual gift is something completely different from a natural talent or whether it somehow overlaps with natural talents.

JASON.

That's something I've wondered about.

KRISTEN.

But how do natural talents play a part in the Spirit-given-ministries view?

DR. MICHAELS.

Certainly God has given each person he has created various abilities and talents—what we call natural talents—that he uses for his glory. But there's nothing unusual about that; both views affirm that's something different. The conventional view, however, teaches that the spiritual activities of the church require an additional layer of spiritual abilities on top of the natural endowments that God has already given.[1]

Jason.

What about this weakness and strength issue that you mentioned? I know you said you'd spend some time on it this afternoon, but couldn't that be a pretty significant implication of what you're teaching?

Kristen.

In what way, Jason?

Jason.

I mean . . . should I expect to always have special enablement for my areas of service in the church, or is it sometimes God's desire that I serve by doing something that I'm truly weak in?

Dr. Michaels.

I think most people who've spent a lot of time in ministry know that God sometimes, though not always, wants us to serve out of our weakness so his glory will become even more obvious through us.

Pastor Cole.

I know there are many aspects of my God-given ministry as a pastor in which I feel weak and insufficient. In fact, I don't know any pastors who feel that they're spiritually equipped to deal with all the different types of issues we encounter. I mean, how many pastors are strong in all the areas that we're called to do—preaching, teaching, evangelism, leadership, mercy, prayers for healing, guidance counseling, grief counseling, marriage counseling, church management . . . and more? We often serve in our weakness but continue to serve because we believe that God has put us in this place of ministry.

KRISTEN.

When I started working in our teen ministry, I felt really inadequate. I didn't believe that I had the ability to relate to these girls and communicate spiritual truth to them, but I've already seen God work through my weakness to draw some of those teenage girls to himself.

DR. MICHAELS.

God in his sovereignty can and sometimes does choose to work through the natural strengths that he's given to us, or to empower us specially for a particular task; but at other times he chooses to use us in our weakness so that his glory might shine through.

JASON.

In other words . . . I may sometimes be called by God to serve out of my weakness.

DR. MICHAELS.

Right.

PASTOR COLE.

You mentioned calling, Jason. That makes me wonder if calling might not be another implication of this discussion. Is there a special calling into ministry for some and not for others?

KRISTEN.

You mean like when people talk about being called to be a missionary or called to be a pastor?

PASTOR COLE.

Right.

Dr. Michaels.

All Christians have been called by God into salvation. And, by their calling into this salvation, they've also been called both to participate in the body of Christ and to participate in what Paul calls "the ministry of reconciliation,"[2] which is helping to bring people into a right relationship with God. Every believer, without exception, pastor and non-pastor, missionary and non-missionary, has been called into the ministry in this sense.

But, as we've already discussed, there are a variety of specific ministries that are assigned by the Holy Spirit to individuals—and these might legitimately be referred to as individual callings that are not the same for everyone. One way of thinking of this issue of calling is that there is a Calling—capital C—into salvation for all believers; a calling—small c—into body life and the ministry of reconciliation, which is also for all believers; and callings—small c with an s on the end—which are individual assignments from the Holy Spirit.[3]

Jason.

So . . . you're saying that when people claim that some are called to ministry, like to be pastors or missionaries, and others are not, this is a distinction that the Bible doesn't make.

Dr. Michaels.

Right. All who know Christ—not just pastors and missionaries—are called into ministry. We're all ministers. But the Bible does still affirm that there are distinctions in roles and ministries. Though everyone is called to ministry in general, not everyone has been assigned the role of pastor-teacher—just as everyone has not been assigned the roles of leadership, mercy, or administration.

PASTOR COLE.

In other words . . . you're saying that there's still diversity among ministry roles within the general unity of a single calling.

DR. MICHAELS.

That's right.

PASTOR COLE.

We're all, in fact, ministers, then—which also helps to break down the clergy/laity distinction that's been such a problem in the history of the church, but it doesn't do away with role distinctions entirely.

KRISTEN.

Are you saying that God expects me to think of myself, and not just the pastor, as a minister?

DR. MICHAELS.

Yes.

JASON.

. . . but that doesn't mean that the pastor doesn't have a specific assignment or group of assignments that others have not been given.

DR. MICHAELS.

That's also correct.

JASON.

Hmm. On a different issue, what about Paul's lists of ministries in 1 Corinthians 12; Romans 12; and Ephesians

4? Do the ministries in his lists include all of the ministries in the church, or do they represent the *kinds* of ministries found in the church?

Dr. Michaels.

The approach that these are spiritual ministries rather than special abilities suggests an answer to this question, too, and is another implication of this alternate approach. The moment we recognize that the items in these lists are ministry assignments rather than special abilities, we enter into a general stream of teaching found in the Bible, and in Paul's writings in particular. We find ourselves comparing the so-called spiritual gifts passages with other passages dealing with roles, stewardships, functions, and ministries. The result is that we quickly become aware that Paul probably intended his lists to be representative, rather than all-inclusive. Although he includes a wide range of ministry possibilities in his lists, there are many other areas of ministry outside of the ones listed in 1 Corinthians 12; Romans 12; and Ephesians 4.[4]

Pastor Cole.

I've been teaching through the book of Philippians, and one example of a ministry that doesn't fit neatly into Paul's lists just came to mind. When Paul was in prison, the church of Philippi sent Epaphroditus to minister to him in his time of need. Paul referred to Epaphroditus as a "co-worker," a "fellow soldier," a "messenger," and a "minister." Paul described what Epaphroditus did as "work" and "service."[5] A lot of other places in Paul's writings, and throughout the Bible, illustrate that there are particular roles and ministries for God's people. In light of all that, we can stop thinking of the sections on the so-called spiritual gifts as isolated sections of Scripture that teach something that's found nowhere else.

DR. MICHAELS.

Right. The list passages should be reunited with this common theme and should no longer be viewed in isolation. You know, in a very important sense, the view that Paul is talking about spiritual ministries rather than special abilities is the more conservative of the two positions because it fits comfortably within a common thread known to us from Paul's writings. The Corinthians, not Paul, were the ones who were focusing on their special, miraculous abilities. Paul's emphasis was that everything should be done to build up the body of Christ, the church.

KRISTEN.

This whole discussion sure makes me want to reread those passages more carefully.

JASON.

I'll be interested in hearing you lay out the biblical case for this view this afternoon. It seems to answer some of my practical questions, but I want to see how you support your case from the Bible.

DR. MICHAELS.

That's fair. Like the Bereans in the book of Acts, you want to check from the Scriptures whether this is, in fact, correct.

PASTOR COLE (*checking his watch*).

Okay, folks. It's about time to get back to the church so we can start the afternoon sessions.

PART TWO

ARGUING THE CASE

The *charisma* granted to each is not so much a supernatural gift as the call of the Spirit to serve the church.[1]

—GEORGE ELDON LADD

THE PRECEDING CHAPTERS were presented as interactive to introduce in a more personal way how most readers of the Bible perceive spiritual gifts. The following chapters in part 2 present argument by argument the biblical case for the alternative approach suggested in this book. The content of each chapter is summarized in a short paragraph at the beginning of each chapter, allowing you to familiarize yourself with the general argument, and offering you the option of not having to read every word on every page.[2]

Think carefully through these chapters, like the Bereans in Acts 17:11, who were "examining the Scriptures daily, to see whether these things were so."[3]

FOUR

On the Meaning of Words

Summary: Much confusion stems from a misunderstanding of the Greek words *charisma* and *pneumatika* in passages such as 1 Corinthians 12, words that are sometimes translated "spiritual gift." This chapter serves as preliminary information for the following two chapters, which deal with the meaning of these words.[1]

WHAT DO WORDS MEAN? For example, what does the word *house* mean?

When you just read the word *house,* if you envisioned an unconnected residence, perhaps with a white fence around the front yard, you wouldn't be alone. But you couldn't use that definition for any of the uses of the word *house* in 1 Chronicles 17. If you looked at a more literal[2] translation, you'd notice that the word *house* is the single most important word in 1 Chronicles 17. In that chapter alone it signifies

- palace
- temple
- any sort of non-tent structure
- family
- future lineage

In that passage, it doesn't mean what *we* think of when we first hear the word *house.*

What does the word *had* mean in the sentence, "Mary had a little lamb"? It seems that everyone knows that it signifies that Mary's pet was a lamb; she was the owner of that lamb. But how do we know that?

What if the sentence were found in a textbook in a veterinary college? Students might imagine a case study of a sheep named Mary who gave birth to a little lamb.

What if it were written by a theologian who was trying to communicate creatively? It could be a reflection on the virgin Mary who gave birth to Jesus, the Lamb of God.

What if the sentence were found in a novel about an older woman named Mary who was dining in a nice restaurant? The word *had* could mean "ate," as in, "Mary had a little lamb, a little beef, a little pork."

But we know as certainly as we know anything that *had* in this sentence means that Mary was the owner of a little pet lamb. How do we know this is the case? We know it because that's the way the word *had* is used in this nursery rhyme.

The word *had* in this example, and the word *house* in the first example, only mean what they mean because of the way they're used. Such is true of all words. Words only mean what they mean because of usage.

When any person in any language uses a word, that person selects a word because it has generally in the past been *used* to mean something similar to what he or she wants to say.[3] But the specific meaning of any word written in any sentence is finally determined by its *usage* in its specific context.[4]

Words, then, do not inherently possess some sort of meaning that determines what a sentence means. A word only has a range of possible meanings that is determined by the way it is generally used. A person selects a word out of that range of possible meanings and then narrows the meaning of the word by putting it into a sentence, which is part of a paragraph, which is part of a piece of literature, which is written in a particular literary type—all of which together contribute to the specific meaning of the word in a particular context. Thus, words are, apart from the contexts in which they are found, weak.

God chose to use a regular language—Koine Greek—with common words to communicate his profound truths to us. But the strength of his revelation comes when the words work together in sentences, and sentences work together in passages, and passages work together in books that are composed in whatever literary type the biblical author chose to write.

To know what a word means in any sentence in the Bible, readers look at the context in which that word is found. If the meaning of the word can't be determined from the immediate passage, the word must be compared to the way the same author uses the word elsewhere in his writings. This is because usage is the key issue in determining what a word means.

What does the word *raise* mean? What does it mean in clauses like "raise children," "raise havoc," "raise wheat," "raise the dead," "raise your voice," or, best of all, "get a raise"?

Raise—and all other words—means what it means because of how it is used in context.

FIVE

Greek Words Don't Solve the Problem (Part 1)

What Does Charisma Mean Outside of 1 Corinthians 12?

Summary: Many people think that *charisma,* no matter where or how that word is used, means "special ability." This chapter argues that *charisma* (outside of 1 Cor. 12) is used in such a variety of ways by Paul that it cannot be a technical term[1] that means special ability.[2]

SPEAKERS OF ENGLISH—and indeed other monolingual speakers— often have a magical view of words that bilingual and trilingual people do not. They assume that words have inherent meanings that determine, in turn, the meaning of a sentence. As discussed in the previous chapter, these people have it backward. The meaning of a word is mainly determined by the way it is used by a given author in a particular literary type.

There's a difficulty in introducing people to the idea that Paul was concerned with ministry assignments rather than special abilities. The difficulty is that many people assume that the Greek word *charisma* actually means "spiritual gift," or "a special Spirit-given ability."[3] If readers of the Bible have never had an opportunity to study biblical Greek themselves, they have no way of verifying this translation, so they assume what they've heard or learned is correct.[4]

But if it is kept in mind that words mean what they mean because of usage, the conversation doesn't have to stop. It's feasible to look at the various places that a word like *charisma* is used and infer the likely meaning of the word from each context. And although the task is easier if readers have a background in biblical Greek, a monolingual person can often figure out the general meaning of a word by looking at the immediate context in which a particular word is found.[5]

So does *charisma* mean a special, Spirit-given ability? After looking at the passages themselves, you'll likely agree that the answer is "no—at least not usually." Apart from one appearance in 1 Peter,[6] *charisma* is used only by Paul in the New Testament. Out of the sixteen times that he uses the word,[7] in six examples *charisma* almost certainly does not signify ability, in four it probably doesn't, and in one the meaning can only be known after a study of 1 Corinthians.

Six Examples in Which *Charisma* Doesn't Mean "Ability"

Example 1:

> For I long to see you so that I may give some *charisma* to you to strengthen you. (Rom. 1:11)

Paul wants to give the church in Rome a *charisma*. Although it's unclear as to what specifically he refers, it's almost impossible to think of it as a special ability. How could Paul give an ability to an entire church? Whatever it means, it doesn't mean ability.[8]

Example 2:

> For the *charismata*[9] and calling of God are irrevocable. (Rom. 11:29)

The context is God's special election of the people of Israel. The concept of ability isn't anywhere in view. *Charisma* in this particular context is usually thought to refer to "the privileges granted to the people of Israel,"[10] although, in light of its connection to the word *calling,* it could signify something nearer to Israel's particular role as a nation chosen by God.

EXAMPLE 3:

> As you also join in helping us through your prayers, that thanks may be given by many persons on our behalf for the *charisma* granted us through the prayers of many. (2 Cor. 1:11)

In context, this word points toward God's graciously rescuing from danger.[11] It doesn't mean ability.

EXAMPLES 4–5:

> But the *charisma* is not like the trespass. For if by the trespass of the one the many died, much more did the grace of God and the gift by the grace of the one man, Jesus Christ, abound to the many. And the gift is not like that which came through the one who sinned; for the judgment that came out of the one trespass resulted in condemnation, but the *charisma* that came out of the many trespasses resulted in righteousness. (Rom. 5:15–16)

Here, *charisma* is being used in reference to God's saving grace through Jesus Christ. It is, in fact, all about God's act of grace in salvation, not about abilities of any sort. This passage and the following support the idea that *charisma* can sometimes be translated as "gift," but this certainly does not mean that it should always be so translated, nor does it even imply that the idea of special abilities should be projected onto the word. To view this passage as the gift of a special ability would be wholly inappropriate.

EXAMPLE 6:

> For the wages of sin is death, but the *charisma* of God
> is eternal life in Christ Jesus our Lord. (Rom. 6:23)

In this example, the *charisma* is not just the saving grace of God; it is one of the specific benefits of saving grace, namely, eternal life. Special ability from the Holy Spirit is nowhere in sight.

In four other verses, *charisma* probably does not refer to a special ability from the Spirit, although such is not as immediately obvious as in the examples above.

FOUR EXAMPLES IN WHICH *CHARISMA* PROBABLY DOESN'T MEAN "ABILITY"

EXAMPLES 1–2:

> Do not neglect the *charisma* in you, which was given
> to you through prophecy with the laying on of hands
> by the council of elders. (1 Tim. 4:14)

> And for this reason I remind you to rekindle the
> *charisma* of God which is in you through the laying
> on of my hands. (2 Tim. 1:6)

Some interpreters read *charisma* here as a special ability that was given to Timothy when Paul and the elders laid hands on him.[12] The main reason for this translation, however, seems to be the presence of the word *charisma*, which, in accord with conventional readings, is assumed to refer to special abilities. That this *charisma* is "in you" in both passages also is viewed by some interpreters as indicating that special ability is in view.[13] But *in you* is used elsewhere in Greek with too much variety to allow it to carry the weight of a special abilities theology.[14] And unless *charisma* can somehow carry the idea all by itself, there is nothing about special abilities in either passage. On the contrary, the verse preceding 1 Timothy 4:14 (v. 13) is a charge to Timothy to "give attention to reading [that is, public reading of Scripture], to exhortation, to teaching," that is, to the carrying out of ministry roles (note also 1 Tim. 4:15–16ff. and 2 Tim. 1:8–14, where there are further charges).

These charges are perhaps why many interpreters—even those who work within a conventional framework—understand the word *charisma* in these contexts to refer to Timothy's appointment to ministry. D. A. Carson, for example, says that "the gift was the ministry to which he [Timothy] was called."[15] Further, the same laying-on-of-hands event seems to be referred to in 1 Timothy 1:18, where Paul says, "This charge I commit to you, Timothy my son, in accordance with the prophecies previously made over you, in order that by them you may fight the good fight."

Paul seems to be saying that he is, in the present, giving Timothy another charge to act in accordance with the prophecies that were made about him at the time Paul and the elders laid their hands on him (cf. 1 Tim. 4:14; 2 Tim. 1:6). Does this not suggest that the initial event mentioned in these letters was itself also a charge entrusted to Timothy, that is, a commissioning to ministry, rather than the passing on of some sort of special ability?[16]

And what does laying on of hands have to do with conferring an ability? Many years earlier, the leaders of the church in Antioch had laid their hands on two men when the Holy Spirit had instructed them to do so: "Set apart for me Barnabas and Saul for the work to which I have called them" (Acts 13:2–3). Paul used *charisma* in a similar way in 1 Timothy 4:14 and 2 Timothy 1:6, again, probably not for the conferring of a special ability on Timothy, but as a reference to the occasion(s) when he was charged or commissioned for ministry.

EXAMPLE 3:

> But I wish that all were as I myself am. However, each one has his own *charisma* from God, one in this, and one in that. (1 Cor. 7:7)

When Paul applies *charisma* to the words "one in this" and "one in that" (literally: "one thus [on the one hand]; one thus [on the other hand]"), he is designating the word *charisma* as marriage (on the one hand) and as singleness (on the other hand).[17] The New Living Translation accurately paraphrases this designation: "God gives some the gift of marriage, and to others he gives the gift of singleness." When we recognize that *charisma* is applied both to singleness and to marriage, it becomes apparent that Paul's use of *charisma* for singleness is probably not a reference to the ability to abstain from sexual activities, as it has often been interpreted; otherwise, then, what ability is the *charisma* of marriage? Is it the ability to engage in marital sex? The parallel application of *charisma* to marriage alongside of singleness makes it unlikely that ability is what Paul had in mind when he used this word.

That ability being unlikely, however, does not mean that one's calling to a celibate life will lack God's enabling. God normally does enable us for whatever he calls us to do. (Refer to the discussion in chap. 18.) Furthermore, Paul's statement comes in a context in which he twice mentions self-control in matters of sexual activity (vv. 5, 9), which may suggest that continence could be a part of what he has in mind. On the other hand, when Paul broadens out into general principles in the heart of this chapter of 1 Corinthians (vv. 17–24), he instructs, "Only, to each as the Lord has assigned, as God has called each, in this way let him walk" (v. 17). In the context of 1 Corinthians 7, *charisma* seems to refer to the present condition (v. 20) or marital calling—that is, married or single—of a person who was called into relationship with Christ (in analogy to circumcised or uncircumcised, v. 18; slave or free, v. 22). What *charisma* is probably referring to in 1 Corinthians 7:7, then, is the calling to the state of marriage or singleness rather than some assumed ability for either.

EXAMPLE 4:

Having *charismata* according to the grace given to us that differ. (Rom. 12:6a)

In Romans 12:6, *charisma* is so closely associated in the context with another Greek word found in verse 4, *praxis*—usually translated as "function"—that it is unlikely that anyone would read *charisma* as special ability if that reader were only looking at Romans 12. On its own, both the link to *praxis* (function) and the nature of the list that follows argue that *charisma,* rather than being used in relationship to special abilities, refers to functions, persons in their functions, and proper attitudes with which the functions should be carried out. Chapter 10 (cf. appendix B) looks closely and carefully at this passage.

First Corinthians 1:7, the last use of *charisma* outside of its five appearances in 1 Corinthians 12, adds little, if anything, to the present discussion at this point because in the former passage it appears that Paul may simply be anticipating his upcoming discussion in 1 Corinthians 12–14, although at the same time he may also be anticipating his discussion of the nature of true wisdom in 1 Corinthians 1:18–2:16. In other words, the context in which *charisma* is used in 1 Corinthians 1:7 offers few indications of its meaning. The meaning of *charisma* in this passage will have to be inferred from a further study of 1 Corinthians as a whole, particularly 1:18–2:16 and chapters 12–14.

Notice the broad range of usage for the word *charisma* in these passages.[18]

Range of usage of *charisma* outside of 1 Corinthians 12

rescue from danger

God's saving grace

the privileges of Israel   eternal life

commissioning for ministry (?)

calling to celibacy or marriage (?)

function (?)

Why did Paul choose to use the word *charisma* in these passages? After all, apart from Paul, who doesn't use it often, *charisma* is not a common word.[19] Why didn't he use a different word?

Paul may have been drawn to use this word because of its formal similarities to the word *charis,* a word that is often—but not always—translated using the English word "grace." *Charis* is, after all, one of Paul's favorite words. He uses *charis* an even one hundred times in his letters, and, in fact, he directly relates the words *charisma* and *charis* in Romans 12:3–8 and 1 Corinthians 1:4–7.[20]

In addition, the *-ma* ending in Greek often (although not always) makes concrete an abstract concept or shows the result of that concept.[21] Thus, Paul may have chosen to use this word so that he could indicate, not grace in general, but practical outworking of God's grace, that is, tangible ways that God expresses his grace.

But the formation and history of a word are not very important in a discussion like this. Why Paul may have used a particular word can only be inferred by looking at the actual passages where he did, in fact, use a word. And when comparing the various uses of the word *charisma* looked at so far, the idea of concrete examples of grace seems to be common to all of them. Each instance is a description of God working out his grace among humans, not in general ways, but specifically, tangibly, observably—as in rescuing from danger, bestowing privileges on the people of Israel, and commissioning people to places of ministry.

These general examples of grace are the common element in all these passages. Thus is provided a conceptual starting point for defining *charisma*, that is, concrete expressions of God's grace or as ways God shows his grace.[22] Should Bible translators, then, translate, using these phrases? On the contrary, a Bible translator should begin with the understanding that the word *charisma* most often indicates observable ways that God shows his grace, and then look for a word or expression in the particular passage being translated that communicates the nature of that particular grace in action.

The next chapter looks at 1 Corinthians 12, where *charisma* is used five times. The context of that passage is all about building up the body of Christ and points toward the ministry roles given to each believer by the Holy Spirit. Expressions such as "ministries of grace," or "works of grace," or perhaps "gifts of ministry" could be used in such a context to translate *charisma* in its plural form (it is always in the plural in these passages). But, there and everywhere, the word *charisma,* like all words, must be defined by how it is used. Usage is crucial to keep in mind—something that is often difficult for monolinguists to remember.

Greek Words Don't Solve the Problem (Part 2)

What Do Charisma and Pneumatika Mean in 1 Corinthians 12?

Summary*Summary:* Even in 1 Corinthians 12, *charisma* is not a technical term meaning "special ability." *Pneumatika,* another key word in the passage, won't solve the problem of meaning either.[1]

ON *CHARISMA(TA)* IN 1 CORINTHIANS 12

THE WORD *CHARISMA* is used in a variety of ways outside of 1 Corinthians 12. Despite that, some people still claim that, for Paul, *charisma* (always in its plural form *charismata* in 1 Cor. 12) is a technical term in 1 Corinthians 12 that means "Spirit-given ability."[2] When the passage itself is examined, however, this claim runs into considerable difficulty. Nor is an incorrect interpretation of *charisma* a minor point. "The wrong understanding of this word has been the root of much misunderstanding of 1 Corinthians 12–14, and its correction is therefore a necessary preliminary to the proper interpretation of the chapters."[3]

It is often assumed that Paul's key word in 1 Corinthians 12–14 is *charismata*, and that he uses it as a technical term for "spiritual gifts." A simple survey of the way he actually uses the word in 1 Corinthians

12 will demonstrate, however, that such an assumption is unfounded. He uses another word, *pneumatika*, to introduce the discussion that begins in 1 Corinthians 12:1 and resumes in 1 Corinthians 14:1.[4] In his lengthy discussion of tongues and prophecy in chapter 14, he doesn't use the word *charismata* at all. Of the five times Paul uses *charismata* in 1 Corinthians 12, three are in the phrase "*charismata* of healing" (12:9, 28, 30), which is obviously a narrow application of the word.

Only two other appearances of the word, then are left—12:4 and 12:31. But notice that *charismata* has to share the stage with two other words in 12:4 since it is one of three words in a triad:

> Now there are distributions[5] of *charismata*, but the same Spirit. And there are distributions of areas of service [*diakoniai*], but the same Lord. And there are distributions of workings [*energēmata*], but the same God who works all things in all persons.[6] (1 Cor. 12:4–6)

If *charismata* were, in fact, Paul's preferred word, as some claim, it seems he would have used it as his key word in verses 4–6. Instead, *charismata* in these verses is merely the first of three terms; it does not stand alone. The most likely explanation is that Paul is using the three words together in these verses to summarize the community activities that build up the body of Christ.[7] The two words that are linked with *charismata* are *diakoniai* ("ministries," "areas of service," "ways of serving"[8]) and *energēmata* ("workings," "activities"), both of which remind the reader that Paul's overall concern in 1 Corinthians 12–14 is with the community-building activities of individual believers in a corporate body rather than with the special abilities to do so.[9]

The last appearance of *charismata* in 1 Corinthians 12 is in verse 31. This verse is usually rendered in English as an imperative; Paul is telling the Corinthians to do something that he wants them to do:

> But earnestly desire the greater *charismata*. (1 Cor. 12:31)

It is far from certain, however, that this verse should be rendered as an imperative, that is, that Paul is telling the Corinthians to "earnestly desire." The Greek form could allow that he is unhappily stating that they are already seeking the "greater" *charismata*—implying that the Corinthians were already striving after the miraculous and spectacular—something that Paul doesn't want them to do.[10] In other words, he could be saying, "You are intensely and wrongly seeking the spectacular activities. Stop it. Let me show you a better way: the way of love."[11]

Still, it appears to be slightly more likely that Paul is using *charismata* as a general word for all the items found in the list immediately preceding, and as an encouragement or command for the Corinthians to make sure the "greater" roles (viewed positively) like apostleship, prophecy, and teaching receive greater emphasis in their congregation.[12] In this case, *charismata* in 1 Corinthians 12:31 would be a summary of all the activities that Paul mentions throughout the chapter. Since Romans 12:6 may also function in a similar summary position in its own context, that leaves two possible examples (and only two) of *charismata* being used by Paul as a summary word for the items that he lists in each passage.[13]

But two things need to be clearly understood. First, a word used in a summary position is not the same as using a word as a technical term, which must have more or less the same meaning each time it is used, at least in a designated context. In light of its variety of uses, even in this chapter, *charisma* clearly does not qualify as a technical term. Second, and most important, in both of these cases (1 Cor. 12:31 and Rom. 12:6) what are summarized are ministry functions or members in those ministries, not abilities, which is the central issue here under discussion. But more evidence for their being ministries will be given in later chapters of this volume that look at the lists themselves.

To recap, *charismata* seems most likely to be used in three ways in 1 Corinthians 12:

1. as a word attached specifically to healing (vv. 9, 28, 30);
2. as one of three words summarizing various community-strengthening activities (v. 4);
3. as a summary word for all these activities (v. 31).

It must be kept in mind that biblical interpreters have struggled with the appearance of *charismata* in both 1 Corinthians 12:4 and 12:31, and have suggested various ways of dealing with them in context.[14] However these are understood by interpreters, it will not do to claim that *charismata* is a technical term that means "special abilities." Based upon the arguments to be presented in later chapters, it could be suggested that *charismata* be translated using expressions such as "ministries of grace," or "works of grace," or "gifts of ministry"[15] in order to incorporate both the idea of ministry and the idea that what has been assigned has been given graciously by God. But those chapters and those arguments are still to come. The goal of the first part of this chapter is simply to point out that the word *charismata* itself does not mean "special abilities."

ON *PNEUMATIKA* IN 1 CORINTHIANS 12–14

If *charismata* cannot fill the role of "special abilities," perhaps, then, *pneumatika*[16] is a technical term that means "special abilities." It is, after all, the word that heads Paul's discussion in 1 Corinthians 12:1, and in 14:1, when he resumes the discussion following his poetic challenge in chapter 13 that the Corinthians pursue love.

A number of difficulties arise, however, with reading *pneumatika* in this way. First, it is used as a noun only twice in the passage (12:1; 14:1). It is as though Paul uses it to introduce the discussion in chapter 12, then to begin the discussion of tongues and prophecy in chapter 14, but otherwise chooses to ignore the word altogether. The way Paul chooses to use *pneumatika* suggests that is not a word he himself wants to use in this context at all; rather, it is a word the Corinthians have been fond of using.

This suggestion is confirmed by the fact that *pneumatika* appears at the beginning of the discussion, and there alone. In 12:1 is the phrase "Now concerning *pneumatika* . . ." Those familiar with 1 Corinthians will know that Paul has been responding to specific questions that arose out of problems in the Corinthian church. With his expression, "Now concerning . . . ," he signals at particular points in the letter that he's responding to questions directed to himself. Examples include the following: "Now concerning virgins . . ." (7:25); "Now concerning idol-food . . ." (8:1); "Now concerning the collection for the saints . . ." (16:1). It is clear from 7:1 that these are responses to something that the Corinthians have written: "Now concerning the things about which you wrote . . ."[17] It looks as if Paul may have begun his discussion with the Corinthians' preferred term and then ignored it until he resumed his topic in chapter 14, at which point he used the word just once more to signal that he was picking up the subject again. Paul then again ignored the word during the lengthy discussion of prophecy and tongues in chapter 14.

It should also be noted that the word *pneumatika* is ambiguous. It is an adjective that usually means something like "spiritual" or "having to do with the spirit (or Spirit)," but is here being used as a noun. As a noun it could mean either "spiritual things" or "spiritual persons."[18] So why do our translations usually read, "Now concerning spiritual *gifts* . . ."? Translators in this case have understood *pneumatika* to mean "spiritual things" and then inferred that the spiritual things that Paul is about to discuss are the spiritual gifts, which they then usually read as special Spirit-given abilities.[19] It should be clear, then, that whatever Paul means by his use of *pneumatika* in 1 Corinthians 12:1 (and 14:1), that meaning must be determined by the context— both literary and situational—of 1 Corinthians 12 and 14. Since *pneumatika* does not clearly mean "special Spirit-given abilities" anywhere else in the letters of Paul, it should not be assumed that it means such a thing in this case unless the context itself suggests such a meaning.

Although it must remain somewhat uncertain, a reasonable explanation for Paul's use of this word can be given. *Pneumatika* was quite likely the Corinthians' favorite word to describe in particular the miraculous activities that had so captivated their interest, particularly the types of activities listed in 1 Corinthians 12:8–10. Paul begins answering their questions using their own favorite word and then moves the discussion in the direction he wants to take it.[20]

Regardless of the exact function of *pneumatika* in this passage, it should nonetheless be clear that its meaning resides not solely in the word, but in the context in which it is found. Many people, especially those unfamiliar with the Greek language, think that particular Greek words themselves somehow take on an instructive role, teaching the theology of the conventional approach, that is, the special-abilities approach. They don't. As has been stated, the words are primarily dependent for their definitions upon the contexts in which they are found.

Stated another way, the isolated words are not the central issue in this discussion. If, however, readers want to know what Paul intended to teach about the entities commonly referred to as "spiritual gifts," it's necessary to look at his explicit statements about his central concerns, and then look at each individual list of "gifts" in the contexts in which they are found. The topic of Paul's central concern is addressed in the following chapter.

SEVEN

Paul's Central Concern

Building Up the Body of Christ Through the Ministries of Its Members

Summary: Paul's central concern in Ephesians 4; Romans 12; and 1 Corinthians 12–14 is the building up of the body of Christ through the ministry roles of its members.

IF THE INDIVIDUAL words themselves aren't the issue, what is?

The issue is whatever Paul tells us it is. It isn't discovered by reading between the lines; it's discovered by reading the lines themselves.

To discover an author's central concerns, begin by looking at whatever the author explicitly says about what he's writing—if such statements exist—and then at how particular details work into that overall framework. This present chapter 7 of this volume is about Paul's central concern; the chapters herein that immediately follow will look at the lists in particular.

As it turns out, Paul tells us in Romans 12; 1 Corinthians 12–14; and Ephesians 4 that with which he is most concerned—and he tells us repeatedly. Take special note of the words in italics:

> And so we, the many, are one body in Christ, and individually members *one of another.* (Rom. 12:5)

> Be devoted to *one another* with brotherly love . . . outdoing *one another* in honor . . . contributing to the needs of the saints. (Rom. 12:10–13)

But to each one is given the manifestation of the
Spirit *for the common good.* (1 Cor. 12:7)

God has arranged the members of the body . . . so
that . . . the members may have the same *care* for one
another. (1 Cor. 12:24–25)

But one who prophesies speaks to men for *edification
and encouragement and consolation.* (1 Cor. 14:3)

So that the church may receive *edification.* (1 Cor.
14:5)

Seek to overflow for the *edification* of the church.
(1 Cor. 14:12)

For you may be giving thanks well enough, but the
other person is not *edified.* (1 Cor. 14:17)

Let all things be done *for edification.* (1 Cor. 14:26b)

So that all may *learn* and all may be *encouraged.*
(1 Cor. 14:31)

With all humility and gentleness, with patience,
showing tolerance *toward one another* in love, being
diligent to maintain the *unity* of the Spirit in the
bond of peace. (Eph. 4:2–3)

For the *equipping* of the saints for the *work of ministry*
leading to the *building up* of the body of Christ until we
all attain to the *unity* of the faith. (Eph. 4:12–13a)

. . . causes the *growth* of the body, leading to the
building up of itself in love. (Eph. 4:16b)[1]

Paul's own statements in these passages reveal what he cares about
most. His central concern is the building up of the body of Christ
through the ministries of each member.

Now notice once again a key motif that ties together Romans 12; 1 Corinthians 12–14; and Ephesians 4: the metaphor of the body (Rom. 12:4–5; 1 Cor. 12:12–27; Eph. 4:4, 12, 16).[2] Note in particular the following verses:

> For just as we have many members in one *body* and all the members do not have the same function, so we, the many, are one *body* in Christ, and individually members one of another. (Rom. 12:4–5)

> For just as the *body* is one and has many members, and all the members of the *body,* though many, are one *body,* so also is Christ. (1 Cor. 12:12)

> God has arranged the *body* . . . so that the members may have the same care for one another. (1 Cor. 12:24–25)

> Now you are the *body* of Christ, and individually members of it. (1 Cor. 12:27)

> There is one *body* and one Spirit. (Eph. 4:4)

> For the equipping of the saints for the work of ministry leading to the building up of the *body* of Christ. (Eph. 4:12)

> From whom the whole *body,* joined and held together by every supporting ligament, according to the working of each individual part, causes the growth of the body, leading to the building up of itself in love. (Eph. 4:16)

The metaphor of the body connects these three passages, as well as the four lists that are in them. It's crucial to notice that thematic links between these three passages are unmistakable, and the body metaphor is the most important link because it is explicit. It's true that in a study of this present kind, each passage must be examined on its own merits—and such will continue as this book progresses. But looking at a passage in isolation and not in relation to other passages that overlap thematically, a grasp of the full picture of what Paul teaches will be ellusive. Nor will such a study connect with the real needs of the church. We who seriously study Scripture must be sensitive to the thematic and conceptual links that tie passages together, such as are in the three passages with which this study is concerned. One of the ways that Paul has flagged for us that the discussions contained in these three passages adequately overlap—and thus can (and should) be studied together—is his use of the body metaphor in each passage.[3]

What does Paul intend to teach using this metaphor? Led by the Spirit, Paul has drawn out this metaphor through a detailed discussion placed right in the heart of 1 Corinthians 12. The answer will come largely, though not exclusively, from there. Actually, Paul's development of the body metaphor constitutes sixteen verses out of the thirty-one total verses in 1 Corinthians 12—more than half. But why does Paul devote so much of his discussion to this subject? It's because the truths that Paul teaches using the body metaphor represent the issues about which he cares most to communicate.

What does he teach using this metaphor?

First, it should be noted that Paul does not talk about special abilities in 1 Corinthians 12:12–27. He neither mentions such a concept nor implies it. To draw a special abilities concept out of this metaphor it must first be assumed that the concept occurs in the surrounding verses, and then it must be read into these verses. The special abilities concept won't be found by looking at what Paul actually says in 1 Corinthians 12:12–27. The absence of an ability concept throughout this metaphor constitutes an argument against the conventional view of spiritual gifts as abilities.

So what is the body metaphor about? The metaphor is about the roles in which the Holy Spirit has placed each individual. Paul says it in these words: "But now *God has placed the members,* each one of them, in the body, just as he desired" (1 Cor. 12:18).[4] The metaphor is not about abilities; it's about roles, functions, ministries. As R. Martin observes, "The body analogy stresses functionality as its chief feature."[5] Then under the central idea of the building up of the body by members in particular roles are a few key supporting concepts. Below is a list of the supporting concepts Paul communicates in his development of the body metaphor in 1 Corinthians 12:12–27.

KEY IDEAS IN PAUL'S BODY METAPHOR: 1 CORINTHIANS 12:12–27

- Unity
  There are no racial or sociological distinctions (v. 13). Unity is based upon our common reception of the Spirit (v. 13).

- Diversity
  There are many individual members (vv. 14, 27).

- Unity in Diversity
  We are members no matter what role we have been assigned (vv. 15–17).[6] There should be no divisions (v. 25).[7]

- Source
  God is the one who has placed the members (v. 18). It is Christ's body of which we are members (vv. 12, 27). The Holy Spirit is the one who has baptized us into this body (v. 13).[8]

- Need
  All the members need each other (v. 21). Members deemed to be weaker are necessary (v. 22).

- Honor
  Members deemed to be less honorable ought to be honored (vv. 23–24).[9]

- Care
  All the members should care for each other (v. 25).
  Members should share both in each other's sufferings
  and in each other's joys (v. 26).

Underlying all of these ideas and influencing the entire discussion is the idea that members in various roles should express care for each other so that the body of Christ is edified.

Key Ideas in Paul's Body Metaphor: Romans 12 and Ephesians 4

Many of the same ideas appear when Paul uses the metaphor of the body in Romans 12 and Ephesians 4, the other two passages besides 1 Corinthians 12 that contain ministry lists. Following are the supporting ideas suggested by Paul's use of the body metaphor in these two passages:

- Humility
  Members of the body should be humble toward one
  another because each has differing functions (Rom.
  12:3–8; Eph. 4:2).

- Unity
  We are one body (Rom. 12:4–5; Eph. 4:4, 13).

- Diversity
  We have many members with differing functions
  (Rom. 12:4–5; Eph. 4:16).

- Edification
  Believers are to be equipped to do ministry so that
  the body of Christ might be built up and grow (Eph.
  4:12, 15).

- Christ the Head
  Christ is the head of the body. Notice that the most

> significant difference between Paul's use of the body metaphor in 1 Corinthians 12 and Ephesians is that in Ephesians (and also Colossians) Christ is the head of the body (Eph. 4:15; cf. 1:22–23; Col. 1:18; 2:19).

Thus, the central idea of these passages, as in 1 Corinthians 12, is that members in their various functions need to aim for unity and the building up of the body.

What, then, is Paul's central concern in all three of these passages? Through his use of the body metaphor and other explicit statements in these passages, Paul shows that he deeply cares that the community of believers is built up as members of that community serve in the roles in which God has placed them.

What is the payoff in understanding Paul's central concern? As readers, our interpretation of the details in a passage will always be influenced by our conception of the overall purpose—or big idea—of a passage. Unless our understanding of the big idea is properly formed, our interpretation of the details will necessarily be skewed. Paul tells us repeatedly where he is going in these passages, using the metaphor of the body as an important focal point. In opposition to the Corinthian Christians' self-centered interest in miraculous activities, Paul says that God has placed each believer in roles of ministry for the purpose of edifying his church. Paul's concerns in Romans 12 and Ephesians 4 are similar at many points. God wants to build up the body of Christ and so has placed individual members in various roles and functions to accomplish this. Paul doesn't encourage his readers to try to discover their special spiritual abilities; rather, he challenges and encourages them to strengthen the community of faith in whatever roles of ministry that God has placed them.

EIGHT

How Paul Uses Lists

Summary: This chapter prepares the reader for the following four chapters, which carefully examine each of Paul's four lists in their contexts (Eph. 4; Rom. 12; and two lists in 1 Cor. 12). Paul's pattern of indicating the nature of a list in words that do not appear as items in a list sets the stage for a proper reading of his four ministry lists.

TRY THIS LITTLE QUIZ. Choose the item in each list below that doesn't quite fit:

1. India, Australia, China, Brazil, Egypt, Spain, Jupiter
2. Joy, faithfulness, hope, humility, love, patience, selfishness
3. Celebrate, sing, rejoice, dance, cheer, grumble
4. Running, walking, jogging, jumping, house

It's obvious that, in each case, the last item doesn't fit the items in the rest of the list. The chapters that follow in this volume examine each of Paul's four lists individually in order to determine what makes each list cohere. In other words, does an ability concept account for what is actually found when looking at Paul's lists, or does another concept hold these lists together? It should first be asked, though, *How does Paul use lists in general* (outside of the four lists that are the focus of this book)? The answer to that question—rather than some preconceived notion about lists—is the starting point for the study of the particular list to be examined.

To arrive at that starting point, every place should be noted where Paul includes a list in his writings, compiling what might be called a list of lists.[1] A list can be characterized as every place in the letters of Paul where he groups together four[2] or more items in a way that could conceivably be considered a list. Some of these groupings are more, shall we say, list-like than others. Consequently, beside each reference in the chart below, I have assigned a value in parentheses to indicate how closely the text adheres to the form, style, and function of Paul's ministry lists (Rom. 12; 1 Cor. 12; and Eph. 4). If the list appears to closely adhere, it receives an A rating. The more dissimilar the list to Paul's ministry lists, the lower the ranking it receives, the lowest being the rank of "H."[3]

THE LIST OF LISTS

Reference: (ranking)

Rom. 1:14 (E)
Rom. 1:28–32 (B)
Rom. 2:17–20 (C)
Rom. 2:21–23 (D)
Rom. 3:10–18 (C)
Rom. 5:3–5 (D)
Rom. 8:30 (D)
Rom. 8:35–36 (C)
Rom. 8:38–39 (C)
Rom. 9:4–5 (C)
Rom. 11:33–36 (H)
Rom. 12:6–8
Rom. 12:9–21 (A)
Rom. 13:7 (C)
Rom. 13:9 (D)

1 Cor. 14:26 (A)
1 Cor. 15:5–8 (C)
1 Cor. 16:13–14 (C)
2 Cor. 4:8–12 (D)
2 Cor. 6:4–10 (C)
2 Cor. 6:14–16 (E)
2 Cor. 7:11 (D)
2 Cor. 8:7 (B)
2 Cor. 11:20 (D)
2 Cor. 11:22–23 (D)
2 Cor. 11:23–29 (B)
2 Cor. 12:10 (C)
2 Cor. 12:20 (C)
2 Cor. 13:11 (D)
Gal. 3:28 (E)
Gal. 4:10 (D)

Col. 2:16 (F)
Col. 3:5 (B)
Col. 3:8 (B)
Col. 3:11 (B)
Col. 3:12–13 (B)
Col. 3:18–4:1 (G)
1 Thess. 5:16–22 (H)
2 Thess. 2:9–10 (D)
1 Tim. 1:9–10 (B)
1 Tim. 1:17 (E)
1 Tim. 2:1 (D)
1 Tim. 2:9 (D)
1 Tim. 3:2–7 (B)
1 Tim. 3:8–12 (B)
1 Tim. 3:16 (H)
1 Tim. 4:12 (C)

Rom. 13:13 (C)	Gal. 5:19–21 (B)	1 Tim. 5:1–2 (E)
Rom. 15:18–19 (E)	Gal. 5:22–23 (B)	1 Tim. 5:9–10 (A)
Rom. 16:25–27 (E)	Eph. 1:21 (D)	1 Tim. 5:14 (C)
1 Cor. 1:12 (D)	Eph. 3:18 (D)	1 Tim. 6:4–5 (C)
1 Cor. 1:30 (E)	Eph. 4:2–3 (B)	1 Tim. 6:11 (B)
1 Cor. 3:12 (D)	Eph. 4:4–6 (B)	1 Tim. 6:15–16 (F)
1 Cor. 3:22 (D)	**Eph. 4:11**	2 Tim. 2:22 (B)
1 Cor. 4:10–13 (C)	Eph. 4:31 (B)	2 Tim. 2:24–25 (B)
1 Cor. 5:11 (B)	Eph. 4:32 (B)	2 Tim. 3:2–5 (B)
1 Cor. 6:9–10 (B)	Eph. 5:22–6:9 (G)	2 Tim. 3:10–11 (B)
1 Cor. 7:29–31 (D)	Eph. 6:12 (C)	2 Tim. 3:16 (C)
1 Cor. 9:1 (C)	Eph. 6:13–17 (C)	2 Tim. 4:2 (B)
1 Cor. 9:20–22 (D)	Phil. 2:1 (B)	2 Tim. 4:5 (B)
1 Cor. 10:7–10 (F)	Phil. 2:2 (B)	Titus 1:6–9 (B)
1 Cor. 12:8–10	Phil. 2:3–4 (B)	Titus 2:2–10 (B)
1 Cor. 12:28–30	Phil. 3:5–6 (D)	Titus 3:1–2 (C)
1 Cor. 13:1–3 (A)	Phil. 4:8 (B)	Titus 3:3 (C)
1 Cor. 13:4–8 (B)	Phil. 4:9 (C)	Titus 3:9 (D)
1 Cor. 14:6 (A)	Col. 1:15–20 (F)	Philemon: None

Many observations could be drawn from a detailed study of Paul's lists. The following six are the most relevant for the present study.

First, Paul likes to use lists, and he uses them in every letter he writes (except Philemon). Depending, of course, on the criteria used for inclusion on a list of Paul's lists, the result will hover around one hundred lists of various kinds in the letters of Paul.

Second, Paul's lists include virtue lists, vice lists, qualifications lists, doxologies, and confessional statements that in some cases may have already been in use before he used them.[4]

Third, at the same time, a clear majority of the lists in Paul's letters appear to have been created by him for the particular needs and issues he was addressing as he wrote.

Fourth, depending upon the conceptual framework that holds together a particular list, the words in a list may all be in the same grammatical form, or may be in mixed grammatical forms. The items in Paul's famous list of the "fruit of the Spirit" in Galatians 5:22–23, for example, are all nouns. Conceptually, the same list can be described as an inventory of attitudes produced by the Spirit and that lead to actions. In contrast, the list in 2 Corinthians 6:4–10 presents an example of mixed forms. Paul begins with a list of eighteen prepositional phrases starting with *in* (for example, "in much endurance"), continues with three prepositional phrases beginning with "by" ("by glory and honor"), and finishes with seven doublets starting with the comparative particle *as* ("as sorrowful yet always rejoicing"). Here is another way of describing the same list: verses 4–5 is a list of hardships; verse 6 is a list of virtues; verse 7 is a list of Paul's spiritual equipment; verses 8–10 is a list of apparent dichotomies. Despite the variety in the list, all the items hold together under the conceptual umbrella of ways that Paul and his band "commend themselves" as servants of God (6:4).[5]

Fifth, lists are not arbitrary. A concept or theme always holds them together. Romans 9:4–5, for example, is a list of the privileges and identification markers of the people of Israel. Romans 13:9 is a list of actions and attitudes that should be rendered to governing authorities. First Corinthians 14:6 is a list of speaking activities in a Christian meeting. Galatians 5:19–21 is a list of the "deeds of the flesh," and 5:22–23 is "the fruit of the Spirit."

For a group of items to be considered a list, then, those items must cluster together under some conceptual umbrella.[6] If, for example, you created a list of apples, you cannot have oranges in the list. If your list is a list of fruit, then, of course, you can have apples and oranges together. It should be assumed, though, that the items in a list are conceptually related to one another unless clear contextual indicators are present that suggest the author intended to change midstream the focus or theme of the list. Readers should always be aware, however, that the concept that they think holds the list together could be too narrow and needs to be broadened or vice versa.

Sixth, and most important, Paul regularly and repeatedly indicates the nature of his list. He does so in words that do not appear as part of the list itself. In the majority of cases (around 80 percent) in which he creates or uses a list, he somewhere besides in the list itself uses explicit words to identify what the list is a list of. For example,

- Romans 1:14 is a list of those to whom Paul is "obligated."
- Romans 8:35–36 is a list of all the things that cannot "separate us from the love of Christ."
- Romans 13:7 is a list of what believers should "pay to all what is due them."
- Second Corinthians 8:7 is a list of the ways that the Corinthians "excel."
- Ephesians 6:13–17 is a list of the "armor of God."
- Philippians 2:2 is a list of activities that the Philippians can do to "make my [Paul's] joy complete."
- Philippians 4:8 is a list of things that the Philippians should "think" about.
- Titus 3:1–2 is a list of what Paul wants Titus to "remind" the Cretan Christians to do.

The importance of this observation is that in each of the four ministry lists that will be studied in the following four chapters of this volume, Paul explicitly indicates how each list should be viewed. These indicators suggest what holds the particular list together and helps to explain why he chose to use a particular list, which is a central concern of this volume. What indicators did Paul include to identify the nature of the four lists that are the central interest of this present study?

1. The list in Ephesians 4:11–12 contains the following indicator: "for the *equipping* of the saints" (v. 12). Paul indicates that this list is a list of equippers that Christ has given to the church.

2. The list in Romans 12:3–8 contains the following indicator: "and all the *members* do not have the same *function*" (v. 4). When considered together with the *charismata* of verse 6, which also summarizes the list (vv. 6–8)—but whose meaning is one of the areas of contention of this book—Romans 12:6–8 should be read as a list of functions and members in their functions.

3. First Corinthians 12:27–31 contains the following indicator: "And God has *placed/appointed* in the church" (v. 28). This indicator works in tandem with *members* in the body metaphor (v. 27). Paul thus indicates that this list should be read as a list of appointments or placements, the first three of which (apostles, prophets, teachers) are members in their appointments.

4. First Corinthians 12:7–11 contains the following indicator: "But to each one is given *the manifestation of the Spirit*" (v. 7). Paul indicates that the list in 1 Corinthians 12:8–10 should be viewed as a list of activities that manifest the Spirit.

The following four chapters of this book examine each of Paul's ministry lists within the contexts in which they are found. The lists will be evaluated from shortest to longest: first Ephesians 4; then Romans 12; then the second list in 1 Corinthians 12; finally the first list in 1 Corinthians 12.[7] This is a reverse of the probable chronological order in which they were written.[8] But this arrangement has been chosen for three reasons.[9] First, this arrangement will allow the following chapters to be of similar length; since only four ministry roles appear in the Ephesians 4:11 list,[10] starting with that passage allows more attention to be given to the ministries of apostles and prophets, which two ministries appear in other lists (such as in 1 Cor. 12:28–30) also under examination.

Second, this arrangement begins with the passages that present the fewest interpretive difficulties (Eph. 4 and Rom. 12)[11] and moves toward the passage that presents the most (1 Cor. 12). Third, this arrangement will help to bring balance to a discussion that has been dominated by ideas derived from the first list in 1 Corinthians 12. It is my conviction that 1 Corinthians 12–14 has been given pride of place in these discussions simply because it is the longest and most detailed. Rather, it could, and probably should be argued that Ephesians 4 and Romans 12 represent more the way Paul usually dealt with spiritual ministries. This is likely so because Ephesians and Romans—out of all of Paul's letters—are the most general and the least situational. And in each of those cases, Paul's lists of ministry assignments come almost immediately after he makes the dramatic shift from the more doctrinal sections (Eph. 1–3; Rom. 1–11) to the more practical sections (Eph. 4–6; Rom. 12–15) of those letters. In contrast, 1 Corinthians is one of Paul's most situational letters. Thus, the probable reason the discussion is the longest in 1 Corinthians is because in that letter Paul is responding to specific problems and questions rather than more generally encouraging believers to build each other up in the faith, as in Ephesians and Romans.[12] This does not mean, of course, that Ephesians and Romans should be pitted against 1 Corinthians since the teachings found in all three letters are in concert with each other, and, indeed, thematically overlap. It does mean, however, that it would be wise to resist the impulse to force-fit the lists in Ephesians or Romans into notions that have traditionally been derived from the list in 1 Corinthians 12.[13]

You as reader may sometimes need to refer to the translations of the list passages found at the beginning of this book as you interact with the discussions in the next four chapters of this volume. You may also wish to have a Bible nearby for looking up references to passages outside of the four list passages. The following four chapters, then, are the heart of this present discussion.

NINE

The Lists in Context (Part 1)

Ephesians 4:11–12

Summary: Ephesians 4:11–12 is a list of equippers that Christ has given to the church. Six reasons support the idea that the items in the list are equipping roles rather than special abilities.

THE LIST ITSELF

And he gave the apostles, the prophets, the evangelists, the pastor-teachers for the equipping of the saints for the work of ministry leading to the building up of the body of Christ. (Eph. 4:11–12)

LOGIC AND FLOW OF THOUGHT OF EPHESIANS 4:1–16

EPHESIANS 4:1 TRANSITIONS between the doctrinal section (chaps. 1–3) and the applicational section (chaps. 4–6) of the book of Ephesians. In 4:2–6, Paul emphasizes the need for humility and for working together to preserve unity of the Spirit. Unity is, in fact, the theme that holds together the first sixteen verses of the chapter (vv. 3, 4–6, 13, 16). Paul emphasizes in this first passage the need to work toward unity (v. 3) through the exercise of humility (v. 2) and delineates the various areas in which those who have been called are united (vv. 4–6).

Paul then moves toward a discussion hovering around the words *give* and *gift* (not *charisma*) (vv. 7–8, 11). He says that grace has been given to individuals (v. 7), and individuals in their ministries have been given (v. 11) as equippers to the church (v. 12). His main point in verses 7–12 is that Christ's purpose for giving grace to individuals and for giving individuals (in their ministries) to the church is that the church might build itself up into a unified, mature body.

Verses 7–16 function for Paul as a unified thought. The list in verse 11 is to be read together with what comes before, particularly verses 7–8. What might make this cohesion less than obvious to a reader of this passage is that one of these verses is an Old Testament quotation (v. 8) and is followed by a two-verse digression about Christ's descent and ascent (vv. 9–10). So how do verses 7–8 lead into verse 11?

Paul says in verse 7, "But to each one of us grace was given according to the measure of the gift of Christ." Paul uses the dual mention of grace in verse 7—with its particular nuance[1] and the mention of the gift of Christ[2] (not *charisma*, but *dōrea*) in the same verse—to move his readers toward the list he presents in verse 11. Moreover, Paul quotes from Psalm 68:18 in verse 8 because it contains the last line "he gave gifts to men," and this also connects with the giving theme in verses 7 and 11.[3] Still, Paul cannot contain himself but digresses into a short comment on the ascent motif found in the same quotation ("when he ascended to the heights . . .") before returning to his topic.[4]

In verse 11, the "he gave" refers not to particular ministries given to individuals (as does the *grace* in v. 7, which has been *given*[5]), but to the persons functioning in their ministry roles.[6] And the recipients of this gift (of these persons in their ministries) are the saints—particularly those saints who are being equipped to do ministry (v. 12). Considering verses 11–12, then, it appears it should not be understood that the apostles, prophets, evangelists, and pastor-teachers themselves are to do the ministry; rather, the function of these persons in their ministries in this passage is the training of the saints to do the work of ministry.[7]

The purpose of such ministry is the "building up of the body of Christ" (v. 12) so that the church will reach a "unity of faith" and maturity (v. 13). The result of this building up, unity, and maturity will be a church that is not led astray by false doctrine and deceit (v. 14) but a church in which truth is spoken (v. 15) and where growth and the building up of the body occurs (vv. 15–16).

WHY THE CONVENTIONAL VIEW DOESN'T WORK IN EPHESIANS 4

There are six reasons why a special-ability reading of the items in the list in Ephesians 4 should not be accepted. Rather, the reading should be viewed as persons in their ministry roles.

REASON 1: SPECIAL ABILITY NEITHER STATED NOR IMPLIED

The idea of special ability is not stated in this passage, nor is it necessary to assume special ability to understand anything in the passage. The entire passage is about the unity, the building up, and the maturing of the church, which is accomplished when persons in their ministries equip believers to do the work of ministry.[8]

REASON 2: REFERENCE IS TO MINISTRY ROLES, NOT SPECIAL ABILITIES

The idea of equipping or preparing under which each of the items in the list is subsumed points toward ministry roles rather than toward abilities to do ministry. One who equips others to do ministry is involved in ministry himself. Perhaps these ministries should, in fact, be referred to as equipping ministries. The idea of equipping, which characterizes this list and holds it together, indicates that Ephesians 4:11 is a list of people in their ministries rather than people who are using special abilities.

REASON 3: "GRACE" HAS BEEN "GIVEN" AS A MINISTRY ASSIGNMENT, NOT AS SPECIAL ABILITIES

The expression "to each one of us grace was given" should cause readers who are familiar with the language of Paul to think about the ministries into which people (Paul included) have been called. In each of the twelve instances that Paul uses "grace" and "given" together in his letters, he always refers his readers to particular ministry assignments in the immediate context. Snodgrass comments on Paul's use of this expression in Ephesians 4:7, "Once again 'grace' has an unexpected meaning. It does not designate saving grace here, but grace for ministry, if indeed the two can be separated. Paul could as easily have written, 'To each of us *ministry* has been given.'"[9] Chapter 13 of this volume takes up this specific literary connection on its own.

REASON 4: ITEMS LISTED ARE MINISTRY ROLES, NOT SPECIAL ABILITIES

The individual items in the list, when found elsewhere in the New Testament, point toward ministry roles or ministry activities rather than abilities to do the ministry.[10]

Apostles (Eph. 4:11; 1 Cor. 12:28–29): The word *apostle* (*apostolos*) is used in the New Testament with greater flexibility than most English readers realize. It can signify people exercising either wide-ranging authority or very little authority, in either long-term or short-term assignments. But in no place where this word is used does any indication appear that there is a special ability attached to being an apostle. Rather, apostleship is always an appointment to a role. It would be difficult—perhaps even humorous—to attempt to formulate apostle into an ability designation, such as an apostolic ability. Apostles of all stripes do the work that they have been appointed to do. There is, of course, nothing new in this observation. Very few commentators attempt to posit an apostolic *ability*. But the recognition of how difficult it is to view apostle as an ability has not yet been incorporated into many people's general understanding of the area usually referred to as spiritual gifts. How, then, can all spiritual gifts be understood as abilities if one of the items in the list is understood not as an ability but as a ministry assignment? This idea of assignment is particularly important because both here in Ephesians 4:11 and in 1 Corinthians 12:28–30 Paul heads his list with "apostles." Shouldn't apostles' functions and roles, rather than some presumed—but unstated at any place in the Bible—ability form the basis for understanding the list that follows?

Prophets (Eph. 4:11; Rom. 12:6; 1 Cor. 12:10, 28–29): Like *apostle*, the word *prophet* is used broadly in the New Testament. In Ephesians 2:20 and 3:5, prophets stand alongside the apostles in the foundational establishment of the church. Elsewhere, prophets sometimes appear in less authoritative, short-term roles (cf. Acts 15:32; 21:9; 1 Cor. 14:29–32). People unfamiliar with the Bible often think of prophets merely as foretellers of events. This, indeed, is one aspect of at least some prophets' roles (Acts 11:28). More commonly in the New Testament, however, prophets are forthtellers who speak messages of revelation from God (1 Cor. 14:29–30) "for edification and encouragement and comfort" (1 Cor. 14:3). In the 1 Corinthians 12:10 discussion of prophecy, it will be argued that prophecy should be viewed as a ministry assignment accompanied by a special enablement. But the argument here emphasizes what is self-evident: that a prophet, like the others listed in Ephesians 4:11, functions in an equipping ministry role. Such a role is consistent with the rest of the New Testament, where prophets execute the community-strengthening ministry of declaring messages from God.

Evangelists (Eph. 4:11): The word *evangelist* is found only three times in the New Testament: Ephesians 4:11; 2 Timothy 4:5; Acts 21:8. What 2 Timothy 4:5 contributes to our discussion is significant: "But you, be sober-minded in everything, endure suffering, do the work of an evangelist, fulfill your ministry."[11] First, in 2 Timothy 4:5 an evangelist is described as one who does a work and not as having a special ability to do the work. Second, Paul immediately adds "fulfill your ministry" and then goes on in verse 6 to explain that he himself had "fought the good fight," thus implying that he had fulfilled his own ministry (cf. 1 Tim. 1:12). Timothy, then, had received a ministry (here described as "your ministry"), and his work as an evangelist certainly would have been included under that heading.[12] We know about "Philip the evangelist" (Acts 21:8, the other appearance of this word) because of the description of his ministry of evangelizing in Acts 8 (note esp. vv. 4, 12, 35, 40). Despite the lengthy narrative of Philip's evangelistic work, a special ability to evangelize is never implied; rather, Philip, like Timothy, had been entrusted with an evangelistic ministry.

Pastor-Teachers (Eph. 4:11): Is Paul referring to two roles here— pastors on the one hand and teachers on the other?[13] Or is he referring to one role—pastor-teachers, who are perhaps pastoring teachers or teaching pastors? Certainly, each ministry is viewed separately in other places in the New Testament (and can be studied separately), but in this case the grammar suggests that they are either a single role or possessing such overlapping boundaries that Paul wants to bring them together rather than separate them as he had the other roles.[14]

For the present study, it is important to recognize that throughout the New Testament outside of the list passages, there is no particular emphasis upon a teaching ability for one to become a teacher. In fact, the only place that in any way connects the idea of ability and teaching is 1 Timothy 3:2, in which a candidate for leadership has to be "able to teach" (*didaktikos*) to become an overseer (1 Tim. 3:2; cf. Titus 1:9)—that is, to become a pastor.[15] But it would be a mistake to interpret this single Greek word in 1 Timothy 3:2 as an inherent power that makes someone a good communicator, as the parallel qualifications list (Titus 1:5–9) makes clear. Titus 1:9 speaks of one who is "holding fast the faithful word which is in accordance with the teaching, so that he will be able both to exhort in sound doctrine and to refute those who contradict." In other words, an overseer/elder must be one who knows doctrine, and, for that reason, is able to instruct in what is right and wrong doctrine. Furthermore, the only other time that *didaktikos* ("able to teach") is used in the New Testament is in 2 Timothy 2:24, which is also about correcting those who err in their knowledge: "The Lord's servant must not be argumentative, but be kind to all, *able to teach . . .* with gentleness correcting those who are in opposition, if perhaps God may grant them repentance leading to the knowledge of the truth." First Timothy 3:2 should not, then, be appealed to as evidence for a special ability of the kind usually described in the conventional view of spiritual gifts. Rather, the ability referred to in 1 Timothy 3:2 is the knowledge of doctrine that is adequate to correct false teaching.[16] Moreover, teaching is not described as an ability elsewhere in the New Testament and it would be remiss to base a theology of spiritual gifts upon a single Greek word that is found outside of Paul's list passages.

To summarize reason 4, each of the individual items in this list fits comfortably with the notion of people in their ministries but not in each case with the idea of special abilities. This is not limited to, but is particularly noticeable in the case of the first item in the list: apostle.

REASON 5: MINISTRY ASSIGNMENT LINK WITH EPHESIANS 3:1–13

The literary links between Ephesians 3:1–13, where Paul describes his own ministry assignment, and Ephesians 4:7–16, where he talks about others in their own ministry assignments, are unmistakable. The two passages are connected by the expression "grace" + "given" (Eph. 3:2, 7, 8 with 4:7); they both speak about unity (3:6; 4:3–6, 13, 16) and of being a minister or doing ministry (3:7; 4:12); mentioned in both sections are apostles and prophets (3:5; 4:11) and evangelizing or evangelists (3:8; 4:11). Moreover, it should not be forgotten that these sections are separated from one another by only two paragraphs consisting of a prayer and a doxology. It could be argued that part of the doctrinal basis for 4:7–16 is Paul's discussion in 3:1–13.

Note that Paul's description of his own ministry assignment in Ephesians 3:1–13 prods readers to view the items in the list of 4:11 as people in their ministries rather than as abilities. Compare "apostles" in 4:11 with Paul's reference to his own apostleship as a "stewardship" in 3:2. Keep in mind, too, that a stewardship is an assignment and a role—no more and no less. Indeed, 3:1–13 is a summary of Paul's apostolic calling.

A further comparison between the passages can be made by contrasting "prophets" in 4:11 with 3:3, where Paul says that his understanding of the "mystery" came to him "by means of revelation" (cf. 1 Cor. 14:30). Paul certainly considered himself among the apostles and prophets to whom the mystery "has now been revealed" (3:5).[17] Also, "evangelists" in 4:11 can be compared with Paul's comment that this "grace was given to preach [euangelizō] to the Gentiles" in 3:8. Although nothing in Ephesians 3 corresponds directly to pastor-teachers in Ephesians 4, these other three connections solidly link those two chapters. These links are significant because they help readers to view the ministry roles of Ephesians 4:11 in relation to Paul's own stewardship as described in chapter 3, which included the ministry roles of apostle, prophet, and evangelist.

REASON 6: KEY TERMS HIGHLIGHT MINISTRY, NOT SPECIAL ABILITIES

The expressions "for the work of ministry" in 4:12 and "as each part does its work" in 4:16 are yet another reminder that Paul's ongoing concern is not with supposed abilities that each member has, but with the various ministries that are building up and bringing unity to the church. O'Brien says about verse 12, "The 'work of ministry' thus corresponds to 'the grace given to each of us' (v. 7), which is the subject of the section."[18]

It's difficult to read an ability concept into Ephesians 4:11. Suppose that this were the only list of its kind in the Bible. Would anybody read the items in this list as special Spirit-given abilities? Everyone would doubtless understand that these were labels of people in their particular ministry roles, and, in particular, people functioning in equipping roles. To understand otherwise requires forcing an ability idea onto this passage. Such would of necessity have to come from outside the passage, as the idea of ability is not found in the passage itself.

TEN

The Lists in Context (Part 2)

Romans 12:6–8

Summary: Romans 12:6–8 lists the diversity of ministry functions, people in those functions, and attitudes that should accompany those functions. Eight reasons are given to support this assertion.

THE LIST ITSELF

Whether prophecy, according to the proportion of faith, whether service, in serving, whether the one who teaches, in teaching, whether the one who encourages, in encouragement, the one who gives, in generosity, the one who leads, in diligence, the one who shows mercy, in cheerfulness. (Rom. 12:6–8)

LOGIC AND FLOW OF THOUGHT OF ROMANS 12

AS WITH EPHESIANS 4:1, Romans 12:1 initiates the second major section of this letter. The first two verses of the chapter transition the reader from the more doctrinal chapters of Romans (chaps. 1–11) to the more applicational ones (chaps. 12–15). With *therefore,* Paul moves the reader from a discussion of "the mercies of God"—that is from a discussion of all God has done through Christ as described in the first eleven chapters of Romans—to an exhortation to offer one's body as a living sacrifice (v. 1) and not be conformed to the world (v. 2). Properly, then, verses 1–2 should be viewed as an introduction to the second major section of Romans rather than simply as an introduction to the following verses, the verses to which this discussion now turns.[1]

Paul introduces this next important section (vv. 3–8) with a call to humility. Everyone, he says, should think properly[2] about themselves in relation to others—certainly not too highly, which is a problem he seems to anticipate. (As we all know, people rarely have a problem with being too humble.) Paul says that such humility is important because God has allotted differing amounts of faith to each person (v. 3).[3]

He then begins the long sentence[4] that continues from verse 4 to verse 8 with an analogy. He compares the physical human body (v. 4) that has many parts (limbs, organs) with the "body" of Christ (vv. 5–8) that has many parts (people in their ministries). The analogy actually consists of three elements, of which the third is the most important: (1) the body is a unity (cf. v. 4 "in one body" with v. 5 "one body in Christ" and "one of another"); (2) the body consists of various members, not just one (cf. v. 4 "many members" with v. 5 "the many" and "members individually one of another"); (3) the members have differing functions (cf. v. 4 "all the members do not have the same function" with vv. 6–8, which is a list of ministry functions that differ [v. 6] from member to member).

Two important shifts take place in the list itself (vv. 6–8). The first shift is from labels of general ministry functions to people in those functions (beginning at "the one who teaches," v. 7). The second is when the corresponding prepositional phrases move from the area or sphere of the ministry to the attitude or way in which the ministry is carried out (beginning at "in generosity," v. 8). (See appendix B for an English-annotated diagram of Rom. 12:4–8.)

What was Paul trying to accomplish when he wrote this important section (vv. 3–8)? His main concern was to encourage an attitude of humility by reminding the Christians in Rome that their functions differed from one another. His main point was not an encouragement to exercise special abilities, although this is how the conventional view often reads at least the second half of this section. Rather, Paul introduces the section discussing humility, then gives a list of various broad ministry functions—as well as the people in these functions and a few attitudes with which these functions should be carried out—in order to encourage humility.[5] Nobody, suggests Paul, does everything, and even those who serve in similar functions still differ in the ways they carry out their ministries.

In verses 9–21 Paul shifts the discussion to practical ways that love should be worked out among believers. Comparing the two sections, verses 3–8 could be described as acting in humility while performing activities that differ from the activities of others—that is, activities that every Christian isn't equally involved in—whereas verses 9–21 could be described as acting in love while performing activities that Christians perform in common—that is, activities that every Christian must do.

WHY THE CONVENTIONAL VIEW DOESN'T WORK IN ROMANS 12:3–8

Given below are eight reasons that a special abilities interpretation of the items in this list should not be accepted. Rather, the items should be viewed as functions, people in their functions, and attitudes with which the ministry functions should be performed.

REASON 1: USE OF THE WORD "FUNCTIONS"

Paul tells us explicitly that he is writing about "functions" (*praxis*, v. 4).[6] His use of this word in this key location is a substantial argument in support of the premise of this book. Paul begins his comparison between the physical body and the body of Christ as follows: "For just as we have many members in one body and all the members do not have the same function . . ." (v. 4). As was pointed out in chapter 8 of this volume, in perhaps 80 percent of the times

that Paul uses a list, he somehow identifies in explicit words what
the items are a list of. He has done the same here with his use of
the words *praxis* ("function") and *charismata* (v. 6). Since *praxis* is the
corresponding word in the analogy (notice the use of "have" before
both *praxis* and *charismata*), shouldn't this particular use of *charismata*
be understood to be indicating a function, as Paul seems to be
saying? Surely such an understanding is preferable to importing an
idea not stated in the text (special ability), then forcing that foreign
idea onto the word *charismata* to interpret the passage. (Readers may
wish to refer to chaps. 5–6 of this volume on the meaning of *charisma*
[plural *charismata*]). Dunn comments about how this key location
of the word *praxis* is often overlooked: "Too little noted is the use
of πρᾶξις, 'acting, activity, function' . . . and in what follows here
Paul thinks of charism as the function of the member, as the act of
ministry rather than as a latent gift which the gifted individual can
call on at will."[7] Paul's use of the word *function* is indeed crucial for a
proper understanding of the list in Romans 12.

REASON 2: USE OF THE BODY ANALOGY

The comparison of the physical body and the body of the
community of believers also indicates that a ministry-functional
reading is more appropriate to the context. Paul begins the comparison
in verse 4: "For just as we have many members in one body and all
the members do not have the same function . . ." Because Christian
readers are so familiar with body terminology, they often, without
realizing it, read verse 4 as though Paul were already discussing the
corporate body in that verse. This is understandable because verse
4 lacks any specific bodily terminology such as foot, ear, or eye as
in 1 Corinthians 12:15–17. But it is certain that verse 4 is about the
human body since Paul is comparing verse 4 with the verses that
follow ("Just as . . . ," v. 4; and "so . . . ," v. 5), and he could not be
comparing the body of Christ with the body of Christ for to do so
does not comprise an analogy.

What is important for our discussion are the labels *members* (that is, bodily limbs and organs) and *functions*. We have already highlighted functions under reason 1 above. Since this is an analogy and Paul is clearly comparing the physical body to the corporate body, it would be well to reflect for a moment on the significance of his use of the label *members*. In short, the designation of "members," because of its close proximity with "function" in the physical body (v. 4), should represent people-in-their-functions in the body-of-Christ verses that follow (vv. 5–8). We know that Paul intended this comparison because in verse 5 he says, "We are one body in Christ"—the "we" being persons in a corporate body (who, as individuals, are the "members" of v. 4).

Special abilities clearly do not work in this analogy. Unless one insists that the word *charismata* alone carries the weight of the special-abilities approach, special abilities are entirely unnecessary for an understanding of Paul's comparison with members of a human body.

REASON 3: UNITY OF THE LIST

There are good reasons to view verses 4–8 as one long sentence rather than as two sentences as they often appear in English translations. (Appendix B deals with this subject in detail.) But when an English speaking person reads with the assumption that Paul is talking about abilities and then reads a translation that begins a new sentence in verse 6, that person might assume that Paul is discussing two separate subjects in verses 4–8—the subject of unity in diversity in verses 4–5 and the subject of spiritual gifts (interpreted as special abilities) in verses 6–8. Granted, reading verses 4–8 as one rather than two sentences indeed strengthens the connection between the verses (see appendix B). Nonetheless, it should be noted that even were the two-sentences argument demonstrated, the second sentence (vv. 6–8) should still be interpreted as a list of functions and as a related, rather than an entirely new idea. As mentioned before, the physical body metaphor of verse 4 has three elements (the oneness, the many-ness, and the differing functions). But whereas the oneness and the many-ness ideas correspond to something in verse 5, the differing functions idea does not appear until verses 6–8. So conceptually—and probably grammatically as well—verses 4–5 must be read together with verses 6–8. Therefore, as has already been mentioned in reasons 1 and 2, verses 6–8 should be read in light of verses 4–5 and should reinforce the conviction that the items in this list should not be viewed as abilities but rather as the functions of the various members.

REASON 4: "GRACE" + "GIVEN" AS MINISTRY ASSIGNMENT

Paul's use of the "grace" + "given" expression, both in relation to himself (v. 3) and in relation to each person (v. 6), should prompt a reader familiar with his language to be alert for a discussion of ministry assignments. This is so because everywhere else Paul uses this combination, he refers his readers to ministry assignments in the immediate context. (Refer to chap. 13 in this volume and the comments on Eph. 4 in chap. 9.)

REASON 5: MOST ITEMS ON THE LIST POINT TOWARD MINISTRIES, NOT ABILITIES

Many of the individual items in the list beg to be viewed as ministry functions rather than as special abilities. Prophecy, as with Ephesians 4, is the only item in the list that of necessity entails a special enablement from God. But even people who are not indwelt by the Holy Spirit sometimes serve others, teach, exhort, financially give, lead, and show mercy. Granted, they have not been "allotted a measure of faith" (v. 3), but the types of service done by those who are indwelt by the Holy Spirit are not wholly different from the types of service rendered by those who are not indwelt. The point of a person's being or not being indwelt by the Holy Spirit is raised simply to highlight that the above activities are not immediately recognizable as requiring divine enablement to accomplish, and so probably should not, in and of themselves, be interpreted as special abilities. Nevertheless, people persist in reading them as abilities when these activities are, in fact, labels for general areas of service, or, as the list progresses, persons in their general areas of service.[8]

The service rather than ability reading can be illustrated by the mention of "the one who leads" in verse 8. Nowhere in Paul's letters are people encouraged to become leaders based upon special abilities that they have. In contrast, 1 Timothy 3:1–13 and Titus 1:5–9 (about qualifications for leadership) are lists of character qualities, not abilities.[9] We know how one gets into a position of leadership because 1 Timothy 3 and Titus 1 tell us, that is, when other leaders recognize the integrity of life and Christian character of a potential leader and then appoint that person to a leadership role, not by a potential leader discovering his leadership ability and then using it.

REASON 6: LOGICAL FLOW OF LIST

Using the conventional view, read in combination with the idea that these verses are two sentences, creates a problem in the logical flow of the passage. In particular, the subtle shift from functions to persons doing those functions in the first part of the pair, including a shift from the first-person plural to the third-person singular, is difficult to reconcile using the conventional view. The difficulty arises because, in the conventional view, there is underlying the entire discussion the assumption that a latent ability has been discovered and should be used by the person doing the ministry. Some translators find themselves in the uncomfortable position of adding an entire clause to verse 6 that does not exist in the Greek, trying to account for this idea that they know must be there. Thus, RSV adds "let us use them"; NIV adds "let him use it"; NASB adds "each of us is to exercise them accordingly." What, though, does it mean to use serving to serve? And once Paul has shifted from functions to persons in their functions, what then? How can one use a person?

Or, as the list progresses, are we as readers just supposed to forget about the suggested insertion "let us use them"?

REASON 7: RELATIONSHIP BETWEEN FUNCTIONS AND PERSONS IN THEIR FUNCTIONS

The ease with which Paul shifts from ministry functions to persons in their ministry functions also suggests that a functional reading rather than a special abilities reading of this list is correct. (This is also true in 1 Cor. 12:28–30, the list to be examined in the following chapter of this volume.) In two out of Paul's four lists, both in Romans 12:6–8 and in 1 Corinthians 12:28–30, he effortlessly— almost without thinking—moves from functions to persons in those functions. This shift makes sense in a functional—rather than special abilities—reading of the passage because of the close conceptual, and sometimes linguistic, relationship between a function and a person in a function. Although this all sounds a bit philosophical, it's not really that difficult. In the English language, if you ask someone what she or he does (that is, her or his function), that person might reply, "I'm an engineer" (the person in the function). If someone says, "I coach the volleyball team at X high school" (the function), this is very similar to saying, "I'm the volleyball coach at X high school" (the person in the function). Most languages, in fact, including Greek, widely use words that serve to express both a function and a person doing a function. In contrast, only on rare occasions do labels for abilities correspond to persons using abilities.[10] The point, once again, is that, in light of the conceptual nearness of functions and persons in their functions, Paul's almost effortless movement from functions to persons in their functions in Romans 12:6–8 (and vice versa in 1 Cor. 12:28–30) suggests that these are probably functions rather than abilities.[11]

REASON 8: PAUL CALLS FOR HUMILITY, NOT USE OF ABILITIES

The main point, or overall conception, of the passage also argues against the conventional view and for a ministry functions reading.

Paul puts this issue on the table immediately when he exhorts his readers (v. 3) "not to think more highly of yourself than you ought to think, but to think with sober judgment." His statement that "all the members do not have the same function" in verse 4 as well as the way he distributes the items in the list under the word *differing* in verse 6,[12] should be a reminder that Paul's main purpose in this passage is to encourage humility among members, not to persuade people to use or exercise their special abilities. This purpose is confirmed as he follows up the passage with a discussion of the practical outworking of humility and love in verses 9–21.

In conclusion, no reader of Romans 12:3–8 would read this passage as referring to special abilities unless told to read it that way. True, it is often assumed that the word *charismata* must indicate special abilities, and it is, of course, recognized that prophecy entails a need for special enabling. Nothing in the passage, though, suggests that the items in this list are special abilities. Rather, they all comfortably fall into the category of ministry functions.

Ministry functions even include prophecy, which is one of the most important ministry assignments described in the New Testament. Readers know of its importance, of course, partially because Paul ranks prophets second only to apostles in 1 Corinthians 12:28. And that list is the subject of the next chapter.

ELEVEN

The Lists in Context (Part 3)

1 Corinthians 12:28–30

Summary: First Corinthians 12:28–30 begins as a list of persons ("members") in their ministries whom God has placed or appointed in the church, then shifts to a list of ministries themselves. Five reasons are given to support this assertion.

THE LIST ITSELF

Whom also, on the one hand, God has appointed[1] in the church . . . first apostles, second prophets, third teachers, then miracles, then *charismata* of healings, helps, administrations, kinds of tongues. All are not apostles, are they? All are not prophets, are they? All are not teachers, are they? All do not do miracles, do they?[2] All do not have *charismata* of healings, do they? All do not speak in tongues, do they? All do not interpret, do they? (1 Cor. 12:28–30)

LOGIC AND FLOW OF THOUGHT OF 1 CORINTHIANS 12

TWO LISTS APPEAR in 1 Corinthians 12 (vv. 8–10 and 28–30), and chapters 11 and 12 of this volume are both devoted to a discussion of 1 Corinthians 12. An examination of the second list (vv. 28–30) follows later in this chapter. Here, though, begins a summary of the logic and flow of thought contained in the entirety of 1 Corinthians 12, rather than of just the verses surrounding the particular lists. Indeed, the entire chapter and, in fact, the whole of 1 Corinthians 12–14, is relevant for understanding the nature of both lists in 1 Corinthians 12.

First Corinthians 12 is well known for its many interpretive difficulties. In order to keep these difficulties from overwhelming the present study, the summary here aims simply to guide the reader into an understanding of the overall flow and sequence of the chapter and does not try to address each of the various problems. Only insofar as these interpretive issues relate to the concerns of this study will they be addressed in the "reasons" sections that follow in this chapter and the next chapter.

One useful way of grasping the main issues in 1 Corinthians 12 is by recognizing that the Corinthians have a set of issues about which they care very much. Paul, however, is concerned about a different set of issues. Simply put, the Corinthian Christians are highly interested in their "spiritual activities" (*pneumatika*);[3] Paul is interested in the ministries that build up the body of Christ. The Corinthians care about the miraculous;[4] Paul cares about ministries allotted by the Spirit, whether or not they are immediately recognizable as miraculous. Verses 1–11 should be read more as Paul's reaction to the Corinthians' intense interest in miraculous activities, and verses 12–31 should be read more as Paul's description of how the body of Christ is supposed to function.[5] In verses 1–11, Paul, of course, asserts his views even as he reacts to the Corinthians, and no doubt some of what he writes in verses 12–31 should be viewed as a response to the Corinthians' aberrations. But there is perceptible movement from reaction to assertion, from response to affirmation as the reader progresses through 1 Corinthians 12.

This suggestion of movement is reinforced by a striking technique of composition: Paul mentions the Holy Spirit eleven times in the first

thirteen verses of chapter 12 and then nowhere again in the second
half of chapter 12, or in chapter 13, or (perhaps) even throughout
chapter 14, where mention of the Holy Spirit would certainly be
expected in a discussion of tongues and prophecy.[6] It's not that Paul
considers the issues he discusses later to be separated from the work
of the Spirit, it's simply that he wants the Corinthians to think more
broadly about ministries, not solely about obvious ways that the
Spirit manifests himself.

That the list in verses 28–30 represents Paul's priorities, and that
the list in verses 8–10 represents the Corinthians' priorities constitutes
the main reason for looking at the second list in the passages before
looking at the first. In verses 28–30 Paul offers a representative list
of ministries, saying that some are more important than others; in
verses 8–10 he draws upon a list of ministries that are sensational and
that cause people to take notice. He presents the list in verses 8–10
first so that he can respond to the Corinthians' overemphasis on the
miraculous and instruct the Corinthians in the proper place of these
ministries in the body of Christ.

A walk through the logic of the passage will be instructive.
Verses 1–3 introduce the subject. Verse 1 signals that Paul is moving
into a new topic and is answering another of the questions that the
Corinthians had addressed to him. Verses 2–3 issue a warning that
any genuine word from the Spirit will affirm the Lordship of Jesus
and that any curse upon Jesus cannot be from the Spirit of God.[7] The
tenor of verses 2–3 reminds us that Paul is responding to problems he
believes are occurring in the Corinthian congregation.

In verses 4–6, Paul connects the three members of the Trinity
("Spirit," "Lord," and "God") with three words that together describe
the various ministry roles distributed to the church: *charismata*,
sometimes translated "gifts"; *diakoniai*, sometimes translated
"ministries" or "ways of serving";[8] and *energēmata*, sometimes
translated "workings" or "activities." Paul seems less concerned that
his readers understand that the ministries to which he is referring
are diverse, and more concerned that his readers understand who

distributed them and how their common source contributes to the unity of the church.

Verses 7–11 list various miraculous ministries of the Spirit that are described under the label of "the manifestation of the Spirit" (v. 7), which, Paul says, have been given "to each one . . . for the common good." That is, certain of the Spirit-given ministries show that the Spirit is particularly at work. These ministries are sovereignly distributed by the Spirit to each person (v. 11).

The heart of the chapter is verses 12–27, Paul's metaphor of the body.[9] Through his use of this metaphor, he emphasizes unity (vv. 12–13), diversity (vv. 12, 14, 27), as well as unity in diversity (vv. 15–17, 25). As with verses 4–6, the sovereign activity of the triune God is emphasized at key points in the discussion: *God* has placed (v. 18) members in the body of *Christ* (vv. 12, 27) by the *Spirit* (v. 13). All parts of the body, including the weaker ones, need each other (vv. 15–22). Weaker members should be shown honor (vv. 23–24) and ought to be cared for (vv. 25–26). Supporting the entire discussion of the body is the idea that the assorted members in their various roles should genuinely show care for each other so that the body is built up.

Finally, in verses 27–31, Paul lists the members of the body of Christ who function in the ministry roles in which God has placed or appointed them. The first three items in this list (v. 28) are persons in their appointed ministries that Paul ranks[10] first, second, and third—apostles, prophets, teachers. Paul then shifts from the persons in their ministries to the ministries themselves—miracles,[11] *charismata* of healings, helps, administrations, and kinds of tongues. In verses 29–30 he uses seven rhetorical questions, each of which in Greek expects a negative answer. In the process, he adds to the list of verse 28 the interpretation of tongues ("All do not interpret, do they?" v. 30). His point in using these seven rhetorical questions is similar to his teaching in his list in Romans 12—that God has appointed people to differing ministries in the body of Christ and the church needs all of them. Paul ends the section by encouraging the congregation to desire earnestly that the greater *charismata* be exercised in their midst.[12]

Although it is possible to discuss 1 Corinthians 12 alone, it nonetheless belongs with 1 Corinthians 13 and 14. Thus, a few comments will be made here about those chapters. In 1 Corinthians 13, Paul delays his specific instructions of how tongues and prophecy should function in a Christian meeting so he can extol the importance of love over and against the sensational, temporary activities that the Corinthians were so interested in. It is worth noting that just after his list in Romans 12:9–21, he introduces the importance of love in action, and in 1 Corinthians 13 he makes a similar point by employing a highly stylized poem of love.[13]

First Corinthians 14 addresses the one miraculous ministry that Paul apparently considered to be most out of balance at Corinth—that of tongues. He gives guidelines for the use of tongues in the assembly and compares it with prophecy, which he considers to be far more useful in a Christian meeting than tongues.

WHY THE CONVENTIONAL VIEW DOESN'T WORK IN 1 CORINTHIANS 12:27–31

Five reasons can be presented as to why a special abilities reading of the items in this list should not be accepted. Rather, the first three items in the list should be viewed as people in their ministry appointments and the last five (plus a sixth in v. 30) as appointed ministries themselves.

REASON 1: GOD'S "PLACEMENT" OF THEM WITHIN THE CHURCH

Paul explicitly states in verse 28 that God has placed or appointed in the church what follows.[14] Shouldn't, then, the list that follows be read as a list of ministry placements, or ministry appointments? Reading the list as such becomes vital considering that the language and structure is parallel to verse 18. Found in the middle of the body metaphor, that verse says, "But now God has placed the members, each one of them, in the body, just as He wanted." It makes very little difference whether we translate this Greek word (*tithēmi*) as "placed" or "appointed"; with either reading, it's clear that Paul's intention is to say that God has placed people in the church to serve in particular ministries, which is another way of saying that God has appointed people to those ministries. If, however, "appointed"—rather than "placed"—is used, as many translations do, care should be taken not to read an official nuance into "appointed," since this list seems to be more functional and less formal, although such distinctions are often overstated.[15] Returning to the main idea, Paul's statement, regardless of the precise nuance, clearly indicates that what follows is a list of ministry placements, or ministry appointments. Such seems almost undeniable, and also is one of the fundamental arguments for the premise of the present study.

To illustrate, let's say that you read an internal memo of a large corporation that started with the words, "The president has appointed in the corporation . . ." What would likely complete the predicate of that sentence? Most of us would assume we were about to read that a particular person had been appointed to a particular task: ". . . John Smith to head up a task force to implement a new marketing plan." We wouldn't expect to see a list of abilities: ". . . has appointed in the corporation leadership, speaking prowess, and forecasting achievements." Similarly, suppose we were to read an advertisement for a college that boasted, "Our school places 98 percent of our graduates within six months of their graduation." You wouldn't assume that the advertisement referred to placing the skills that their graduates had learned: "Our school places leadership, computer literacy, and marketing savvy." Rather, you'd assume that the advertisement referred to the positions that the graduates accepted in the workforce: "Our school places managers, accountants, and marketing specialists." So it is with 1 Corinthians 12:28: "God has appointed/placed in the church . . ." What follows are people who serve in the places of ministry to which God has appointed them.

REASON 2: LIST OF MEMBERS, NOT ABILITIES

Consider verse 27, which immediately precedes the list: "Now you all[16] are the body of Christ and individually members of it." In light of verse 27, verse 28 can also be read—at least the first three items in the list—as a list of members, that is, body parts, rather than as abilities. Verse 27 is thus an important verse in the context because it summarizes the entire body metaphor that comes before (vv. 12–26), and makes the transition into the following section, which contains the list (vv. 27–31). Indeed, almost all translations rightly begin the new section with verse 27 and thus signal its relevance for understanding the list that follows. Moreover, it is a grammatical necessity to read verse 28 in light of verse 27, because in Greek verse 28 begins with a relative pronoun, "whom" *(hous)*—a pronoun that also functions as the direct object of the verb but is usually left out of our English translations in order to avoid awkwardness. Nevertheless, this pronoun connects the verses and makes it imperative that these verses be read together, rendering it appropriate that the list that follows be read as a list of members rather than as a list of abilities.

REASON 3: THE BODY METAPHOR

Flowing out of the above insight and related to it is the recognition of how important is the flow of thought contained in the whole of 1 Corinthians 12, particularly the relevance of reading this list in light of Paul's extended analogy in verses 12–26 between the human body and the body of Christ. As mentioned in chapter 7, the body metaphor is all about the various roles into which God has placed people. It is necessary to read the list in this light because, among other things, the "God has placed" terminology found both in verses 18 and 28 pulls these passages together. Since there is no hint of special abilities in the body metaphor, and it is indefensible to introduce the idea if nothing suggests it, the reader should also be reticent to introduce special abilities as the organizing framework for the list in verses 28–30.

REASON 4: MOVEMENT FROM MINISTRY TO PERSONS IN THOSE MINISTRIES

The noticeable shift in the passage from persons in their God-appointed ministries to the ministries themselves once again argues that ministry rather than ability should be the organizing idea of the list. Such has already been argued in the discussion of Romans 12, since Paul does something similar there. It is intriguing that in two out of four of Paul's lists (Rom. 12:6–8; 1 Cor. 12:28–30) he shifts midpassage either from ministries to persons in their ministries (as in Rom. 12:6–8), or from persons in their ministries to the ministries themselves (as here in 1 Cor. 12:28–30). The ease with which he makes the shift between persons and ministries argues for a close conceptual link between the idea of an appointment to a ministry and the ministry itself. It was shown in the previous chapter on Romans 12:6–8 how this argument works more fully. Here, suffice it to add that the movement is not one-way—Paul can move from ministries to persons (so Rom. 12:6–8) or from persons to ministries (as here, in 1 Cor. 12:28–30), which indicates even more strongly how close were these concepts in his mind. This easy shifting between persons and ministries once again suggests that ministries, rather than abilities, is the conceptual framework that holds together this list, 1 Corinthians 12:28–30, and Romans 12:6–8.[17]

REASON 5: SOME OF THE LISTED ITEMS THEMSELVES

Some of the listed items themselves argue against a conventional reading of this passage. When Paul starts his list with apostles, prophets, and teachers—and gives priority to them—it cannot help but remind his readers of his very similar list in Ephesians 4:11–12, "And he gave the apostles, the prophets, the evangelists, the pastor-teachers." The same three items—apostles, prophets, and teachers—are found there in the same order. Only evangelists (found a mere three times in the entire New Testament) and pastors (found in this sense only in Eph. 4:11 among Paul's writings) are missing from the list in 1 Corinthians 12:28–30.

That apostles, prophets, and teachers appear in both lists suggests two things. First, three ministries were thought of by Paul as most important for the church, namely, the apostolic ministry, prophecy, and teaching. When after the list he tells the Corinthians to desire earnestly the greater *charismata* (v. 31), he may be referring more particularly to these three. Second, in 1 Corinthians 12:28–30 Paul is drawing up a list that is somewhat similar to the list in Ephesians 4:11.[18] Such is confirmed by his comments before each list that God has given to, or has placed in, the church persons in their ministries. This might also imply that in both places he is thinking along similar lines and that these first three items in 1 Corinthians 12:28, as in Ephesians 4:11, should be thought of as persons (in their ministries) that God has placed in, and thus given to, the church.[19]

In addition to these three not likely being meant as abilities, it is highly unlikely that helps and administrations would be thought of as abilities were it not for the mere assumption, based upon the influence of the conventional view, that these must be abilities. Each, rather, seems to point toward some sort of administrative role. There is disagreement about the exact nature and extent of authority (or lack thereof) of these roles, but there seems to be some merit, as J. Knox suggests, in linking helps and administrations with the roles of deacons and overseers respectively.[20] Regardless of the exact connotation of helps and administration, Fee hits the nail on the head when he comments regarding administration that "it would be a far cry from what Paul had in mind" to think of this item as "administrative skills."[21] In other words, it is unnecessary to read skills or abilities into helps and administration when there is no reason to do so.

The only other items in verse 28 are miracles, *charismata* of healings, and kinds of tongues. Verse 30 adds interpretation of tongues when Paul says, "All do not interpret, do they?" Since these are inextricably linked with the list found earlier in the chapter (vv. 8–10), it is preferable to look at those items in the contexts in which they were first introduced. To those the following chapter now turns.

TWELVE

The Lists in Context (Part 4)

1 Corinthians 12:8–10

Summary: First Corinthians 12:8–10 is a list of ministries that manifest the Spirit. Various arguments are presented that the items in the list can be viewed both within the narrower category of Spirit-given abilities and within the broader category of Spirit-assigned ministries.

THE LIST ITSELF

> For to one is given a word of wisdom by the Spirit, and to another a word of knowledge according to the same Spirit, to another faith by the same Spirit, to another *charismata* of healings by the same Spirit, and to another workings of powers, to another prophecy, to another discerning of spirits, to another types of tongues, to another interpretation of tongues. (1 Cor. 12:8–10)

THE LOGIC AND flow of thought of this passage has already been summarized in the previous chapter. This present chapter looks at the nature of this first list in 1 Corinthians 12 and at arguments for viewing the list items both in the narrower category of abilities and in the broader category of ministries. More particularly, it will be proposed that abilities should be understood as a subset of ministries. O'Brien's comment on this passage summarizes it well: "In 1 Corinthians 12:4–11 the 'varieties of gifts' are the diverse ministries allocated by the Spirit and the ability to exercise them."[1]

The reader will remember that, in the summary of 1 Corinthians 12 at the beginning of the previous chapter, the first list in 1 Corinthians—the list before us (vv. 8–10)—represents the activities in which the Corinthians were most interested, whereas the latter list in 1 Corinthians 12 (vv. 28–30) is more representative of the way Paul wanted to present these issues. It could be said that list 1 (vv. 8–10) represents the Corinthians' vision of the church and list 2 (vv. 28–30) represents Paul's vision of the church. List 1 is what the Corinthians were pursuing; list 2 is what Paul was pursuing. List 1 contains the more exciting ministries; list 2 is a representative mix of various ministries.[2] Paul seems to affirm a valid place for the exercise of each of the items in this first list (vv. 8–10), but presents them primarily because he intends to minimize their importance and argue for the necessity of each member ministering to one another in the roles that God has assigned to each, even if those ministries appear more mundane.

ARGUMENTS FOR MIRACULOUS SPIRIT-GIVEN ABILITIES

The conventional approach views the list in 1 Corinthians 12:8–10 as a list of Spirit-given abilities, and in one sense that is a valid perspective—at least for this list. But there are two aspects of this particular list that stand out as different from Paul's other lists. First, for all the items in this list, the power of the Holy Spirit is obvious when these activities occur. For this reason, these items are grouped together and are referred to as the "manifestation of the Spirit."

Second, for the items in this list, enablement is a prerequisite for the activities. In some of the other ministries found in Paul's other lists (for example, administration, service, teaching), enablement is not as noticeable and the activity can be done, at least to some degree, through the employment of natural abilities.[3] Such is not the case for the items in 1 Corinthians 12:8–10, for which an obvious ("manifestational") work of the Spirit is necessary to even think about performing these ministries. And since enablement is obvious for the items in this list and inextricably linked with the activity, it seems a proper perspective to view them, at least on one level, as Spirit-given abilities. Arguments for the validity of viewing the items in this list through the lens of ability are listed below, followed by arguments for viewing them through the broader perspective of ministries.

ABILITY ARGUMENT 1: THE MANIFESTATION OF THE SPIRIT

The organizing description for the list is the expression "the manifestation of the Spirit." This expression, as it stands, suggests less the idea that the list is a list of abilities (although it does suggest that) and more that the items in the list particularly manifest, or show, the Spirit.[4] Notice also in this regard the preponderance throughout the list of expressions like "by the Spirit" that serve to emphasize the noticeable activity of the Spirit. It is thus probably valid to infer that when the Spirit manifests in the life of a believer, that believer is able to do something that could not otherwise have been done and thus the expression points toward an ability idea.

ABILITY ARGUMENT 2: EMPHASIS ON THE MIRACULOUS

A surface reading of this list will immediately alert a reader that it is, at the very least, more miracle oriented than any of Paul's other lists. Healings, miracles (literally, "powers"), certain aspects of prophecy, discernment of spirits,[5] tongues, and interpretation of tongues stand out to most readers as being of a class that is more miraculous than many of the items in Paul's other lists (esp. Eph. 4:11 and Rom. 12:6–8). Although attempts have been made to view some of the items in 1 Corinthians 12:8–10 as more mundane ("word of wisdom," say, as a wise word; "word of knowledge" as knowing doctrine; "faith" as a private matter), it is unlikely that this is the correct way to view any of them.[6]

Knowledge, for instance, is linked in 1 Corinthians 13:8–9 into a triad with tongues and prophecy—and contrasts with love—which strongly suggests that this knowledge is of a more spectacular type. Moreover, 1 Corinthians 13:2 introduces four items, each of which has parallels in the list of 1 Corinthians 12:8–10: (1) "Prophecy," which, at least sometimes, appears overtly miraculous; (2) "I know all mysteries," which parallels "word of wisdom"; (3) "knowledge," which parallels "word of knowledge"; (4) "faith so as to remove mountains," which, of course, parallels "faith."[7] Particularly significant is that the content of knowing in 1 Corinthians 13:2 is "all mysteries," and faith is of such a kind that mountains get removed, each of which suggests a more visible and manifestational sort of activity. When other items, along with knowledge, in a list are so, one should assume that "knowledge" is also overtly miraculous, particularly as it contrasts with the general activity of love. For these reasons, it is far more reasonable to view each item in the 1 Corinthians 12:8–10 list as overtly Spirit-manifestational, even if one can imagine other less manifestational ways to construe a few of the items. Mutually supportive of this manifestational idea is the connection between the "manifestation of the Spirit" in 1 Corinthians 12:8–10 and the "demonstration of the Spirit and of power" idea in 1 Corinthians 2:4–5, which points to an empowering for these items (cf. "power of God").

ABILITY ARGUMENT 3: THE MISSING ITEMS

Notice the items that are missing from the list: apostles, helps, administration, teaching, evangelist, service, exhortation, giving, leading, mercy. None of these items from Paul's other lists are particularly breathtaking, whereas every item in the list of 1 Corinthians 12:8–10 can be plausibly interpreted as overtly manifestational and inextricably linked with Spirit enablement.

What is missing from the list, in itself, suggests that the nature of the list is that of more awe-inspiring ministries of the Spirit, which, along with its constant link with the enablement of the Spirit, suggests that these items can be viewed as Spirit-given abilities.[8]

In light of these observations, there is, indeed, a probability that, were Paul able to comment today on whether the particular items in the list of 1 Corinthians 12:8–10 are abilities, he would respond, "Yes, they all require ability from the Holy Spirit to do them. But I really want you to view them as taken together with all the ministries that God has given to the church." To that issue the section below now turns.

ARGUMENTS FOR MINISTRIES: WHY THE CONVENTIONAL VIEW IS INADEQUATE IN 1 CORINTHIANS 12:7–11

Even granting that the items in this particular list could be described as abilities, plain indicators in the text point to viewing them as ministries, the same as has been argued for Paul's other lists. More precisely, Paul is incorporating the items in this list—which the Corinthians viewed as abilities—into the larger category of ministry roles and functions. Stated yet differently, the list in 1 Corinthians 12:8–10 can be viewed as abilities that are also a subset of all the activities that Paul categorizes as ministries, as already diagrammed in chapter 2 of this volume:

All are ministries

Some are also abilities
(1 Cor. 12:8–10)

Just as

- *House pets* is a subset of *animals*;
- *Ball sports* (basketball, soccer, etc.) is a subset of *sports*;
- *Two-person professions* (piano moving, doubles ice skating) is a subset of *professions*;
- *Thinking games* (chess, Scrabble) is a subset of *games*.

The list in 1 Corinthians 12:8–10, then, is a subset of Paul's broader category labeled as ministry roles or ministry assignments. This list is different, however, from Paul's other lists insofar as Spirit-given ability is necessary for performing these activities. But one of the reasons that Paul even includes this list here is to communicate to the Corinthians that they have focused too narrowly on the special-abilities aspect of this list. He wants them to recognize the ministry focus, that is, the part that each person's ministry plays in the building up of the body of Christ. A number of indicators in this passage suggest that such is what Paul was thinking. Following are arguments that the items in this list (vv. 8–10) should not be read merely under the more narrow abilities category but also should be read under the broader ministries category.

MINISTRY ARGUMENT 1: PROPER EMPHASIS ON CHARISMATA

The abilities view usually isolates the word *charismata* out of verses 4–6, arguing that the items in verses 8–10 should also be read under the heading of *charismata*.[9] But if the contention presented earlier is correct—that those three words (*charismata*, sometimes translated "gifts"; *diakoniai*, sometimes translated "ministries"; and *energēmata*, sometimes translated "workings") work together to describe the various ministries that are distributed to the church[10]—it will not do to pull out *charismata*, load on it the entire ability theology, and then use that idea to interpret the list that follows solely as Spirit-given abilities. Rather, the three words together appear to have been chosen by Paul to introduce his discussion of activities that strengthen the community of faith. Nor should readers fail to factor in nuances suggested by his choice to include "ministries" (v. 5) and "workings" (v. 6) in parallel with *charismata* in verses 4–6.[11] These two words certainly suggest a ministry and functional focus for everything he discusses in the chapter, including this list.

MINISTRY ARGUMENT 2: PROPER UNDERSTANDING OF BODY ANALOGY

The list under current study is followed by Paul's metaphor of the body (vv. 12–27). The importance of this metaphor for understanding 1 Corinthians 12 has already been discussed.[12] The body metaphor is, indeed, the heart of 1 Corinthians 12 and its longest section, taking up, as it does, half of the chapter. Since the metaphor comes on the heels of this list, it appears that Paul is trying to draw focus away from the more sensational ministries that are found in this list and focus on how each member of the body in its given role is necessary and should be honored. The connection between the body metaphor and the previous list is cemented grammatically through an explanatory conjunction (*gar*) that is usually translated "for." As Fee states, "The 'for' with which this sentence begins indicates that what follows is intended to offer further explanation of the point made in verses 4–11."[13]

In addition, Paul uses a comparative conjunction (*kathaper*), which "regularly introduces an analogical comparison, and means *even as* or *just as*."[14] Although the connecting words are sometimes omitted in English translations, they help us to see the connection with the previous discussion and the analogical nature of the metaphor that follows. And what do we learn from Paul's use of this metaphor? The members of the body have roles that need to be valued by all so that unity is maintained.

MINISTRY ARGUMENT 3: PROPHECY AND TONGUES

The extended discussion of prophecy and tongues in 1 Corinthians 14 makes the case that Paul views—and wants the Corinthians to view—prophecy and tongues as ministries that are to build up the body of Christ. Paul's discussion of these two items in 1 Corinthians 14 serves as a guide toward viewing these as ministries, not merely as abilities. Consider each in turn.

Prophecy. Paul exhorts the Corinthians to desire earnestly to prophesy (14:1). He explains, "But one who prophesies speaks to men for edification and encouragement and comfort" (14:3). Each of these three items—edification, encouragement, and comfort—suggests the ministry aspect of prophecy. Paul simply states in verse 4 that "one who prophesies edifies the church." Furthermore, he says in 14:24 that when everyone prophesies, an unbeliever who comes into their midst "is convicted by all, he is judged by all, the secrets of his heart are shown, and thus falling on his face he will worship God." In 14:31 Paul says, "For you can all prophesy one by one, so that all may learn and all may be encouraged." Each of these statements in 1 Corinthians 14 highlights the ministry focus of prophecy.

Moreover, the mention of prophets or prophecy in each of the four of Paul's ministry lists suggests both the importance of this activity to Paul and that the list in 1 Corinthians 12:8–10 can be read, like these other passages, as a list of ministries.

Tongues. In some ways, Paul's discussion of tongues in 1 Corinthians 14 provides one of the strongest pieces of evidence that he wants to include all the items in this list (1 Cor. 12:8–10) under the framework of ministry. Tongues is, after all, more than almost any other item in the list, easiest to view not as a ministry. It appears that the Corinthians themselves failed to focus on the ministry aspect of tongues but focused on its sensational nature and that they were able to speak in tongues. They extolled their special ability, but it was not contributing to the ministry of the church. In fact, it was having a detrimental effect on both the internal ministry (14:6, 8, 11–12, 17) and the outreach (14:23) of the church, and Paul was evidently upset about it. It is not that Paul altogether opposed the use of tongues—quite to the contrary. For he writes, "Now I would like all of you to speak in tongues, but even more that you would prophesy" (1 Cor. 14:5). He comments on his own participation—"I thank God, I speak in tongues more than all of you" (14:18)—and later instructs the congregation "do not forbid to speak in tongues" (14:39). But he certainly wants to minimize the importance of tongues when the Corinthians assemble, regulate its use, and emphasize that the activity of tongues-speaking is valid for the building up of the body of Christ only if a tongue is interpreted.

Thus, when the congregation meets together, the only way for tongues to function as ministry is when the tongues are interpreted. So Paul says, "greater is the one who prophesies than one who speaks in tongues, unless he interprets, so that the church may receive edifying" (14:5). That Paul tries to bring a use of tongues into balance should not, however, preclude his thinking that there is ministry value in tongues when they are interpreted. He states that the purpose of these "spiritual things"—tongues included—is "the edification of the church" (14:12). Thus, Paul says that the one who speaks in a tongue should pray that he may interpret (14:13). He wants other people to share in the praise that would be offered through tongues (14:16–17) so they also can be edified (14:17). Tongues are included among the various activities done during a worship service to which Paul exhorts, "Let all things be done for edification" (14:26).

So what should be the response when someone asks, "Is tongues really a 'ministry'?" If ministry is defined, as it has been throughout this book, as any activity, whether performed long-term or short-term, that builds up the body of Christ, then tongues without a doubt qualifies as a ministry. Paul's drawing direct connections in the verses referenced above between tongues and edification of the church demonstrates the ministry aspect of tongues. Although a tongue may be spoken for only twenty seconds, if it is interpreted it becomes ministry because the hearer is edified as he or she shares in the praise offered by the tongues-speaker.

In 1 Corinthians 14, Paul's emphasis on ministry orientation is clear in regard to both prophecy and tongues. Shouldn't, then, the ministry orientation of these activities be recognized in 1 Corinthians 12:8–10?

MINISTRY ARGUMENT 4: "WORKINGS OF POWERS"

The list in 1 Corinthians 12:8–10 includes the expression "workings of powers." The word sometimes translated "workings" is *energēmata*, the same word as is found in the third position in the triad of verses 4–6 as one of the three words that together describe the activities of a congregation. It points toward the activity of doing miracles, which is why *energēmata* is sometimes translated simply as "activities."[15] And it, thus, suggests the possibility of reading the items in the list functionally.

MINISTRY ARGUMENT 5: MOVEMENT FROM MIRACULOUS TO FUNCTIONALITY

Finally, the movement in the chapter toward the list at the end of 1 Corinthians 12 (vv. 28–30) encourages us to view the items in this list (vv. 8–10) also as ministries. These two lists contain nine items each; five of them overlap, although the form and order is different.[16] Since these items are found in the more functional list in verses 28–30, some sort of functionality can be understood as well in verses 8–10. It is true that the Corinthians were not very concerned about the ministry focus of these items, and Paul probably drew up the list in verses 8–10 so he could correct their overemphasis on their abilities. But he is trying to send the Corinthians a message of how these activities ought to be viewed as he works his way through this chapter to its end, which suggests that Paul viewed the items in the list in verses 8–10 under the category of ministries as well.[17]

When my two daughters were in elementary school, my wife and I would play a game with them at the dinner table that we called "categories." We'd begin listing particular items and they would have to identify the category. "Apples, oranges, bananas, peaches."

They would cry out, "Fruit." "Math, science, reading, writing." They would moan, "School subjects." In each list considered in the previous four chapters of this book, the likely nature of each list has been identified by means of indicators within the lists and their surrounding contexts, rather than by importing foreign concepts about what those lists should be. It seems conclusive that each item in each list somehow fits into the category of ministry— either ministry assignments themselves or people in those ministry assignments. Reading this book, you are certain to be wondering how putting these insights into practice might affect what we do in the church today. Practical implications and applications will be discussed toward the end of this book. Before placing these passages into the context of Paul's general theology, though, and applying insights to our present day, it is first necessary to examine one more noteworthy argument for these passages being viewed as ministry assignments rather than abilities.

THIRTEEN

"Grace" That Has Been "Given"

An Important Connection

Summary: The literary connections of "grace" + "given" found both in the list passages and elsewhere in Paul's writings indicate that ministry assignments rather than special abilities are Paul's central concerns in the list passages.

THE CONVENTIONAL VIEW of spiritual gifts as abilities disconnects the list passages (Eph. 4; Rom. 12; 1 Cor. 12) from the rest of Paul's letters. It does so because Paul doesn't make a Christian's abilities the focus of his discussion anywhere else.

But significant literary and thematic connections do exist between the list passages and other sections in Paul's letters. These parallels in language and theme allow movement between the list passages and other passages in Paul and broaden the understanding of his concerns in the list passages.

To underscore the importance of thematic parallels, an analogy will be helpful. Most people drive the same route every day to and from work. Similarly, most of my college students sit in the same seat every time they come into the classroom. Something similar often occurs at the level of communication. The thoughts of humans move down familiar, well-worn trails, and we often express those thoughts in similar ways. The way I answer questions in the classroom, for example, reflects that I've answered a particular question before in a previous semester. I tend to explain things in similar ways, citing similar passages, employing similar language, and rehashing well-worn and proven illustrations. Paul does the same. Whenever he talks about particular God-given ministries, he tends to rely on certain patterns of communication. One of these, an expression that Paul uses repeatedly, is particularly significant to the present discussion.

The single most important of such connections is Paul's use of "grace" (*charis*) in conjunction with "given" (*didōmi*).[1] This expression is particular to Paul, and whereas he uses it repeatedly, no other New Testament writer uses it.[2]

What is notable for this current study is that in every case that Paul uses the "grace" + "given" combination he discusses particular ministry assignments in the immediate context, either his own assignment or those of others. This connection is a substantial observation in its own right and constitutes a potent argument that Paul's similar use in the list passages infers similar concepts there.[3]

First, notice the central role that the combination of "grace"+ "given" plays in two of the list passages—Ephesians 4 and Romans 12.

- Ephesians 4:7: "But to each one of us *grace* was *given*."
- Romans 12:3: "for through the *grace* that has been *given* to me I say."
- Romans 12:6: "but having *charismata* that differ according to the *grace* that has been *given* to us."

Also relevant is 1 Corinthians 12:7: "But to each one is *given* the manifestation of the Spirit for the common good."[4]

Second, observe the clear literary parallels in the following phrases also written by Paul:

- Romans 15:15: "because of the *grace* that was *given* to me by God."

- 1 Corinthians 1:4: "because of the *grace* of God that was *given* to you in Christ Jesus."
- 1 Corinthians 3:10: "according to the *grace* of God that was *given* to me."
- 2 Corinthians 8:1: "the *grace* of God that has been *given* in the churches of Macedonia."
- Galatians 2:9: "and recognizing the *grace* that was *given* to me."
- Ephesians 3:2: "the stewardship of the *grace* of God that was *given* to me."
- Ephesians 3:7: "according to the gift of the *grace* of God that was *given* to me."
- Ephesians 3:8: "To me, the least of all the saints, this *grace* was *given*."
- 2 Timothy 1:9: "according to his own purpose and *grace* that was *given* to us in Christ Jesus."[5]

In a few other places, as well, Paul uses "grace" and "given" together in his letters, but those listed above are the only instances that possess structural similarities to the list passages.[6] The structural parallels force a more careful consideration of the thematic relationships of these passages to one another.

Looking more closely at each of these passages in turn, notice the discussion of particular ministries that enters each of these passages whenever Paul uses the "grace" + "given" expression. Sometimes the ministries are his own; sometimes they are the ministries of others.

ROMANS 15:15–19

> But I have written to you boldly in part so as to remind you—on account of the *grace* that was *given* to me by God, that is, to be a minister of Christ Jesus to the Gentiles, serving as a priest the gospel of God—that the offering of the Gentiles might become pleasing, sanctified by the Holy Spirit. Therefore I have reason

> to boast in Christ Jesus in what I have done for God.
> For I am not bold to speak of anything except what
> Christ has accomplished through me leading to the
> obedience of the Gentiles—in word and deed, in
> the power of signs and wonders, in the power of the
> Spirit—so that from Jerusalem and round about to
> Illyricum, I have fully preached the gospel of Christ.
> (Rom. 15:15–19)

As stated explicitly in this passage, the grace of God that was given to Paul is his ministry assignment to preach the gospel to the Gentiles. He refers to this assignment in various ways as (1) being a minister, (2) serving as a priest, (3) what he has done for God, (4) what Christ has accomplished through him, and (5) fully preaching the gospel. These are all references to Paul's central ministry assignment, which chapter 16 of this volume will address in more detail. This passage strongly supports the assertion that each time Paul uses the "grace" + "given" combination in his letters, he has God-given ministries on his mind. Moreover, the grace that Paul is describing is not simply general favor upon him; it is the grace of placing him into ministry.

1 Corinthians 1:4–7

> I thank my God always for you because of the *grace*
> of God that was *given* to you in Christ Jesus, that
> you have been made rich in him in every way, in all
> speech and in all knowledge, just as the testimony
> of Christ was established among you; so that you do
> not lack in any *charisma*[7] while you eagerly await the
> revelation of our Lord Jesus Christ. (1 Cor 1:4–7)

This passage probably anticipates to some degree the discussion that Paul will take up in 1 Corinthians 12–14. The "grace" + "given" connection is present here (as in Eph. 4 and Rom. 12) as is the use of the word *charisma* (as in 1 Cor. 12 and Rom. 12), establishing a literary connection between the passages. But as was already stated in the study of the word *charisma* in chapter 5 of this volume, Paul speaks too generally in 1 Corinthians 1:4 for the word *charisma* to indicate clearly on its own whether he in this passage is pointing toward special abilities (the conventional view) or spiritual ministries.

Paul does, however, refer to ministry activities when he mentions "speech/word" in verse 5 and the "testimony of Christ" in verse 6. His mention of "knowledge" in verse 6 could be anticipating "word of knowledge" in 1 Corinthians 12:8 (cf. the "knowledge" of 13:2, 8, 12), but could also be in anticipation of the discussion of true wisdom in 1:17–2:16. So although this passage adds less to the current argument than any of the other "grace" + "given" passages, it should be remembered that Paul does refer twice to particular ministries in this passage when he mentions "speech/word" and "the testimony of Christ" (and perhaps a third time if the knowledge he is thinking of is in the form of a "word of knowledge," cf. 1 Cor. 12:8). Such supports the central contention of this chapter that every time Paul uses the "grace" + "given" combination, in the immediate context he is talking about particular ministry assignments.

1 CORINTHIANS 3:10–13

> According to the *grace* of God that was *given* to me as a wise master builder I laid a foundation, but another builds on it. But let each one be careful how he builds upon it. For no one is able to lay a foundation other than that which is laid, which is Christ Jesus. But if anyone builds upon the foundation with gold, silver, precious stones, wood, hay, straw, each person's work will become obvious, for the Day will reveal it since it will be revealed by fire and the fire will test the kind of work each person has done. (1 Cor. 3:10–13)

The grace that has been given to Paul is the assignment to the role of a wise master builder. He describes his work of ministry using the metaphor of laying a foundation. He describes the ministry assignments of others as building upon the foundation and as the work each person has done. Special abilities play no part in this passage. The issue for Paul relates to a particular ministry that he has been given as a foundation-layer and the particular ministry assignments that have been given to others as workers on the building.[8]

This passage, like the others now being looked at in this chapter, sheds light on the list passages. In the other passages, as here, Paul's concern is the ministries given to each by God.

2 Corinthians 8:1–7

> Now I make known to you, brothers, the *grace* of God that has been *given* in the churches of Macedonia; that in much testing of affliction, the abundance of their joy and their depth of poverty has overflowed into the wealth of their generosity. So I bear witness that they gave according to their ability and beyond their ability—of their own accord—with much insistence begging us for the *grace* and the sharing of the ministry of the saints. And not only as we had hoped, but they *gave* themselves first to the Lord and to us through the will of God, resulting in us encouraging Titus that as he had already begun, so also he should finish this *grace*. But just as you abound in everything, in faith and in word and in knowledge and in all eagerness and also in our love for you, abound also in this *grace*. (2 Cor. 8:1–7)

The grace that Paul examines in this immediate passage—and, indeed, throughout 2 Corinthians 8–9—is a ministry of sacrificial giving.[9] It is not an ability to give; it is the ministry of generous sharing that Paul has in mind. English translations regularly translate the word *grace* at various points in this passage with phrases like "gracious work" or "act of grace."[10] In the immediate context, the ministry Paul encourages is described as (1) an overflowing into the wealth of generosity, (2) giving beyond one's ability, (3) sharing in the ministry of the saints, (4) finishing this grace, and (5) abounding in this grace. The remainder of chapters 8–9 describes this collection for the poor in Jerusalem as (1) a ministry of supplying their need (8:14), (2) a grace that is being ministered (8:19), (3) the ministry for the saints (9:1), and (4) the ministry of service (9:12). This last description and the three verses that follow it at the end of 2 Corinthians 9 (vv. 12–15) are second in importance only to 8:1–7, partly because 9:12–15 are at the end of the broader discussion and partly because of the expressions Paul clusters together there. In 9:12–15, the designations "ministry of service," "ministry," and "grace of God upon you" all work together in the crescendo with which he concludes this discussion of the ministry of generous giving. There can be little doubt that the gracious work that Paul refers to in chapters 8–9 of 2 Corinthians is a ministry of giving—a sacrificial sharing of one's goods for others who are in need.[11]

It should not escape notice how the ministry of generous giving in this passage informs Paul's more general description of the same type of activity, which is found in the middle of one of his ministry lists: "the one who gives, with generosity" (Rom. 12:8). Should not this particular extended example of a ministry of generosity in 2 Corinthians 8–9 be used in understanding the little undefined phrase in Romans 12?

GALATIANS 2:7–9

> But, on the other hand, seeing that I had been en-
> trusted the gospel to the uncircumcised, just as Peter
> had been to the circumcised (for he who worked
> through Peter in his apostolic ministry to the cir-
> cumcised also worked through me to the Gentiles),

> and recognizing the *grace* that was *given* to me, James
> and Cephas and John, who were considered pillars,
> gave to Barnabas and me the right hand of fellowship
> in order that we [might go] to the Gentiles and they
> to the circumcision. (Gal. 2:7–9)

The line "I had been entrusted the gospel to the uncircumcised"
is conceptually parallel to the later line "the grace that was given
to me." That is, in this passage the grace that Paul says he had been
given by God was an assignment to take the gospel to the Gentiles.
This particular ministry of Paul is described as (1) an entrusting of
the proclamation of the gospel to the Gentiles, (2) an apostleship/
apostolic ministry, and (3) a going to the Gentiles. The central focus
on his ministry assignment is clear in this passage and, because of its
literary connection to the list passages, encourages us to read those
passages as ministry assignments.

EPHESIANS 3:1–2, 7–8

> For this reason, I, Paul, the prisoner of Christ Jesus
> on behalf of you Gentiles—if indeed you have heard
> of the stewardship of the *grace* of God that was *given* to
> me for you. . . . Of this gospel I was made a minister
> according to the gift of the *grace* of God that was *given*
> to me according to the working of his power. To me,
> the least of all the saints, this *grace* was *given* to preach
> the incomprehensible riches of Christ. (Eph. 3:1–2,
> 7–8)

The "grace" + "given" combination is found three times in this
passage. That by itself is striking. Here, Paul describes the grace
that he was given as (1) on behalf of the Gentiles, (2) being made a
minister of the gospel, and (3) preaching the incomprehensible riches
of Christ. But even beyond these, perhaps the most remarkable aspect
of this passage is not what is found in these immediate verses but

what is of note in the parallel between Ephesians 3:2 and 3:7, both set in the same context of Paul's own ministry calling. There is a parallel in the middle parts of these two verses that suggests that the first (3:2) can be used to expand upon what Paul means by the "gift of the grace" in the second (3:7). The parallels can be seen in English, and accurately represent the same parallel structure in Greek.

3:2	the steward-ship	of the grace	of God	that was given	to me
3:7	the gift[12]	of the grace	of God	that was given	to me

It appears that, in light of the structural parallel between these two verses, "the gift of the grace of God that was given to me" should be understood as a stewardship or managerial assignment. Such an understanding is developed more fully in the surrounding verses, where it is learned that Paul's stewardship is the responsibility to proclaim that the Gentiles share in the gospel of Jesus Christ (vv. 3–6, 9–10).[13] That was his primary ministry assignment; that was his calling.

This Ephesians passage is important in another way. Not only does the "grace" + "given" combination occur three times, contextually, it is very close to Ephesians 4, one of the list passages in which Paul says that not only has a ministry of grace been given to him, but it is also true that "to each one of us grace was given" (Eph. 4:7).

2 TIMOTHY 1:6–11

> For this reason I remind you to rekindle the *charisma* of God which is in you through the laying on of my hands. For God has not given us a spirit of fear, but of power and of love and of good judgment. Therefore do not be ashamed of the testimony of our Lord or

> of me his prisoner, but suffer with me for the gospel according to the power of God, who has saved and called us with a holy calling, not according to our works but according to his own purpose and *grace* that was *given* to us in Christ Jesus from all eternity, but now has been revealed by the appearing of our Savior, Jesus Christ, who abolished death and brought life and incorruptibility to light through the gospel, for which I was appointed a preacher and an apostle and a teacher. (2 Tim. 1:6–11)

The grace that was given to all believers in this passage is the holy calling that both brings us to salvation and leads us into ministry. The person who is involved in such a calling (1) is not ashamed of the testimony of the Lord, (2) suffers for the gospel, and (3) works within the purpose of God. In Paul's case, the outworking of the calling was his appointment as (1) a preacher, (2) an apostle, and (3) a teacher. This passage forges together the ideas of calling into salvation and calling into ministry. In Timothy's case, the calling into ministry was a *charisma* that had been given to him through the laying on of Paul's hands. As mentioned in chapter 5 of this volume, it is more likely that this *charisma* was Timothy's commissioning for ministry rather than the granting of some unnamed ability. Regardless, the "grace" + "given" combination here, as everywhere else, is found in a context in which Paul emphasizes particular ministries.

In short, although Paul uses *grace* in a wide variety of ways in his letters—to indicate mercy, or kindness, or blessing, or thanks— whenever he uses *grace* together with *given* he has in mind ministry assignments—either his own or those of others. This mindfulness is true outside the list passages, as this current chapter has demonstrated, and it is also true inside the list passages. When Paul refers to the grace that has been given to him, he is reflecting upon the amazing reality that God chose to take a person such as he—one who formerly persecuted the church—and put him (of all people) into a place of ministry, even the ministry of taking the gospel to the Gentiles. Similarly, when Paul applies this expression to all believers, he is reminding them of the incredible grace that God has shown in calling each person into a place of ministry.

The passages looked at in this chapter and the list passages are all part of Paul's ongoing concern that the members of the community of faith serve in their God-appointed ministry roles to strengthen the church. The so-called spiritual gift passages should not remain disconnected from other aspects of Pauline theology. They are part of a central theme—the theme of ministry—that weaves itself through the letters of Paul.[14] The list passages are informed by these other passages. And what do these other passages relate? They relate Paul's central concern that believers in Christ carry out the spiritual ministries that they have so graciously been given by God.

FOURTEEN

"But What About . . . ?"

Addressing Potential Objections

Summary: Four potential objections—the language of given-ness and having, the issue of talents, English usage of the word *gift,* and the role of 1 Corinthians 12:8–10—are raised and addressed in this chapter.

BEFORE LOOKING AT the relationship of the spiritual ministries approach to other broader themes in the letters of Paul, it is only fair to pause and consider some possible objections to this view. These are ordered in this chapter from least likely to most likely to be a concern for someone studying the evidence for the spiritual-ministries approach presented so far in this book.[1]

THE LANGUAGE OF GIVEN-NESS AND HAVING

Someone might object that the language of given-ness (Rom. 12:3, 6; 1 Cor. 12:7–8; Eph. 4:7–8, 11) and having (1 Cor. 12:30; 13:2; 14:26; Rom. 12:6), which is found in the list passages, suggests the idea of ability. This concern may seem especially pertinent to those who have walked in circles where people are regularly asked which spiritual gifts they have, or have been encouraged at some point to try to determine which spiritual gifts God has given to them. It must be pointed out, however, that a ministry *is* both something that an individual has, and something given by God. Furthermore,

Paul regularly uses the language of *giving* and *having* elsewhere in his letters in a variety of ways, and rarely in reference to abilities.

Consider first the language of giving. In addition to the items listed in the "grace" + "given" verses highlighted in the previous chapter (a distinctive Pauline expression indicating ministries) many other things are, according to Paul, given by God, and it is not clear that in any of these cases these things should be understood as abilities. What does Paul say that God gives?[2] The following chart outlines all the different things for which Paul uses the language of giving.

the Holy Spirit (Rom. 5:5) (as a pledge, 2 Cor. 1:22; 5:5)	earnestness (2 Cor. 8:16)	a stewardship to preach the Word of God (Col. 1:25)
Jesus Christ himself (for our sins, Gal. 1:4; as a ransom for all, 1 Tim. 2:6; for us, Titus 2:14)	[help] "to the poor" (2 Cor. 9:9)	retribution (2 Thess. 1:8)
perseverance and encouragement (Rom. 15:5)	apostolic authority (2 Cor. 10:8; 13:10)	eternal comfort and good hope by grace (2 Thess. 2:16)
service roles (1 Cor. 3:5)	a "thorn in the flesh" (2 Cor. 12:7)	peace (2 Thess. 3:16)
hair as a covering (1 Cor. 11:15)	the promise that is by faith (Gal. 3:22)	[not] a spirit of cowardice but of power and love and good judgment (2 Tim. 1:7)
honor to the members that lack honor (1 Cor. 12:24)	a spirit of wisdom and revelation in the knowledge of Christ (Eph. 1:17)	mercy (2 Tim. 1:16, 18)

the "body" of a tree (as a metaphor of the resurrection body, 1 Cor. 15:38)	strengthening with power through his Spirit in one's inner person (Eph. 3:16)	understanding (2 Tim. 2:7)
victory through Jesus Christ (1 Cor. 15:57);	gifts [of persons in their ministries] (Eph. 4:8, 11)[3]	repentance (2 Tim. 2:25)
the ministry of reconciliation (2 Cor. 5:18);	a "word" to proclaim with boldness the mystery of the gospel (Eph. 6:19)	and Paul himself (as a person being "given" to Philemon, Philem. 22)[4]

Few of these examples could be interpreted as the giving of special abilities.[5] It should not be assumed, therefore, that the mere presence of the language of giving suggests the special-abilities view in, say, 1 Corinthians 12.

An even more pronounced (and longer) list would emerge if a chart were drawn up for every time that Paul uses the word translated in these texts as "have" or "has." Perhaps a more efficient way of seeing the many ways this word was used both inside and outside the New Testament would be to list the various categories in which this word was used in Greek, found in the most widely used standard Greek-English dictionary.[6] (In his letters, Paul himself uses this word in all these various ways except one.)

1. to possess or contain—*have, own*
2. to stand in a close relationship to someone—*have, have as*
3. to take a hold on something—*have hold (to), grip*
4. to carry/bear as accessory or part of a whole—*have on*

5. to be in a position to do something—*can, be able*
6. to have an opinion about something—*consider, look upon, view*
7. to experience something—*have*
8. as a connective marker—*to have* or *include in itself, bring about, cause*
9. in special combinations (that is, when used in combination with particular other words)
10. to be in some state or condition
11. to be closely associated—*hold fast, be next to, be next*

Further, I've examined every instance in which Paul uses this word (143 verses). And unless I've overlooked an example, I can find no clear instance in which *have* is used in a sentence that—even when taken as a whole—suggests the idea of "possessing a special ability."[7] Rather, it appears more likely that a Western consumer mentality has predisposed us to associate the English word *have* with something that we own or possess, even though it is used in many other ways in Paul's letters. Even if it occasionally does indicate possession, it is precarious with no clear examples in Paul's letters that associate *have* with an ability concept, to project such a concept onto the passages now under study. Moreover, even if an example were demonstrated outside the list passages, such a concept couldn't be assumed to be present in a list passage unless that passage itself suggested such a use. If truth be told, *have* is one of the most flexible of all words in both Greek and English. Recall, for instance, how chapter 4 of this volume illustrated that *had*, in "Mary had a little lamb," could potentially mean "possession of," "giving birth to," or even "eating" the lamb. Neither the language of given-ness, then, nor the language of having, should be taken as indicating the special-abilities view without other evidence to support such.[8]

TALENTS

People do have natural talents, do they not? If natural talents are taken to mean capacities or abilities that have been given by God to people at birth, then the answer seems clearly to be yes.[9] In theology, such giving is an aspect of what is usually referred to as "common grace." Capacities or abilities given by God to believers and unbelievers alike are one way God demonstrates his grace to the world. Examples of natural abilities might include a communication skill, or the ability to administer a large project, or a particularly good musical ear—some aspects of which God gives at birth and some aspects of which God develops through our upbringing and environment. Calvin comments that "all of us have a certain aptitude. . . . Hence, with good reason we are compelled to confess that its beginning is inborn in human nature."[10] We can gladly affirm that all people have special capacities that come as a result of God's dispensing his grace. What is being argued in this book is not that people lack special abilities (given by God as part of common grace), but rather that the items Paul includes in his ministry lists of Ephesians 4:11–12; Romans 12:6–8; and 1 Corinthians 12:28–30 should not be viewed under the category of special abilities;[11] rather, they should be categorized as lists of ministry assignments that God has given to believers and to the church through those believers.

Beyond natural abilities, we can also affirm that God regularly empowers believers to overcome sin, to proclaim the good news, and to serve the body of Christ. But as will be developed more fully in chapters 17–18, such enabling is a general empowering that God frequently—although not always—gives when he calls us to do something; it's not a special enablement that Christians can use when they discover that they have it.

What about the parable of the talents in Matthew 25:14–30? Doesn't that parable teach that God has given everyone special abilities that they must use? No, a talent is a measurement of monetary value, originally the weight of a precious metal. In a similar way, the word *pound* was originally a measurement of weight in English but today designates a specific amount of money in the United Kingdom. Newman says that a talent is a "Greek coin with value of 5,000–6,000 denarii."[12] (A denarius is a "Roman silver coin equivalent to the day's wage of a common laborer.")[13] That a talent is an amount of money is also obvious in a parable that is about trading talents (v. 16), gaining more talents (vv. 16–17, 20, 22), and the possibility of giving talents to a bank from which to earn interest (v. 27). A likely reason English speakers become confused about the meaning of a biblical talent is because they are so accustomed to using the word *talent* to mean a special ability or skill, they often unwittingly read this idea back into the parable.[14] So, too, the confusion over the English word gift described in the following section. It's easy to read a foreign idea back into a passage when an English word has two meanings.

In any event, in the parable of the talents, a distinction is made between what is given and the abilities of the slaves. Thus, "to one he *gave* five talents, to another two, to another one, each *according to his own ability*" (v. 15).[15] Furthermore, if somehow Jesus was, in fact, referring to people's abilities, how could one person's ability be taken away and then given to another (v. 28)? It is not the purpose of this current study to discuss the overall interpretation of this parable,[16] but whatever the conclusion about its interpretation, it should be noted that the talents in this parable merely signify amounts of money, and, without clear contextual evidence, it cannot be assumed that Jesus' point was to teach about a person's abilities simply because the word *talent* was encountered in the reading.

ENGLISH USAGE OF THE WORD GIFT

English usage appears to have played a far more important role in the way we think about the so-called gifts than most people realize. No one would likely verbalize an objection to the premise of this book based upon English usage. Nonetheless, usage seems to be a pervasive influence on people's intuitive sense of whether Paul could actually use gifting language as a reference to a ministry assignment. Thus, usage is addressed here.

The word *gift* in English is used in two ways, as the following definitions from *Webster's Dictionary* illustrate (only two uses for *gift* appear even in the unabridged dictionary). The first definition is "a special or notable capacity, talent, or endowment either inherent, acquired, or given by a deity." In other words, one definition of *gift* in English is a special ability. The second and broader definition is "something that is voluntarily transferred by one person to another without compensation."[17] An example of the second would be a birthday gift. We should note that Bible translators who translate using the word *gift* are referring primarily to the second definition (the more basic of the two) that a gift is simply something freely given by God.[18] It is not difficult, though, to understand how the first definition—that is, relating to talents and abilities—influences the thinking of English speakers. To think clearly about this subject, however, readers will have to remind themselves again and again that gifting language in and of itself does not even suggest special abilities. It merely refers to the free transfer of something from God to his people.

After dozens of conversations with people, I've concluded that the widespread use of two meanings for the word *gift* in English (and some other languages) has created an environment in which the conventional view appears reasonable. It also represents a fundamental reason that so many people have accepted the special-abilities view. But English usage should never determine how we read a text that was originally written in Greek. So although English usage of the word *gift* presently plays a substantial role in people's assumptions about and acceptance of the conventional view, such usage needs to be once and for all exposed and set aside in future discussions of this topic. The only way to do so successfully in most cases is to steer clear of the use of the word *gift* when discussing the entities that Paul lists in Ephesians 4; Romans 12; and 1 Corinthians 12.[19] English usage should not determine how we interpret the Bible. (See appendix C for a discussion of gifting language in English Bible translations.)

First Corinthians 12:8–10 as the Starting Point for Everything Else

This may be the most important of possible objections with which to interact because it appears to represent the procedure pursued by many who enter into a study of the so-called spiritual gifts. Many people assume that Paul wrote these passages simply to teach about the subject of spiritual gifts, which are often viewed from the start as special abilities. Since Paul's most extensive discussion of the subject is 1 Corinthians 12, that chapter is considered to be the natural starting point for any study. When reading this chapter, the first list to appear is 1 Corinthians 12:8–10. Since at least some of the items in that particular list appear to require special ability because of their miraculous nature, it is inferred that this list must be a list of Spirit-given abilities. Moreover, since 1 Corinthians 12:8–10 is one of four lists of spiritual gifts, it is assumed that the other three lists must also be lists of abilities. Thus, the ability concept present in 1 Corinthians 12:8–10 determines the way the other three lists are read, even though none of the other three lists fits well into the ability mold.[20]

Such a determination will not do, however, because it lacks sensitivity both to the reasons Paul wrote to the Corinthians and to the differences between the lists in their contexts, forming the foundation of two misdirected assumptions. Further consideration of these issues are sprinkled throughout earlier chapters of this book, especially chapters 9–12.

The first assumption is that Paul wrote 1 Corinthians 12–14 simply to teach people about spiritual gifts, similar to the way someone today might instruct an adult Bible class or youth group about the nature and use of spiritual gifts. But Paul is clearly reacting to the Corinthians' overzealousness for flashy miraculous activities such as miracles, healings, prophecy, and, especially, tongues. This is confirmed (1) by the direct movement out of a list of activities that manifest the Spirit (1 Cor. 12:7–11) into the body metaphor (1 Cor. 12:12–27, which is all about the ministry roles of each member), (2) by the placement in chapter 13 of a carefully inserted poem extolling love over sensational activities,[21] and (3) by the way Paul challenges tongues-speakers to get under control while encouraging activities that edify (1 Cor. 14). Paul is not dispassionately teaching a seminar on spiritual gifts to the Corinthians; he is writing in order to counterbalance what he perceives to be an overemphasis on the miraculous.

The second assumption of those who interpret the other lists as abilities is that such an interpretation is warranted via the abilities idea in 1 Corinthians 12:8–10. This assumption also falters for a couple of reasons: (1) all four lists differ from one another in regards to whether they are ministries, persons in their ministries, or a combination of both; (2) each list contains somewhat differing indicators—words like *equipping, functions, appointed/placed*—that reflect the nature of the list. Such does not mean that the lists are unrelated to each other. There is, indeed, significant conceptual overlap between lists, as has already been argued. The items in all four lists are linked together by the broader concept of ministries God has given to the church.[22] Only by using the ability concept derived from 1 Corinthians 12:8–10 can the conventional view maintain the assertion that all the items in all the lists are abilities only. As has been seen in previous chapters of this volume, many indicators are present in the contexts of each list, arguing against this notion and supporting the central premise of this book—that Paul wants believers to serve in the ministries into which God has placed them to strengthen and build up the church.

To close this chapter with an analogy, imagine a university that sponsors a wide range of sporting activities. The track team, however, is famous for a long line of outstanding runners who have broken many speed records. Imagine further that the school sends out three different newsletters that, altogether, include the following four lists of university-sponsored sporting activities:[23]

Newsletter 1		Newsletter 2	Newsletter 3
List 1	*List 2*	*List 3*	*List 4*
Cross-country running	Basketball players	Long-distance running	Basketball players
Long-distance running	Long-distance runners	Playing football	Long-distance runners
Middle-distance running	Tennis players	Wrestlers	Tennis players
Sprints	Middle-distance running	Soccer players	Wrestlers
	Playing soccer	Tennis players	
	Playing baseball		
	Running cross country		
	Sprinting		

If you were to receive the newsletters that included these four lists, you might well observe that all the people who do the activities in list number 1 possess the ability to be fast. It would certainly not be legitimate, however, to look at list 1 and then conclude from your observation that the other three lists are lists of fast-ness. That conclusion would be inaccurate because lists 2, 3, and 4 are not lists of fast-ness. List 4 is a list of persons in their activities while lists 2 and 3 are mixed lists of activities and persons in their activities. (List 1 itself is also a list of activities, but activities of a type that require a participant to have the ability to be fast.) List 1, however, shouldn't determine how the other three lists are read. In the same way, it is not legitimate to use 1 Corinthians 12:8–10 as the solitary lens through which 1 Corinthians 12:28–30; Romans 12:6–8; and Ephesians 4:11–12 are interpreted.

PART THREE

BROADER
CONNECTIONS

FIFTEEN

Ministry and Service in the Letters of Paul

Summary: The spiritual-ministries approach re-connects the list passages (Eph. 4; Rom. 12; 1 Cor. 12) with Paul's general teaching on ministry and service in a way that the conventional view does not.

As HAS BEEN SEEN, numerous reasons can be offered for viewing the so-called spiritual gifts primarily in the category of ministries rather than in the category of abilities. It is important, however, not just to look at these arguments in their immediate contexts, but also to integrate what has been learned from the list passages with other related themes in the letters of Paul. In other words, Paul's teaching about particular ministry assignments are woven together with other theological themes in his letters. The strands of teaching are not separate from one another; they intertwine and reinforce one another. Four biblical-theological themes must be understood in order to arrive at a balanced reading of Paul's teaching in Ephesians 4; Romans 12; and 1 Corinthians 12–14.

This chapter and the chapter that follows explores what Paul teaches about ministry and service in general and about his own central ministry assignment. The two subsequent chapters look first at Paul's general teaching about the Holy Spirit and then more particularly at his theology of empowering and weakness in ministry. It will be argued that the spiritual-ministries approach fits comfortably with these other Pauline themes, whereas the conventional approach to spiritual gifts does not.

Paul viewed every Christian as a minister. In his thinking, the ministry—as well as particular ministries under the general category of ministry—is not limited to a select few, but is the privilege and responsibility of every believer. As one author notes, "The New Testament writers consistently refused to make any distinction between an official ministry of a selected person or group and that of any believer."[1]

Paul teaches that, from the Old Testament period to the New Testament period, the conditions under which ministry is carried out have changed. In 2 Corinthians 3, ministry performed under the new covenant is contrasted with old covenant ministry. The contrasts include the following:

The Ministry of the Old Covenant	The Ministry of the New Covenant
Written on stone tablets (3:3)	Written by the Spirit on our hearts (3:3)
The letter [of the law], which kills (3:6)	The Spirit, who gives life (3:6)
Fading glory of first covenant (3:7, 11)	Far greater glory (3:8–11)
"Ministry of condemnation" (3:9)	"Ministry of righteousness" (3:9)
Temporary (3:13)	Permanent (3:13)
A "veil" when old covenant is read (3:14–15)	The "veil" is removed in Christ (3:14, 16)
Bondage (3:17)	Liberty (3:17)
Loss of heart (3:12; 4:1)	Boldness; we don't lose heart (3:12; 4:1)

Two chapters later, Paul refers to this new covenant ministry as the "ministry of reconciliation" (2 Cor. 5:18). He is primarily describing, of course, his own calling and ministry in these chapters, but his use of plurals ("we," "us") indicates that he intends to include his co-workers and probably others who perform apostolic ministry (cf. 1 Cor. 3:5–10; 4:1). By extension he includes anyone who carries the appeal that people be reconciled to God through Christ, who died on behalf of them.[2] The ministry of reconciliation is, in fact, the responsibility of every believer.

The paradigm for all ministry is Christ's own ministry and teaching about servanthood. Although we might have expected Paul to make comparisons with the Old Testament temple service of priests and Levites, his letters make very few and only tentative connections with these ideas (with one notable exception, Rom. 15:16).[3] Rather, Paul seems to write in conscious continuity with what Jesus taught and modeled about servanthood. Jesus taught that the greatest among his disciples are the ones who become as servants to others, wholly unlike the benefactors, the leaders, and the great men of the world who expect others to serve them while they recline (Matt. 23:11; Mark 10:42–44; Luke 22:24–26). Christ himself modeled what it is to serve (Matt. 20:28; Mark 10:45; Luke 22:27; John 13:1–15). Christ carried his servanthood, as Paul records, even to the point of death (Phil. 2:7–8).

Common in Paul's language is "ministers of . . ." (or "servants of . . .").[4] He refers to himself and to those working in new covenant ministry as "ministers of a new covenant" (2 Cor. 3:6). Some of the descriptions that he uses are "ministers of God" (2 Cor. 6:4), "ministers of Christ" (2 Cor. 11:23; Col. 1:7; 1 Tim. 4:6), and "ministers of righteousness" (2 Cor. 11:15). Reminiscent of his ministry lists, Paul describes himself as a minister of the gospel (Eph. 3:7; Col. 1:23; cf. 1 Cor. 3:5) and of the church (Col. 1:25).

Paul's letters are full of general instructions on how all believers are to serve one another (Gal. 5:13). He emphasizes the general characteristics and actions of believers through these "one another" descriptions. Followers of Christ are to love one another (Rom. 12:10; 13:8; 1 Thess. 3:12; 4:9); show preference for one another (Rom. 12:10; Phil. 2:3); act in unity and humility toward one another (Rom. 12:16; Phil. 2:2–5; Eph. 4:2); build up and show care for one another (Rom. 14:19; 1 Cor. 12:25; 1 Thess. 5:11); show tolerance to one another (Rom. 14:13; 15:7; Eph. 4:2; Col. 3:13; 1 Thess. 5:13), admonish (Rom. 15:14), speak truth (Eph. 4:25; Col. 3:9) and forgive one another (Eph. 4:32); speak in psalms, hymns, and spiritual songs to one another (Eph. 5:19; Col. 3:16); and comfort and encourage one another (1 Thess. 4:18; 5:11). Such instructions permeate Paul's letters and also illustrate the attitudes that should characterize relationships among members of Christ's body. The activities mentioned in this paragraph are not individual ministries that differ from believer to believer (as in the ministry lists); these are activities that all believers must do. Humility, love, and genuine concern should undergird all ministry in the church.

Paul was passionate not only about ministry taking place member to member; he also wanted to build up the body of Christ by bringing new believers into the community of faith. In Paul's letters (2 Cor. 4:1–6; 2 Tim. 4:5), the preaching of the gospel is itself viewed as part of a believer's servanthood. Paul was so passionate about the gospel being spread that he could rejoice even when some who preached were preaching with wrong motives (Phil. 1:15–18). This tolerance should not be taken as implying that motives and attitudes in general weren't important to Paul. Quite the contrary. Just as ministry to one another is to be performed with the right attitude, Paul teaches that the gospel ministry should avoid error, impurity, deceit, flattery, greed, and glory seeking, and should be characterized by gentleness, affection, a desire to please God rather than people, and a sharing of one's very life (1 Thess. 2:3–8).

In addition to general principles for ministry in the body of Christ, dozens of specific areas of ministry are mentioned or alluded to in Paul's letters. Chapter 19 of this volume, in fact, presents a list of all the ministries mentioned in the letters of Paul, so that list will not be duplicated here. As part and parcel of his teaching about ministry, that list, though, actually belongs in this chapter alongside other descriptions of his understanding of ministry. Since, however, that list leads us so effectively into practical implications and applications, it has been left to the final section of this book, where the practical dimensions are addressed specifically. But reaffirmed here is what has already been noted in earlier chapters—that, in Paul's understanding, each believer has been given particular areas of ministry, whether short-term or long-term, whether spontaneous or planned, that are for the building up of the body of Christ. Paul would consider someone who didn't know this to be impoverished in his or her Christian life.

Paul's letters are filled with metaphors for ministry. That the vast majority of metaphors for ministry in the New Testament are found in Paul's writings demonstrates how important this topic was to him and how deeply he had thought about it. (Examples of these metaphors can be found in chap. 19.)

Furthermore, Paul mentions by name dozens of people in his letters, both men and women, who were obviously co-laborers in some way with him in ministry. (Again, see chap. 19 for a few examples.) Paul taught and modeled that ministry is to be done as a community activity.

So how does all this general teaching about ministry in the letters of Paul relate to the central premise of this book—that the list passages are actually pointing toward ministry assignments as the primary category rather than abilities? Simply put, the spiritual-ministries approach reintegrates the list passages (1 Cor. 12; Rom. 12; Eph. 4) into Paul's more general theology of ministry and service. That theology might, in fact, be analogous to a musical piece played by an orchestra, with the list of spiritual ministries in the list passages analogous to the cello section; they both fit within the whole. The cello section blends together with the other instruments in communicating a unity in the musical piece. If the cello section were replaced by a few electric guitars connected to a large amplifier, the sound of the guitars, while exciting, would not blend with the other instruments in a classical orchestra. Such a substitution would, in fact, draw attention away from the music, and people would leave the performance discussing the guitars, rather than reveling in the music. So, too, the list passages viewed through the lens of the conventional (special abilities) approach leaves many people today talking a lot about spiritual gifts (as abilities) and focusing much less on mutual ministry in the body of Christ.

In the conventional approach, the topic of spiritual gifts has often been treated as a separate subject in Paul's thought and undue attention has been focused upon it. Long overdue, however, is the reintegration of Paul's teaching about the individual ministries mentioned in the list passages into his general teaching about ministry. One of the most important aspects of Paul's understanding of ministry—indeed, a topic about which he is clearly very passionate—is his own calling to ministry. So much of his understanding of the nature of ministry seems to have been formed out of the backdrop of his own ministry assignment. This theme will be briefly explored in the following chapter.

SIXTEEN

Learning by Example:

Paul's Central Ministry Assignment(s)

Summary: Paul's own ministry assignment(s) is one extended example of the various ministries that have been given to individual believers; it is not a topic to be separated from his teaching on the so-called spiritual gifts.

WHEN PAUL WAS a young adult traveling to Damascus to persecute Christians, he encountered the resurrected Christ (Acts 9). It was through this encounter with Jesus the Messiah that he was converted and called into ministry (Acts 9:15–16). Paul never, ever got over his commission. He was passionately committed to the ministry that he had received from the Lord, as Luke records in Paul's farewell speech to the Ephesian elders: "But I do not consider my life of any value nor as precious to myself, so that I may finish my race and the ministry that I received from the Lord Jesus, to testify to the gospel of the grace of God" (Acts 20:24).

Paul believed and communicated throughout his letters that he had received a central ministry assignment from the Lord, as well as a number of smaller, related ministries.[1] Along with comments throughout his letters, Paul reflected on the particulars of his central ministry assignment in greater length in two passages: Romans 15:14–21 and Ephesians 3:1–13. In Romans 15 he teaches the following:

- Paul's ministry was a "grace that was given" to him from God (v. 15);
- He was "to be a minister of Christ Jesus to the Gentiles" (v. 16);
- Paul's offering to God of believing Gentiles is comparable to the sacrifices a priest would offer up to God (v. 16);
- The offering of the Gentiles would be "sanctified by the Holy Spirit" (v. 16);
- Paul's work is described as "what Christ has accomplished through me" (v. 18);
- The intended result of Paul's proclamation was "the obedience of the Gentiles by word and deed" (v. 18);
- Paul's preaching was accompanied "by the power of signs and wonders, by the power of the Spirit" (v. 19);
- Paul's goal was "to preach the gospel, not where Christ has already been named, so that I would not build on another person's foundation" (vv. 20–21).

In short, according to Romans 15:14–21, Paul's ministry was to proclaim the Good News and bring Gentiles to obedience to Christ in places that had not yet heard the message.

The second main passage in which Paul reflects on his central ministry assignment is Ephesians 3:1–13. Ephesians 3 focuses more on the content of the message Paul preached, and the following is learned about his central ministry assignment:

- Paul viewed his ministry as a "stewardship" (v. 2) "of God's grace" (v. 2);
- It was "given" to Paul (v. 2) "for the sake of you Gentiles" (vv. 1, 2);
- Paul refers to his message as a "mystery" that had been made known to him "by revelation" (v. 3) and

into which he had particular "insight" (v. 4). It had been revealed to Paul as also to the "holy apostles and prophets in the Spirit" (v. 5);

- This was something new; other generations did not understand it (v. 5);
- The content of the mystery was that "Gentiles are co-heirs and co-members of the body and co-partakers of the promise in Christ Jesus through the gospel" (v. 6);
- Paul was made a "minister" of this gospel (v. 7) "according to the gift of God's grace which was given" to him (vv. 7–8, cf. v. 2);
- Paul was "to proclaim to the Gentiles the incomprehensible riches of Christ" (v. 8) and "to bring to light the administration of the mystery" that had been hidden (v. 9).

In short, according to Ephesians 3:1–13, Paul's central ministry assignment was to proclaim openly to the Gentiles the formerly hidden message that they, too, could be sharers in the promise of Christ.[2] Such, then, was Paul's central ministry calling. When he referred to himself as an apostle, it often seems that he was simply using shorthand to refer to his calling to share this good news with the Gentiles (Rom. 1:5; 11:13; 1 Cor. 1:1; 2 Cor. 1:1, etc.).

Further, his understanding of his calling was written in short form in Galatians 1:15–16, comprising the first half of a continuing sentence: "But when God, who had set me apart from my mother's womb and called me through his grace, was pleased to reveal His Son in me so that I might preach Him among the Gentiles . . ."

Paul was passionate about his calling and radically dedicated to carrying it out. In his own words, he was "compelled" by the love of Christ (2 Cor. 5:14). He commented elsewhere, "for I am under compulsion; for woe is me if I do not preach the gospel," a ministry that he refers to as his "stewardship" (1 Cor. 9:16–17; cf. Eph. 3:2).

His entire life was consumed with carrying out this calling. Later in his ministry, he could reflect on his life and say "so that from Jerusalem and round about as far as Illyricum I have fully proclaimed the gospel of Christ" (Rom. 15:19).

It is doubtless no exaggeration to say that almost everything Paul did in the area of ministry hovered around this central ministry assignment; it was his single-minded objective. Still, other related areas of ministry are obviously important to Paul and part and parcel of the various ministries given to him. These include, among others,

- prayer for the churches (Rom. 1:8–10; 2 Cor. 13:7–9; Eph. 1:15–19; 3:14–19; Phil. 1:3–11; Col. 1:9–12; 2 Thess. 1:11–12; 2 Tim. 1:3; Philem. 4–7).
- encouragement/exhortation, seen by us especially in his letters.
- teaching (1 Tim. 2:7; 2 Tim. 1:11; Col. 1:28).
- defending the integrity of the gospel against false teachers (Gal. 1:6–9; Phil. 3:2; Col. 2:16–23; 1 Tim. 4:1–5; 2 Tim. 4:1–4), including those who would challenge Paul's apostolic calling (2 Cor. 11:12–15).
- miracles and healings (Rom. 15:18–19; 2 Cor. 12:12; Gal. 3:5; 1 Thess. 1:5; cf. Acts 19:11–12).
- evangelism (Rom. 15:18–20; Eph. 3:8–10; 6:19–20).
- mentoring (2 Tim. 2:2 and esp. throughout the Pastoral Letters; note also all the co-workers Paul mentions in his letters).
- modeling for others how to live out one's faith (1 Cor. 4:16–17; 11:1; Phil. 3:17; 2 Thess. 3:7–9).[3]

At the same time, it is also clear that no individual, even the apostle Paul, could fill every role (1 Cor. 12:29–30; Eph. 4:11); otherwise Paul's illustration of unity and diversity in the corporate body would be meaningless.

Paul as Example

But to what degree is Paul's own activity of ministry an example and model for us? Wasn't Paul unique? In short, in a narrow sense Paul viewed his own ministry and work as unique, but in a broader sense he viewed his ministry as an example to be followed. The uniqueness of his ministry is primarily located in the way he received his calling to ministry (directly mediated by the Lord) and the authority that he believed came with his ministry as an apostle (cf. Gal. 1–2; 2 Cor. 10:8; 13:10; 1 Thess. 2:6; 4:2). The broadness of his ministry is evident in Paul's eagerness, even insistence, to use himself as a model for ministry.

First Corinthians 3–4 is one illustration of Paul's intention to use his own ministry (and to some degree, those of Apollos and Cephas/Peter) as an example that should be imitated. Paul viewed the Corinthians as the beneficiaries of his ministry (3:9–10; 4:1, 15) and, at the same time, people who should model their lives and ministries after his own. His statement, "Therefore I urge you, be imitators of me" in the context under current discussion (4:16),[4] comes in the same overall discussion of his own "planting" ministry (3:6) and the "watering" ministry of Apollos (3:7). (Some of the Corinthians obviously had been negatively comparing Paul to Apollos and Cephas [1:12; 3:22]). But Paul's intention in these chapters was not to write just about his own ministries—or those of Apollos or Cephas, for that matter. He wanted to challenge the Corinthians about the "work" (3:13–15) that "anyone" or "each one" does (3:10, 12–15), which will on the final day be tested by fire (3:13–15). He adds, "I have applied these things to myself and Apollos for your sakes" (4:6). These two chapters indicate that Paul wanted to use himself as an example of faithfully doing the work to which God had called him (4:1–4), even though he was at the same time asserting the validity of his ministry and authority in relation to the Corinthians (3:9; 4:15).

Similarly, in Philippians, Paul says, "Brothers, join in imitating me, and observe those who walk according to the pattern you have in us" (3:17). Later in the same letter he says, "The things you have learned and received and heard and seen in me, practice these things" (4:9). This modeling certainly included for Paul virtuous attitudes (3:15; 4:8), but it was not merely limited to attitudes; it also included modeling in activities (ministries) such as preaching and defending the gospel (1:7, 12–18), encouraging others in the Lord (2:1, 19–24), visiting those in prison (2:25–30), reconciling believers who were not getting along (4:3), and sharing in others' afflictions through monetary gifts (4:14–18).[5]

Another example of Paul's viewing his performance of ministry as that which should be imitated is found in Paul's relationship to the Thessalonians as taught in 1 Thessalonians. He says to the Thessalonian believers, "You also became imitators of us and of the Lord" (1:6).[6] The modeling of Paul and his co-workers Silvanus and Timothy (1:1) included the preaching of the gospel through words (1:5; 2:2, 9), exhortation and encouragement (2:3, 11; 3:2–3; 4:18; 5:11), and the sharing of their very lives (2:8).[7]

One striking instance of Paul as example brings this current discussion into dialogue with earlier chapters in this volume and to the particulars of his ministry assignment found in Ephesians 3:1–13, which was explored earlier in this chapter. Paul's discussion of his own ministry assignment in Ephesians 3 contains literary and thematic connections with Ephesians 4 that suggest strongly some aspects of modeling.[8] Paul knew that the young churches he founded would be watching his example and modeling their lives, to some degree, after his own. He was keenly aware of the educational effect of example.

How, though, does knowing about Paul's view of his own central ministry assignment(s) argue for the premise of this book, namely, that his lists in 1 Corinthians 12; Romans 12; and Ephesians 4 are primarily lists of ministries rather than lists of abilities? The answer, as in the preceding chapter, is that Paul's own ministry is one example of the types of ministry assignments that God has given to each and every person he has indwelt by his Spirit. As can be clearly concluded from the preceding discussion, Paul's own ministry assignments did not belong in a wholly different category from the ministries that he says are given to each believer. Rather, Paul is a model of one person to whom God gave specific ministry assignments, centering particularly on his call as apostle to the Gentiles. All believers have been given, as had Paul, various ministries through which we as Christians are to build up the body of Christ. Our particular assignments may be different from Paul's, but they are Spirit-given assignments nonetheless, and they are absolutely necessary for the health of the community of believers.

The list passages (Eph. 4; Rom. 12; 1 Cor. 12) are one element of Paul's overall teaching about ministry in the body of Christ. They are not a separate area of Pauline theology—as if there were two subjects, that is, ministry and spiritual gifts—although the lists are often treated that way in the conventional approach. Rather, there is one subject—the subject of ministry in the body.

SEVENTEEN

The Holy Spirit in the Letters of Paul

Summary: The heart of Paul's teaching about the Holy Spirit is not spiritual gifts. He focuses far more on the Holy Spirit's work in salvation and sanctification. In the study of Paul's letters, a reorientation of emphasis away from the spiritual gifts and toward these central emphases is needed.

AT THIS POINT it is not unreasonable to ask, *Does not the Holy Spirit empower believers when they serve the body of Christ?* Under the influence of the conventional view, many believers have become accustomed, after all, to thinking of spiritual gifts as empowerments. An acceptance of the spiritual-ministries approach might, then, raise such a question. It is true that the Spirit usually does empower believers to do whatever ministry he calls them to do, but such an empowering is no different from the general empowering God gives for whatever a Christian needs, not a special empowering that is uniquely tied to specific ministries in the church. God has sent his Spirit to give believers the power they need, not only for effective ministry, although that is truly the case, but also for overcoming sin, producing spiritual fruit, and praying and worshipping effectively.

But a discussion of Spirit empowering puts the cart before the horse. (See the following chapter in this volume for an examination of empowering for ministry.) First it is necessary to advance in a general understanding of what Paul taught and emphasized about the Holy Spirit, and in perspective on how his teaching about spiritual ministries fits in with his other teaching about the Holy Spirit. Although Paul's teaching on the Holy Spirit to first-century churches is situation-specific (and so is usually not laid out systematically), he reveals in his numerous—but often brief—comments about the Spirit that he has thought deeply about the person and work of the Holy Spirit.[1]

The goal of this chapter is to lay out briefly Paul's teaching, in general, about the Holy Spirit. Doing so has the partial goal of laying the groundwork for the more specific look at his teaching on the power of the Spirit and the theme of weakness in chapter 18 to follow.[2] Indeed, understanding the foundational emphases of Paul's teaching about the Holy Spirit will lead to understanding that the special-abilities approach to spiritual gifts moves away from what Paul really cared to communicate about the Holy Spirit, and will bring the reader's understanding of the Holy Spirit and his activities back into balance with Paul's central emphases.[3]

There are two areas that, more than any other, Paul emphasizes in his teaching about the Holy Spirit. The first is the Holy Spirit's work in salvation. From Paul's letters, we learn the following about the Spirit and salvation. God has given the Holy Spirit as a gift (Rom. 5:5; Gal. 3:5; 4:6; 1 Thess. 4:8) to each person who believes in Christ (Gal. 2:3–5; 3:14; Eph. 1:13–14). The evidence that we as believers truly belong to Christ is, in fact, the presence of the Spirit (Rom. 8:9, 14), who testifies with our human spirits that we are children of God (Rom. 8:16). The work of the Holy Spirit at salvation can be variously described as the baptism into one body (1 Cor. 14:13), the sending forth of the Spirit into our hearts (Gal. 4:6), the pouring out of the love of God into our hearts (Rom. 5:5), the giving of life (2 Cor. 3:6), inward circumcision (Rom. 2:29), the washing of regeneration and renewing by the Holy Spirit (Titus 3:5; cf. 1 Cor. 6:11), receiving the Spirit (Gal. 3:2), and indwelling by the Spirit

(Rom. 8:9; 1 Cor. 3:16; 2 Tim. 1:14). Access to God is through Christ in one Spirit (Eph. 2:18). Freedom from condemnation is mediated to us through the Spirit (Rom. 8:1–2). It is the work of the one Spirit that breaks down racial and social barriers (1 Cor. 12:13). Each person who believes is sealed with the Spirit (2 Cor. 1:22; Eph. 1:13; 4:30). This sealing represents a pledge that God will fully accomplish in the future all that he has promised to do (2 Cor. 1:21–22; 5:5; Eph. 1:14). Finally, Paul seems to assume in his letters that true salvation always leads to sanctification in the life of a believer, and this sanctifying work is a work of the Spirit (cf. 2 Thess. 2:13).

This last point leads naturally into Paul's other main emphasis when he teaches about the Holy Spirit, namely, the work of the Spirit in sanctification. Sanctification in this context refers to growth in holiness in the life of a believer. This emphasis is even more pronounced in Paul's writing than is the work of the Holy Spirit in salvation and probably constitutes the gravitational pull of Paul's teaching about the Holy Spirit. In Paul's teaching about the Holy Spirit, then, his emphasis is on the work of the Spirit in salvation and sanctification, but especially in sanctification, with an important aspect of that teaching being the cooperation with this work by believers who walk in the Spirit. While an extended look at this topic would be edifying, this present volume addresses spiritual ministries and not, except in a general way, the work of the Holy Spirit in the life of a believer. Therefore, the brief summary that follows will suffice for the current purpose.

First to be summarized is what the Holy Spirit does in sanctification, followed by how we as believers cooperate with the Holy Spirit in the process.

The grounding action for freedom from sin is Christ's atonement on the cross (Rom. 8:2–3), but that freedom is actualized for the believer through the ministry of the Spirit (Rom. 8:2, 4). The Holy Spirit leads us as believers (Rom. 8:14), and releases us from fear (Rom. 8:15). The Spirit testifies with our human spirits that we are children of God (Rom. 8:16). The Holy Spirit helps us when we don't know how to pray by interceding for us according to the will of God (Rom. 8:26–27; cf. Eph. 6:18). Worship and prayer are both done by the Spirit (Phil. 3:3; Eph. 6:18). The Holy Spirit works on the conscience of a believer (Rom. 9:1). The power of the Holy Spirit is the means through which we have hope (Rom. 15:13), and, indeed, through which all the fruit of the Spirit, beginning with love, is produced (Gal. 5:22–23; cf. 1 Thess. 1:6).[4] Maturing (or "perfecting"; cf. Gal. 3:3) is by the Spirit. The Spirit contends against the flesh[5] (Gal. 5:17) and releases us from the law when we are led by him (Gal. 5:18). The Holy Spirit fills us (Eph. 5:18). The Holy Spirit helps his people to guard the treasure that has been entrusted to them (2 Tim. 1:14). In short, sanctification is empowered "by the Spirit" (2 Thess. 2:13). Thus, Paul prays in Ephesians 3:16, "that he would grant you . . . to be strengthened with power through his Spirit in your inner being."[6]

Although sanctification is truly a work of the Spirit, believers can and must cooperate with the Spirit. We as believers do this by "setting our minds," or thinking constantly, on the things of the Spirit (Rom. 8:5). In so doing, we experience peace from the Holy Spirit (Rom. 8:6; 14:17). Since the Holy Spirit leads us, presumably we cooperate with the Spirit by allowing him to lead us and by following his lead (Rom. 8:14; Gal. 5:18). Paul says that the Spirit's leading successfully resists both the pull of the flesh and the pull of the law in our lives (Gal. 5:16–18, 23). When we pray, we pray "in the Spirit" (Eph. 6:18; cf. Rom. 8:26–27). Because we are sons (Rom. 8:15; "children" in v. 16), and, it would seem, because the Spirit dwells within us and motivates us to it, our prayer should be that of love, affection, and the intensely personal response, "Abba, Father!" (Rom. 8:15). We also cooperate with the Holy Spirit by allowing the Spirit to empower us to overcome sin in our lives. We are to glorify God in our bodies, which are temples for the Holy Spirit, by avoiding sexual immorality (1 Cor. 6:12–20; 1 Thess. 4:1–8). We should avoid "grieving" the Holy Spirit of God (Eph. 4:30) through unedifying talk (Eph. 4:29), bitterness, anger, and the like (Eph. 4:31). In general, we put to death the deeds of the body "by the Spirit" (Rom. 8:13; cf. 6:11–14). Since the promise is that those who walk by the Spirit "will not carry out the desire of the flesh" (Gal. 5:16), we must not "sow" to the flesh but rather to the Spirit (Gal. 6:8). Inasmuch as life was given by the Spirit, now we must "walk by the Spirit" (Gal. 5:16, 25). As a general characterization of our lives, we are to be "filled with the Spirit" (Eph. 5:18). Finally, "through the Spirit by faith" we wait for the hope of righteousness (Gal. 5:5).

In addition to the Holy Spirit's work in salvation and sanctification, there are other activities of the Holy Spirit that Paul seems keen to address. These include the Holy Spirit's work in revelation and illumination (1 Cor. 2:6–16; Eph. 3:5; 1 Thess. 4:8; 1 Tim. 4:1), the Holy Spirit as evidence that a new covenant age has dawned (2 Cor. 3:4–18; Gal. 3:14; 5:18, 23; Eph. 3:5),[7] the Holy Spirit as the promise of what God will do in the future (Rom. 8:11, 16–17, 23; 15:16; 2 Cor. 5:5; Eph. 1:13–14; 4:30; Gal. 5:5), and the Holy Spirit as the basis for fellowship among believers (2 Cor. 13:14; Eph. 2:22; 4:3–4; Phil. 2:1; 1 Thess. 5:19).[8] Each of these activities is important to Paul, but none is so emphasized by Paul as his teaching about the Holy Spirit's work in salvation and, even more so, in sanctification.

In contrast to this rich teaching about the Holy Spirit that regularly surfaces throughout Paul's letters, in the list passages the Holy Spirit plays a prominent role in the immediate context of the "manifestation of the Spirit" list (1 Cor. 12:8–10) but a less explicit role in the context of the other lists (1 Cor. 12:28–30; Rom. 12:6–8; Eph. 4:11). This is not to deny that Paul almost certainly understood that the grace that had been given to him was, as is apparent in so many of his discussions of ministry,[9] mediated by the Holy Spirit. It is to point out that, except in the list in 1 Corinthians 12:8–10 (which coheres under the concept of the items' manifesting the Spirit), Paul does not emphasize the Holy Spirit in these passages the way he does in passages such as Romans 8, Galatians 5, 1 Corinthians 2, or 2 Corinthians 3.[10] The somewhat light use of explicit references to the Holy Spirit in some of these ministry passages would not be noticeable were it not for Paul's insistence on mentioning the Holy Spirit in so many other passages throughout his letters. Clearly, the focal point of Paul's discussion of the Holy Spirit is not the so-called spiritual gifts but is the work of the Holy Spirit in salvation and sanctification.

Paul exhibits a rich understanding of the work of the Holy Spirit throughout his letters. The emphasis in our day on spiritual gifts (as abilities) pulls the focus away from Paul's central emphases. The current prominence given to individuals' special abilities in our generation has often caused believers to miss out on the richness of a theological and profoundly practical theme in Paul. A reemphasizing of Paul's own emphases on the Holy Spirit, both in our teaching and, indeed, in our lives, is long overdue.

EIGHTEEN

Empowering and Weakness in the Letters of Paul

Summary: God in his sovereignty usually empowers us, as believers, for the ministries to which he calls us, but sometimes he wants us to serve out of our weakness. The concept of serving out of weakness does not fit well with the conventional view.

GEORGE W. BUSH, in his acceptance speech for a second term of office as the president of the United States, said, "Do not pray for tasks equal to your powers; pray for powers equal to your tasks."[1] Believers praying for tasks equal to their powers might be an appropriate summary of the conventional view of spiritual gifts. Rather than praying for tasks equal to their powers, perhaps they should, in fact, be praying for powers equal to the tasks to which God has assigned them.

Let us assume for the moment that we've already decided not to base our decisions of which ministries to get involved in upon which spiritual abilities we have (the conventional view). Rather, we've decided to ask God to guide us into ministry assignments and pray for strength to do what he has called us to do (the spiritual ministries approach). Making this decision still leaves us with a question. Can we assume that God will always give us the strength to do the ministries into which he leads us? It seems to be a generally true statement (see discussion below) that, according to Paul's letters, the Holy Spirit regularly empowers us not only for a life of holiness, as seen in the previous chapter of this volume, but for ministry as well. But strong evidence in Paul's letters also suggests that he understood that God in his sovereignty would sometimes allow us to minister out of our areas of weakness, not just out of our strengths. How, though, does Paul's position on weakness and strength work together and how do they relate to the premise of this book? This chapter begins with a brief look at Paul's teaching about empowering for ministry, and then summarizes Paul's teaching about weakness. The result will serve as one more argument that the conventional view has misread Paul's teaching about spiritual gifts.

EMPOWERING FOR MINISTRY IN THE LETTERS OF PAUL

It is clear, according to the letters of Paul, that all aspects of a believer's life are to be empowered by God through the Holy Spirit. There is no spiritual activity whatsoever that can be done in a spiritually effective way apart from the Spirit's work. We cannot grow in sanctification apart from the empowering of the Spirit, nor can we do ministry unless God empowers us to do so. Since some of the focus of the previous chapter was on empowering for sanctification, the focus of the first section of this chapter will be on empowering for ministry. Nor will the argument in this current chapter be limited to passages that particularly mention the Holy Spirit, as was so in the previous chapter, since the Holy Spirit is sometimes not mentioned directly in passages about empowering for ministry, even though those passages are relevant to the current argument.

What did Paul believe about empowering for ministry? Paul, of course, attributed his ability to do signs and wonders to divine empowering (Rom. 15:18–19; 1 Cor. 2:4–5; 12:7–10; 2 Cor. 12:12;

Gal. 3:5; 1 Thess. 1:5). But he also saw the whole of his ministry and, indeed, particular aspects of that ministry, as divinely empowered as well: "I thank Christ Jesus our Lord, who has strengthened me, because he considered me faithful, placing me into service" (1 Tim. 1:12). Paul commented that his ministries of proclamation, admonition, and teaching were all "according to his power, which works within me" (Col. 1:28–29). Similarly, when he had to make his first public defense in Rome, he declared, "But the Lord stood with me and strengthened me, so that through me the message might be fully proclaimed" (2 Tim. 4:17). Furthermore, Paul understood that he had been enabled by God to comfort others because he had received comfort from God during his own afflictions (2 Cor. 1:5–7). Even the ministry of church discipline is done by him in the context of "the power of our Lord Jesus" (1 Cor. 5:4–5).

What is true of Paul in this case is also true of others. He encourages the Corinthians with his statement that, in the context of their ministry of giving, God "is able to make all grace abound to you, so that always having all that you need, you may overflow into every good deed" (2 Cor. 9:8).[2] It is "in the strength of his might" that believers also are "able to stand firm against the schemes of the devil" (Eph. 6:11; cf. 6:13, 17). The "weapons" of spiritual warfare have divine power (2 Cor. 10:4). Paul prayed for the Thessalonian believers, too, that God would "fulfill . . . the work of faith with power," suggesting that he expected a work of faith to be accompanied by power (2 Thess. 1:11). In the context of Timothy's own ministry, Paul says to Timothy, "God has not given us a spirit of fear, but of power and love and of good judgment" (2 Tim. 1:7). He makes various comments in a number of places to the effect that God gives the power needed for "every good work and word" (2 Thess. 2:17; cf. Col. 1:10–11; Eph. 3:20; Phil. 2:12–13).

It thus seems clear that Paul prayed and expected God regularly and in an ongoing way to empower Paul's own ministry and the ministries of others. This empowering does not seem to be a different kind from that which is needed for a life of sanctification;

all aspects of a believer's life are to be empowered by God through the Holy Spirit. How, then, do these references to "empowering" reconcile with Paul's theme of weakness in his letters to the church in Corinth?

WEAKNESS IN MINISTRY IN THE LETTERS OF PAUL

> And Caspian knelt and kissed the Lion's paw.
> "Welcome, Prince," said Aslan. "Do you feel yourself sufficient to take up the kingship of Narnia?"
> "I—I don't think I do, Sir," said Caspian. "I'm only a kid."
> "Good," said Aslan. "If you had felt yourself sufficient, it would have been a proof that you were not."[3]

Paul most often uses the terminology of weakness in the context of ministry, but such is not always the case. He speaks of weakness, for example, in our praying and the need for help from the Holy Spirit when we pray (Rom. 8:26–27), or he refers to simply as "the weak" those who need to grow spiritually (1 Thess. 5:14), or to Abraham's not becoming "weak in faith" (Rom. 4:19), or to bodily weakness (1 Cor. 15:43). He has dedicated discussions about the "strong" and the "weak," also, in Romans 14 and 1 Corinthians 8–10. But those references, and indeed all of these others, are largely separate from the theme under current discussion.

As stated above, most of Paul's use of weakness terminology comes in the context of ministry. Perhaps most significant in this regard is that the church receiving the most instruction on spiritual gifts—the church in Corinth, actually, receiving correction—is also the church that received almost all of Paul's comments on weakness in ministry. To speak of a theology of weakness in Paul's letters is, in fact, to speak of his teaching about weakness in the letters to the

Corinthian church (1 and 2 Corinthians), since those are the only letters in which he develops this theme to any significant degree.

The reason Paul's theology of weakness is so pronounced in his letters to Corinth is because a lot of people in the Corinthian church seem to have been complaining that Paul was, among other things, weak, and he felt that he had to respond to their complaints. It appears that some (but only some) of these complaints were incited by people who had come in from the outside and who were questioning Paul's authority so they could move in and get some of that authority for themselves. Other complaints may have been from people who were exploring whether to join the Christian movement but were unconvinced by Paul. And probably still other complaints may have been from regular members of the church. If we look at Paul's comments in the Corinthian letters, we can infer the types of complaints against him. Other complaints besides those listed below were probably lodged, but the ones listed here all intersect in some way with Paul's comments on the theme of weakness and more readily lead to an understanding of his teaching about weakness. It appears that some in Corinth were making comments such as,

- Paul isn't a very effective communicator. His speaking ability is contemptible (cf. 1 Cor. 2:1–4; 2 Cor. 10:10; 11:6).
- Paul's arguments are foolish. He isn't as sharp as some of the philosophers I've heard (cf. 1 Cor. 1:18–2:13).
- He doesn't look the part of an apostle (cf. 2 Cor. 5:12; 1 Cor. 4:11).
- A true apostle of Christ wouldn't experience the kinds of hardships that Paul does (cf. 1 Cor. 4:8–13; 2 Cor. 6:3–10).
- Other apostles get financial support for what they do. Paul doesn't take any money from us at all (cf. 1 Cor. 4:12; 9:1–18; 2 Cor. 11:7–9; 12:13).

- Paul doesn't keep his promises. He said he was going to come visit us again (cf. 2 Cor. 1:15–24).
- Paul hasn't given us any tangible proof that Christ actually speaks through him (cf. 2 Cor. 13:3).
- He doesn't see visions and receive revelations like the others (cf. 2 Cor. 12:1).
- Paul talks big in his letters, but in person seems rather weak (cf. 2 Cor. 10:1, 10; 13:3–4).

Paul responds in a variety of ways to such accusations. One of the key ways is by making comments about the true nature of foolishness (and wisdom) and weakness (and strength). He wants the Corinthian Christians to understand that their appraisal of him, and indeed of weakness in general, is wrong. Following is a short summary of Paul's comments to the Corinthians on the theme of weakness in the context of ministry (but only as a subtheme of his total response to the detractors in Corinth).

Paul declares that God uses the foolishness of the message to save those who believe (1 Cor. 1:21). God has deliberately chosen the foolish things of the world to shame the wise, and the weak to shame the strong, and the "nothings" to shame the "somethings" (1 Cor. 1:27–28). There is no ground for boasting (1 Cor. 1:29–31), except in Christ (1 Cor. 3:21–23). This apparently needed to be heard in an environment where boasting was a problem (1 Cor. 5:2, 6). Paul appears to have made a conscious decision while in Corinth to focus particularly on the message of a crucified Messiah (1 Cor. 2:2). One wonders whether he made this decision after his mostly unsuccessful attempt to reach the "wise" philosophers at Athens (cf. Acts 17:15–34; 1 Thess. 3:1). But as Christ was crucified in weakness, so Paul was content to minister out of weakness (2 Cor. 13:2–4).

God has allowed Paul and his co-workers (1 Cor. 4:9, 11–13) to be a spectacle to the world in their sufferings (1 Cor. 4:9) and to become fools for Christ's sake—weak and without honor (1 Cor. 4:10). Paul presses the point home with some sarcasm: "We have become as the scum of the world, the refuse of all things" (1 Cor. 4:13). He seems to have viewed his sufferings as a badge of honor and as indicating the genuineness of his apostolic calling (2 Cor. 6:3–10, esp. v. 4, "commending ourselves").

The basic virtues that undergird his theology of weakness are humility and faith (cf. 1 Cor. 2:5; 4:6–7, 21; 2 Cor. 1:9; 5:7; 10:1; 12:7). In contrast to his detractors, who were into power and prestige, Paul hoped to encounter in Corinth simplicity and purity toward Christ (2 Cor. 11:3). Rather than lording over their faith (2 Cor. 1:24), Paul dealt with the Corinthians "in weakness and in fear and in much trembling." (1 Cor. 2:3). He wanted his open and honest attitude to commend himself to their consciences (1 Cor. 4:2). Paul interspersed his entire discussion about weakness and foolishness with comments about true power. True power isn't found with those who perceive they are strong, but with those who know they are weak (1 Cor. 2:4; 4:19–21). Similarly, the way to become wise is by first becoming foolish (1 Cor. 3:18).

When Paul uses the metaphor of clay jars in 2 Corinthians 4:7, the jar is apparently a metaphor of weakness. It is within this fragile container "that the greatness of the power is of God and not from ourselves" (2 Cor. 4:7). The weaknesses and sufferings of Paul (2 Cor. 4:8–9), it seems, opened up the way for the life of Jesus to be powerfully manifested in and through his life (2 Cor. 4:11). At one point Paul bursts out, "Who is adequate for these things?" (2 Cor. 2:16). These passages, then, taken as they are, in a context of the gospel ministry, indicate that God sometimes calls one to minister out of one's weakness. In the chapter of 2 Corinthians that follows, Paul himself answers the question he asked about adequacy: "Not that we are adequate in ourselves to consider anything as from ourselves, but our adequacy is from God" (2 Cor. 3:5).

Paul says that true strength comes not from comparing oneself with others, who only compare themselves with each other; it is God who commends and gives a sphere for ministry (2 Cor. 10:12–18; cf. 12:6). Paul doesn't seem even to mind being viewed among the

Corinthians as unapproved[4] or weak as long as they end up doing what is right and grow strong in the faith (2 Cor. 13:5–9). Paul implies that sometimes to reach the weak, one must oneself become weak (1 Cor. 9:22; cf. 2 Cor. 11:29).

Although in one section Paul repeatedly uses the language of boasting (starting in 2 Cor. 11:1 and tapering off in the middle of chap. 12), it appears that he is very uncomfortable displaying his qualifications and would never have done so if he hadn't felt driven to it by all the criticisms of his detractors (2 Cor. 11:21; 12:11). So he takes on the tone and demeanor of his detractors in order to mitigate their criticisms (2 Cor. 11:12). Still, he clearly would much rather talk about the weakness and sufferings that he endured to carry out the ministry God had given him (2 Cor. 11:30; 12:5).[5]

The most important passage for understanding Paul's thinking about weakness is 2 Corinthians 12:1–10 (esp. vv. 9–10). He had been given a thorn in his flesh[6] to keep him from exalting himself after seeing (or participating in) an amazing vision. Paul asked the Lord three times (likely in three separate periods of prayer) to take the thorn away. The Lord responded by reminding him of two precious truths:

1. "My grace is enough for you" (v. 9);
2. "Power is perfected in weakness" (v. 9).

Paul's response to such a revelation is to "boast" gladly about his weakness so that the power of Christ may dwell in him (v. 9). Furthermore, if this is how God works, writes Paul, he is "content" with weakness and difficulties, "for when I am weak, then I am strong" (v. 10). According to him, weakness is the path to spiritual power.[7]

It is significant that, as a bridge to the two lists found in the Corinthian letters, the weakness theme leads right back into the heart of 1 Corinthians 12, that is, to the section between these two lists. In 1 Corinthians 12:22–23 Paul says, "On the contrary, the parts of the body that seem weaker are necessary, and those parts of the body which we think less honorable we clothe with the greater honor." Although in context this is an analogy with parts of the human body, Paul's basic point is clear: the ministries of the weaker members are needed for the health of the church.

With the preceding discussion in mind, once again the question is posed. Paul assumes that when God calls believers to an area of ministry he will empower us for ministry. How, then, does that assumption reconcile with his own insistence that God works through our weakness?

The answer is twofold. First, God always wants believers to serve out of humility, dependence, and trust with an understanding that we as believers are, in fact, weak and need his empowering for any effective spiritual ministry. Second, God in his sovereignty usually, although not always, empowers us when he calls us to serve, but sometimes he calls us to serve in an area where we sense that we are weak and are less than effective. Paul's own ministry well illustrates this kind of service. Although elsewhere he describes his preaching and teaching ministry as "according to his power which works within me" (Col. 1:28–29), in the context of the Corinthian church (cf. 2 Cor. 11:6) Paul seems aware of weakness in preaching and teaching—they certainly viewed him as inadequate as a speaker (cf. 2 Cor. 10:10). Even though it is clear that preaching and teaching were two of the ministry assignments given to him by God (1 Tim. 2:7; 2 Tim. 1:11), it appears from his ministry at Corinth that God sometimes wanted Paul to preach and/or teach in situations where he was not always powerful and effective as a preacher and/or teacher.

But why might God ask believers sometimes to serve out of weakness rather than strength? There are at least three reasons, all of them found in the Corinthian letters. First, as has already been discovered, God's power "is perfected in weakness" (2 Cor. 12:9). God may choose to do his work of power, to continue the teacher illustration, not by making a particular teaching session powerful, but by showing that he himself is powerful through the one who has received this teaching assignment, even though the teacher is teaching out of weakness.[8]

Second, God might ask us as believers to serve out of our weakness so that he can do something, not just through us, but in us. Remember, his goal for us is not just to use us but also to do a work of transforming power in us. Paul said in 2 Corinthians 12:9, "Most gladly, therefore, I will rather boast about my weaknesses, so that the power of Christ may rest upon me."

Third, Paul explained that the main reason God allowed him to suffer affliction in Asia was "so that we would not trust in ourselves, but in God who raises the dead" (2 Cor. 1:9). Similarly, God may sometimes allow us in a small way to suffer as we serve in areas of weakness so that we will learn to trust in him, deeply and radically.

Have you ever been in a place of ministry where you were confident that God wanted you there, and at the same time felt that you were serving out of weakness? I frequently hear people relate such experiences from their own ministries. But how do those experiences align with the conventional view of spiritual gifts—that God gives us abilities (strengths) that we have to discover, and that our places of service should be determined by those abilities? The short answer is that it doesn't align at all with the conventional view. Paul's numerous comments on weakness in the Corinthian letters argue against the conventional view of spiritual gifts as abilities but fit quite comfortably with the so-called spiritual gifts actually being God-given ministries. God sometimes wants us to serve out of our weakness, not just out of our strengths.

An apt way to conclude this chapter is with this challenge from Henry and Mel Blackaby: "So never put limits on how God can use your life. Obey almighty God and trust that He knows what He's doing in your life. Don't look at your abilities and natural talents alone and serve only in the areas you feel competent. If you do, you'll eliminate yourself from significant arenas of service."[9]

PART FOUR

IMPLICATIONS AND APPLICATIONS

NINETEEN

Early Church Ministries in the Letters of Paul

THE ITEMS IN Paul's list passages (Eph. 4:11–12; Rom. 12:6–8; 1 Cor. 12:8–10, 28–30) are not meant to be comprehensive, but rather representative. Although the four lists overlap at a number of points, no two are alike, and not one of the lists contains all the ministry assignments that are included on all four lists. Was the church in Corinth impoverished because Paul failed to list evangelist or mercy among the ministry roles he mentions? "Evangelist," after all, appears in Ephesians 4:11 and "one who shows mercy" in Romans 12:6–8.

Two lists include, among some of their more particular entries, items that, rather than as concrete examples, should be viewed as general descriptions of ministries (i.e., Rom. 12:6–8; 1 Cor. 12:28–30): "service" (Rom. 12:7), "one who leads" (Rom. 12:8), "one who shows mercy" (Rom. 12:8), "helps" (1 Cor. 12:28), and "administrations" (1 Cor. 12:28). These entries seem more general, whereas other items on the lists would be more easily recognized as particular examples of specific ministries.

The spiritual ministries contained in Paul's list passages, then, belong in a category with other ministry assignments that are found in the documents of the earliest days of the church. The chart included in this chapter is an attempt to compile a comprehensive list of anything that might reasonably be considered a ministry assignment in the first-century church. It also serves partially as a transition into application and partially to set Paul's ministry lists in a proper context. The chart does the latter by providing concrete examples of ministries in the letters of Paul. The following chapter 20 of this volume contains a chart of concrete examples of ministries from all the other New Testament writings that describe the period after the ascension of Christ and coming of the Spirit (Acts, General Letters [Hebrews–Jude] and Revelation). No doubt this list is missing a few items that arguably could have been included, and may include some items that one could argue do not belong. But the goal is to include as many early church examples of specific ministries that can be found in the New Testament and thus to offer a fairly comprehensive list of early church ministries as a reference point for moving into implications and applications.

More specifically, the goal is to list concrete examples of early church ministries—particular activities that were done with a view to the building up of the church (like teaching or pioneer missionary work)—rather than general virtues that should characterize all believers (like love or joy). Nevertheless, some might prefer to see such examples as "hospitality" on a list of more general Christian virtues, but such appear on this list because of their nature as particular activities that strengthen the church.[1] Simply because, however, there's a somewhat fuzzy line between ministries and Christian virtues does not diminish the value of drawing up such a list and using it as a point of reference.

You, as reader, do not need to take in all the items on this list (or on the list in the following chapter). Rather, you can skim the list to become familiar with the types and extent of the various ministries in the letters of Paul (and in the following chapter, outside the letters of Paul). These lists will help you to think more broadly about the types of ministries that God may be assigning to you.[2] This is why the chart is included at this point before more general implications and applications are drawn. The most significant implication of this study is that all believers should be dedicated to serving in the various roles into which God has placed them, and in so doing, building up the community of faith. If you want to know what is meant by a ministry, the following list will prove to be of significant value. The chart begins with examples of ministries found outside of the four list passages in the letters of Paul.

CONCRETE EXAMPLES OF MINISTRIES IN THE LETTERS OF PAUL (OUTSIDE OF THE LIST PASSAGES)

Proclamation of the gospel (Rom. 1:9, 15–16; 10:14–15; 1 Cor. 1:21–23; 2:1, 4; 9:14–18, 23; 2 Cor. 1:19; 4:2–6; 5:11; 11:7; Gal. 1:11–12, 16; 4:13; Eph. 6:19–20; 1 Thess. 2:1–12), sometimes viewed as the passing on of apostolic teaching (1 Cor. 15:1ff.; 2 Thess. 2:15; 2 Tim. 2:2) or being witnesses of the resurrection (1 Cor. 15:15–17)	Apostleship (Rom. 1:1, 5; 1 Cor. 9:1–5; 15:7–9; 2 Cor. 11:5; Gal. 1:17–19; 1 Thess. 2:6), including Paul's own ministry calling (Rom. 15:16–21; Gal. 2:7–9; Eph. 3:1–13; Col. 1:25)[3]	Prayer and petition (Rom. 1:9–10; 12:12; 1 Cor. 14:15; Eph. 6:18–19; Col. 4:12; 1 Thess. 1:2; 3:10; 1 Tim. 2:1–2, 8; 2 Tim. 1:3; Philem. 4)
Encouragement, strengthening, refreshing, exhortation (Rom. 1:12; 1 Cor. 16:17–18; 2 Cor. 7:13; Col. 4:11; 1 Thess.	Generous financial giving to those who are poor, both believers and unbelievers (Rom. 12:13; 15:25–27, 31; 1 Cor. 13:3;	Overseeing a case of church discipline (1 Cor. 5:3–5; 2 Cor. 10:6; 13:2; 2 Thess. 3:14–15; Titus 3:10), including the

2:3, 11; 3:2; 5:11; 5:14; 1 Tim. 1:16; 4:13; Philem. 7)	16:1–4; 2 Cor. 8:1–9:15; Gal. 2:10; Phil. 4:14–19; 1 Tim. 6:18)	restoration of those who have repented (2 Cor. 2:5–11)
Hospitality (Rom. 12:13; 1 Cor. 16:6; 1 Tim. 3:2; 5:10; Titus 1:8; Philem. 22)[4]	Pioneer work/ church planting (Rom. 15:20–21; 2 Cor. 10:14, 16)	Holding church meetings in your house (Rom. 16:5; 1 Cor. 16:19; Col. 4:15; Philem. 2)
Baptizing (1 Cor. 1:14–17)	Reminding believers of what they have already learned (1 Cor. 4:17)	Financially supporting mission work (1 Cor. 9:14)
Various signs and wonders (Rom. 15:19; 2 Cor. 12:12; 1 Thess. 1:5)	Ministry by example; modeling (1 Cor. 4:16; 11:1; 2 Cor. 5:11; 1 Thess. 1:5–7; 2:8–10; 2 Thess. 3:7–9; 1 Tim. 4:12; Titus 2:7)	Teaching (1 Cor. 4:17; 14:26; Gal. 6:6; Col. 1:28; 1 Thess. 5:12; 1 Tim. 1:5; 2:7; 2:12; 3:2; 4:11, 13, 16; 5:17; 6:2; 2 Tim. 1:11; 2:24; 3:10)
Acting as a mediator among believers in difficult situations (1 Cor. 6:5; Phil. 4:2–3; Philem. 8–21)	Prophecy (1 Cor. 13:2, 8–9; 14:1–6, 22–33, 37; 1 Thess. 5:20; 1 Tim. 1:18)	Knowledge (1 Cor. 1:5; 13:2, 8–9; 2 Cor. 11:6)
Tongues (1 Cor. 13:8; 14:1–33, 39–40)	Interpretation of tongues (1 Cor. 14:13, 27–28)	Faith (1 Cor. 13:2)

Martyrdom (1 Cor. 13:3; Phil. 1:20–24; 2 Tim. 4:6)[5]	Praying/singing/ blessing in the spirit/Spirit and with the mind (1 Cor. 14:15–16)	Sharing a psalm in a meeting (1 Cor. 14:26)
Receiving and delivering a revelation (1 Cor. 14:26; Gal. 2:2)	Bringing comfort (2 Cor. 1:4–7; 7:6; Eph. 6:22; 1 Thess. 3:7; 4:18)	Letter-writing (2 Cor. 7:8; 10:9–10; 2 Thess. 2:15)[6]
Suffering for Christ as ministry (2 Cor. 4:7–10; Phil. 1:12–18; 1 Thess. 1:8; 2 Tim. 1:8; 2:9; 3:11; 4:5)[7]	Rebuke/admonition (Rom. 15:14; 2 Cor. 7:8–12; 12:19; 13:10; Gal. 2:11–14; Eph. 1:28; Col. 1:28; 4:17; 1 Thess. 5:14; 1 Tim. 5:1, 20; 2 Tim. 2:14; 3:16; 4:2; Titus 1:13; 2:15; 3:10)[8]	Being responsible for handling with integrity money collected from the church (2 Cor. 8:18–21)
Escorting believers as they travel from place to place (2 Cor. 8:19–20; cf. 1 Cor 16:11–12)[9]	Apologetic ministry—defense of the faith (2 Cor. 10:4–5; Phil. 1:16)	Working for one's own needs to serve others (2 Cor. 11:8–9; 1 Thess. 2:9; 2 Thess. 3:8)
Restoring (on a personal level) someone who has been caught in sin (Gal. 6:1; cf. 2 Tim. 2:25–26)	Equipping the saints so they can do the work of the ministry (Eph. 4:12)	Speaking an edifying word according to the need of the moment (Eph. 4:29)

Using psalms and hymns and spiritual songs to teach and admonish one another (Eph. 5:19; Col. 3:16)	Relaying information about how someone is doing, often for encouragement (Eph. 6:21; Phil. 2:19; Col. 4:7–9; 1 Thess. 3:6–7)	Serving as an overseer/elder (Phil. 1:2; 1 Tim. 3:1–7; 5:17; Titus 1:6–9)
Serving as a deacon (Phil. 1:2; 1 Tim. 3:8–13) or deaconess (Rom. 16:1–2; perhaps 1 Tim. 3:11)	Ministering to someone in prison (Phil. 2:25–30; 2 Tim. 1:16–17; 4:9–11; Philem. 13)	Carrying and delivering a money gift from a church (Phil. 4:18; 2 Cor. 8:19)
Correcting false doctrine (Gal. 1:6–9; Col. 2:8–23; 2 Thess. 2:3; 1 Tim. 1:3–7; 4:1–6; 6:3–5, 20–21; 2 Tim. 2:14–19, 23; 3:1–9; 4:3–5; Titus 1:9–13)	Helping the weak (1 Thess. 5:14); assisting those in distress (1 Tim. 5:10)	Administering the distribution to widows who are cared for by the church (1 Tim. 5:9–10, 16)
Evaluating prophetic utterances (1 Thess. 5:21; 1 Cor. 14:29)	Public reading of Scripture (1 Tim. 4:13)	Preaching (1 Tim. 5:17; 6:2)
Mentoring (1–2 Timothy, esp. 2 Tim. 2:2; Titus)	Doing the work of an evangelist (2 Tim. 4:5)	Defending the faith before secular courts (2 Tim. 4:16)
Appointing elders (Titus 1:5)	Older women teaching younger women (Titus 2:3)	Helping traveling missionaries (Titus 3:13)

If the various items from the lists Paul has drawn up himself were added to the above chart (Eph. 4:11–12; Rom. 12:6–8; 1 Cor. 12:8–10; 28–30), it would quickly become evident that they belong there, as they could have easily been incorporated into that list.

Apostle (1 Cor. 12:28, 29; Eph. 4:11)	Prophet/prophecy (1 Cor. 12:10, 28, 29; Eph. 4:11; Rom. 12:6)	Teacher/teaching/ pastor-teacher (1 Cor. 12:28, 29; Rom. 12:7; Eph. 4:11)
Evangelist (Eph. 4:11)	Miracles (1 Cor. 12:10, 28, 29)	Healings (1 Cor. 12:9, 28, 30)
Helps (1 Cor. 12:28), serving (Rom. 12:8), giving (Rom. 12:8), mercy (Rom. 12:8)	Leadership (Rom. 12:8) and administrations (1 Cor. 12:28)	Exhortation (encouragement) (Rom. 12:8)
Word of wisdom and word of knowledge (1 Cor. 12:8)	Faith (1 Cor. 12:9)	Distinguishing between spirits (1 Cor. 12:10)
Tongues (1 Cor. 12:10, 28, 30)	Interpretation of tongues (1 Cor. 12:10, 30)	

Beyond these concrete examples of early church ministries, Paul's letters are filled with a few dozen metaphors for ministry. Here are only six examples (a more complete list can be found in the note).[10]

- Agricultural: Planting or watering (1 Cor. 3:6–8; 9:11)
- Commercial: Managing what was entrusted to one as a steward (1 Cor. 4:1; 9:17; Eph. 3:2; Titus 1:7)

- Military: Serving as a soldier (1 Cor. 9:7; 2 Tim. 2:3–4)
- Familial: Serving in the furtherance of the gospel like a child serving his father (Phil. 2:22)
- Architectural: Doing the work of a builder (Rom. 15:20; 1 Cor. 3:10–15)
- Domestic: Serving as a slave of Christ (Rom. 1:1; 1 Cor. 7:22; 2 Cor. 4:5; Gal. 1:10; Eph. 6:6; Phil. 1:1; 2 Tim. 2:24; Titus 1:1)

Paul's letters are also filled with general expressions for service to the Lord, such as serving the church (Rom. 16:1), striving together for the faith of the gospel (Phil. 1:27), fulfilling one's ministry (2 Tim. 4:5), and many references to doing the work of the Lord.[11]

Moreover, Paul mentions various people who were obviously co-workers with him on some level and who were involved in particular ministries, although often it is not known specifically what they were doing. Examples include Phoebe, "a servant/deacon of the church which is at Cenchrea . . . for she has also been a helper of many, and of myself as well" (Rom. 16:1–2); the household of Stephanas, who "have devoted themselves to ministry to the saints" (1 Cor. 16:15); Tychicus, "the beloved brother and faithful servant and co-slave in the Lord" (Col. 4:7; cf. Eph. 6:21); Euodia and Syntyche, "these women who have shared my struggle in the gospel" (Phil. 4:3); Epaphras, "our beloved co-slave, who is a faithful servant of Christ on our behalf" (Col. 1:7); and Archippus, to whom Paul said, "Pay attention to the ministry which you have received in the Lord, that you may fulfill it" (Col. 4:17).

It is of interest that if someone were to compare this list of ministries found in the letters of Paul with a list drawn up from other post-Pentecost New Testament literature, that person would discover substantial overlap between the lists. In other words, the ministries Paul mentions in his letters are activities that happened not solely in his sphere of ministry, but belong together with all the ministries that were functioning in various places among first-century believers in Christ.

Although most everything in this book to this point has focused on the letters of Paul, a chart of other post-Pentecost New Testament ministries is presented in the following chapter. Taken together, these charts will round out the understanding of the types of ministries that first-century Christians were involved in and thereby aid believers in considering how to minister to one another in the twenty-first century.

TWENTY

Early Church Ministries Outside the Letters of Paul

As has been seen from the chart in the preceding chapter, Paul's lists of ministry assignments fit into a general list of ministries found in his own letters. They fit comfortably as well into a general list of ministries from the other post-Pentecost writings of the New Testament.[1] As mentioned in the previous chapter, you as reader can skim through the chart presented in this chapter to see the types and extent of various ministries mentioned in the New Testament. Doing so is one means of considering and praying through how and where you should serve.[2]

Concrete Examples of Ministries in the Early Church (Outside of the Letters of Paul)

Public proclamation of the gospel (Acts 2:37–41; 3:12–26; 4:31; 8:5, 12, 25; 9:20; 10:34–43; 11:19–21; 13:5, 15–41; 14:1, 3, 7, 25; 16:10; 16:28–34; 17:13, 18; 18:4, 19, 27–28; 19:8–9; 20:25; 21:8;

Prayer (Acts 6:4; Heb. 13:18; James 5:14–18; Jude 20; Rev. 8:4), including corporate prayer (Acts 1:14; 4:24–31; 12:5, 12; 13:2–3; 14:23; 16:25; 20:36; 28:8–9)

Sharing of money and property with believers in need (Acts 2:45; 4:32–37; 5:1–11; Heb. 13:16; James 2:15–16), including sharing with other believers or churches at a

22:1–21; 26:19–20; 28:17–28, 30–31), often described as being witnesses (Acts 1:8, 22; 23:11; 26:16; Heb. 2:3; 1 Peter 5:1)	with fasting (Acts 13:2–3; 14:23)[3]	distance (Acts 11:29–30; 12:25)
Baptizing (Acts 1:8; 8:12, 38–39; 10:47–48; 16:15, 33; 18:8; 19:5; 22:16)	Apostleship (Acts 1:25; 1 Peter 1:1)	Speaking in tongues (Acts 2:4–13; 10:44–46; 19:6)
Prophecy (Acts 2:17–18; 13:1; 15:32; 19:6), including but not limited to predictive prophecy (Acts 11:27–28; 21:4, 9, 10–11; 27:21–26, 31, 33–34)	Apologetic ministry/arguing the truth of the message (Acts 6:10; 9:22, 29; 17:1–4, 18–34; 18:4–5, 19; 18:27–28; 19:8–9; 1 Peter 3:15)	Sharing the gospel one on one or in small groups (Acts 8:27–37; 10:34–43; 16:14–15, 31–34; 24:25)
Signs and wonders (Acts 2:43; 5:12; 6:8; 8:6, 13; 14:4; 19:11; Heb. 2:4)	Healing (Acts 3:1–10; 5:15–16; 8:7; 9:32–35; 14:8–10; 19:12; 22:13; 28:8–9; James 5:14–15)	Defense of the faith before authorities (Acts 3:5–12; 7:1–53; 26:1–32)
Casting out demons (Acts 5:16; 8:7; 16:16–18; 19:12)	Suffering for Christ (Acts 5:40–41; 12:4; 16:19–25)[4]	Distributing food among needy believers (Acts 6:1–6)

Ministry of the Word (Acts 6:4)	Martyrdom (Acts 7:54–60; 12:2; Rev. 2:13; 6:9–11)[5]	Admonishing and rebuking (Acts 8:20–23; 20:30)
Commissioning of someone to ministry, to apostolic/ missionary work (Acts 9:15–16 with 22:14–15; 13:3) and to eldership (Acts 14:23)	Helping believers who have been persecuted (Heb. 13:3), including helping them escape from their persecutors (Acts 9:25; 17:10, 14), washing their wounds (Acts 16:33), acting as a spokesperson for the group being persecuted (Acts 17:7–9), and ministering to those in prison (Acts 24:23; Heb. 13:3)	Encouraging and strengthening of believers (Acts 11:23; 14:21–22; 15:32, 41; 16:5, 40; 18:26; Heb. 3:13; 10:24–25) and exhortation (Acts 20:1–2)[6]
Speaking on behalf of a believer to another believer (Acts 9:26–27; 11:1–18)	Doing deeds of kindness (Acts 9:36), including making clothes for people (Acts 9:39)	Raising the dead (Acts 9:36–43; 20:9–10)
Hospitality (Acts 9:43; 16:15; 16:34; 17:7; 18:7; 21:7, 17; 28:14; Heb. 13:2; 1 Peter 4:9)	Receiving and sharing a vision (Acts 2:17; 10:9–16, 23; 16:13–15)	Being a support person on a missionary team (Acts 10:23; 13:5)

Breaking down ethnic barriers (Acts 10:34–43; 13:46–49)	Standing with someone at a defense before believers (Acts 11:12)	Teaching believers as an ongoing ministry (Acts 11:26; 13:1; 15:32; 18:11; Heb. 5:12; James 3:1)
Carrying and distributing money or food for those struck by famine (Acts 11:30; 12:25)[7]	Missionary work—going to other places (Acts 13:2ff.)	Spiritual warfare/power encounter (Acts 13:8–12; 16:16–18)
Personal follow-up after public proclamation (Acts 13:43)	Visiting places of past ministry, whether of one's own ministry or those of someone else (Acts 11:22–23; 14:21–22; 15:36)	Serving as an elder/overseer (Acts 14:23; 20:28; 1 Peter 5:1) or other leader (Heb. 13:17); shepherding the flock (1 Peter 5:2)
Reporting back about what God has done on a missionary trip (Acts 14:27; 15:3; 21:19)	Wrestling through and deciding on an important doctrinal issue proposed by leaders (Acts 15:6–29)	Carrying and delivering a decision made by leaders (here the apostles; Acts 15:22, 30; 16:4)[8]
Letter-writing (Acts 15:23–29; 18:27; 1 Peter 5:12)	Singing hymns of praise to God (Acts 16:25)[9]	Starting a new small group or church of believers (Acts 16:40; 17:34)

Escorting believers as they travel from one place to another (Acts 10:23; 17:15; 20:4–5; 21:5, 16; 28:15)[10]	Working as a tentmaker for one's own support and the support of others on the ministry team (Acts 18:3; 20:34–35)	Bringing greetings to a church (Acts 18:22; 21:7, 19)
Explaining the way of God more fully to someone who only has partial understanding (Acts 18:26; 19:4)	Preaching in a church setting (Acts 20:7, 27), including giving a charge to church leaders (Acts 20:17–35)	Ministry through example/modeling (Acts 20:35; 21:26; Heb. 6:12; 13:7; 1 Peter 2:12; 3:1–6; 5:3)
Visiting orphans and widows in their distress (James 1:27)	Turning back and restoring someone who has committed sins (James 5:15, 19–20), or those who are doubting (Jude 22–23), including prayer in such situations (1 John 5:16)	Countering false teaching (2 Peter 2:1–22; 1 John 2:26–27; 4:1–6; 2 John 7–11; Jude 3–19; Rev. 2:6)
Supporting people who are traveling ministers (3 John 8)[11]	Putting to the test those who call themselves apostles but are not (Rev. 2:2)	

As in Paul's letters, sometimes outside of his letters general expressions for ministry are found, such as "speaking" (1 Peter 4:11), "serving" (1 Peter 4:11), or "the work and the love which you have shown toward his name in having ministered and in still ministering to the saints" (Heb. 6:10). Paul seems to be unique, however, at least among the New Testament letter-writers, in extensively using metaphors for ministry, many dozens of which appear in his epistles.[12] In comparison, relatively few metaphors for ministry appear in the New Testament letters not written by Paul.[13]

The charts drawn up in this chapter and in the previous chapter together offer a comprehensive list of New Testament ministries (post-Pentecost). It is in this broader list of ministries that Paul's ministry lists, which have been under study in this book (Eph. 4:11–12; Rom. 12:6–8; 1 Cor. 12:8–10, 28–30), sit most comfortably.

The ministries found in the charts in these two chapters can be used to suggest the types of ministries that should be taking place among believers for the building up of the church in our day. This is not to say, of course, that every activity found in these two charts is transferable into the present day; some may be particular to the immediate situation in which they were first done. Not all believers today, for example, have been called in a vision to preach in Macedonia, although Paul himself received such a vision and calling at a particular time on his second missionary journey (cf. Acts 16:9–10). Nor is it to say that, as believers, we should limit ourselves to the specific ministries found in these charts, although these ministries are comparable to most of the types of ministries that will be done in churches today. But as God moves us into long-term ministries, such as teaching, and short-term ministries, such as an edifying word for the need of the moment (Eph. 4:29), each of us will build up the body of Christ and bring glory to him.

TWENTY-ONE

What Difference Does It Make?

Significant Implications of the Spiritual-Ministries Approach

CHAPTER 3 OF this volume introduced a few implications of the premise of this book so that readers would be aware of the relevance of the spiritual-ministries approach as they read subsequent chapters. The present chapter simply summarizes a number of the more significant implications of viewing the spiritual gifts primarily in the category of ministry assignments rather than in the category of special abilities. Moreover, in a number of instances, the implications highlight practical weaknesses in the conventional view while underlining the relevance of the spiritual-ministries approach.

NATURAL ABILITIES OR SPECIAL ABILITIES?

Those working within the conventional view struggle to answer this question: Are their "gifts" special and unique abilities that they did not possess before conversion or are they intensifications of natural talents that they already had before conversion? This difficulty is eliminated if Paul's concern is ministries.

COMPREHENSIVE OR REPRESENTATIVE?

Proponents of the conventional view often pose another question: Are Paul's lists (Eph. 4:11–12; Rom. 12:6–8; 1 Cor. 12:8–10, 28–30) comprehensive of all possible Spirit-given abilities, or are there other abilities beyond these lists? (Examples might include such "gifts" as music or martyrdom.) But once it is understood that the items on the lists belong together with all the ministries mentioned in the letters of Paul (see chap. 19), and indeed with all the ministries mentioned in the New Testament (see chap. 20), it is clear that the lists must be representative rather than comprehensive. It is clear that Paul himself did not intend his lists to be comprehensive; each list Paul compiled is, after all, different from the other lists. Thus, as brothers and sisters in Christ, our place can be affirmed and our involvement encouraged in the whole spectrum of ministries that strengthen the body of Christ.

ONE MINISTRY OR MANY?

Another difficulty for proponents of the conventional view is deciding whether Christians have only one special ability or whether they have more than one. But once it is understood that the primary category for these items is ministries rather than abilities, this question is readily answered: Everyone will have at least one ministry, but many will have more. Paul, as mentioned before, was "a preacher and an apostle and a teacher" (2 Tim. 1:11; cf. 1 Tim. 2:7), he performed miracles and healings (Acts 19:11–12), he was an evangelist (Eph. 3:1–13), and he was a tongues-speaker (1 Cor. 14:18). Other New Testament people, similarly, have a variety of ministry roles. Each Christian should definitely be involved in at least one ministry, but the Lord usually assigns Christians to various ministries on various levels.[1]

NO EXCUSES

Ephesians 4:7 says "to each one of us" grace is given. Although Paul's understanding of grace is rich, wide, and varied, his use of the "grace" + "given" combination, as has already been argued in chapter 13, evidently points toward God's extension of grace in giving someone a place of ministry. The significance for the current discussion is that Paul emphasizes that such grace for ministry has been given "to each one." Similarly, in 1 Corinthians 12:7 and 12:13, he again uses the language of "to each one."[2] Unlike the conventional view, in which one could potentially have an ability and not use it—or not even know that one has it—in the spiritual ministries approach, God simply assigns each believer to at least one area of ministry, and probably to more in most cases. This means that each person who belongs to Christ should be actively involved in the work of the ministry on some level.

One woman I know almost dropped out of teaching women's Bible studies just before her first teaching session because she was struggling to get over her fear of public speaking. In the process, she began to question whether she was actually gifted to teach (that is, the conventional view). The irony was that for a long time leading up to this struggle, she'd sensed a strong calling to just such a teaching ministry, perhaps even as her central life ministry. As it turned out, she confronted her fear and began teaching regularly, to the great blessing of many women (herself included). Because of the conventional view of gifts as abilities she perceived her lack of ability as an excuse for not entering a particular ministry, even though everything else pointed her in that direction. She wouldn't have been tempted to use this excuse if she'd been reading these gifts as ministry callings, since she was already convinced of God's leading.

No Soloists

Note the way that Paul distributes the ministries in Romans 12:6–8, using the word *differing* (v. 6) along with the "everyone does not" rhetorical questions at the end of 1 Corinthians 12. Both devices point toward the idea that nobody alone can or should try to do everything. Every member is to do the work of the ministry; it's the business not of just pastors and those in leadership positions (Eph. 4:11–12).

SHORT-TERM OR LONG-TERM?

Another discussion commonly heard in special abilities circles is whether the gifts are lifelong, or whether they come and go. But once the gifts are understood to be ministry assignments, and when they are read in conjunction with all of the other ministries mentioned in the letters of Paul (and beyond), it becomes far more plausible to view some as long-term—sometimes even lifelong—ministries, and some as short-term—or even spontaneous—ministries. If the activity in question is one that builds up the body of Christ, it is, indeed, a ministry, and it can be either long-term or short-term. Note, however, that the ministry itself does not necessarily determine whether it is short-term or long-term; certain ministries, such as ministries of leadership, are generally longer-term whereas some ministries, such as speaking an edifying word or speaking in a tongue, are usually shorter-term. But someone could conceivably speak in tongues repeatedly over a long period of time (cf. 1 Cor. 14:18) or could be in a leadership role for a relatively short time. Length of ministry presents no problem for the spiritual-ministries approach, which affirms that the ministries can be either short-term or long-term.

MINISTRIES OF LEADERSHIP

One implication of the spiritual-ministries view concerns leadership. Spiritual ministries implies that, although every member is called to ministry, only some of those assignments are to positions of leadership. Conventional readings can sometimes have the effect of flattening out notions of leadership, suggesting that on the basis of everyone's having been given gifts, then everyone is equal and leadership thus unnecessary. Such a conclusion is related partly to the view put forth by certain New Testament scholars asserting that there was no hierarchy in the early church—at least the first generation of the church was entirely "charismatic."[3] But the spiritual-ministries approach affirms the presence of ministries of leadership alongside all the other ministry positions, such as the "overseers and deacons" of Philippians 1:1. Moreover, just as 1 Corinthians 12:28–30 and Romans 12:6–8 include roles of leadership along with non-leader ministries in the same list, so today leadership ministries and non-leadership ministries exist side by side.

LACK OF ABILITY FOR LEADERSHIP?

The conventional view can sometimes open a theological door for a person's not submitting to the authority of God-appointed leadership. On a recent trip overseas, I counseled with a Christian brother who did not want to submit to the newly appointed local pastor of his church. The pastor it seems had been challenging this brother on a couple areas of sin that he was harboring and unwilling to confess. During one conversation, he commented that he didn't believe that this local pastor possessed the gift of leadership. But it appeared to me that the recalcitrant brother was using the abilities view as a cover for his unwillingness to listen to someone whom God had appointed as part of the spiritual leadership in his life. We should keep in mind that nowhere does Paul suggest that a person should be appointed as a leader because of particular abilities; rather, according to 1 Timothy 3 and Titus 1, people are appointed to leadership roles in the church because of their quality of character.[4]

WHO GETS THE GIFTS?

The spiritual-ministries approach also resolves another question: To whom are the gifts given? Although it seems apparent from Paul's own statements that these ministry roles are given to individuals (1 Cor. 12:7, 11; Rom. 12:3–8), it seems equally clear that the people in those ministries are given to the church (Eph. 4:11–12; 1 Cor. 12:18, 28). But the conventional view usually reads these gifts merely as abilities given to individuals. So when someone with this mindset approaches Ephesians 4:11–12, that person must either force-fit that passage into an abilities mold or declare that what is given to individuals is an ability, but what is given to the church are the persons in their ministries. Amazingly, and simply under the influence of the conventional view, Ephesians 4:11–12 is often said to portray persons who have been given special abilities to be in the roles listed. The result in conventional-view circles is an almost exclusive discussion of personal abilities—which must, of course be "used"—with almost a complete lack of emphasis on the idea that people who serve in their ministry roles are themselves a gift given to the church. As discussed in chapters 10 and 11 of this current volume, the line for Paul between a ministry assignment and a person in his or her ministry assignment is very thin. The spiritual-ministries approach fits comfortably with Paul's teaching that God has given ministries to individual believers, and those individual believers in their ministries have been given to the church. Ephesians 4:11–12, which is a list of persons in their ministry roles, often causes problems in the conventional view, as, indeed, should Romans 12:6–8 and 1 Corinthians 12:28–30, which, in part, list people in their ministries.

Spiritual Gifts as Guidance?

Proponents of the conventional view often encourage Christians to try to discover their special abilities as a way to help in decision making, analogous to the way aptitude and personality tests are used in career counseling to help people know what career to pursue. The implication, usually unstated, is that if God has given you some sort of special ability, this must be one way he is letting you know what he wants you to do.[5] In contrast, an approach that views these items on Paul's lists as ministries would encourage believers to seek out what God wants them to do in ministry in the same way as they seek out what God would want them to do in any area of life (see chap. 22).[6]

GOD-FOCUSED OR HUMAN-FOCUSED?

The conventional view can sometimes have the effect of focusing our attention upon the gift (viewed as an ability) rather than on God, who is the Giver. But if, in fact, what has been given is an assignment to do ministry, the only proper response is what the slaves in Jesus' parable in Luke 17:10 said after serving: "We are unworthy slaves; we have only done that which we ought to have done."

HUMILITY

The Corinthians, as is well known, were enamored of their special abilities. In their case, their abilities to perform such miracles as healing, prophecy, and tongues were foremost in their minds. In response to this lack of humility, Paul redirected them to the fact that God had placed each of them in necessary roles as members of his body (1 Cor. 12:12–27). The inordinate attention placed in our day upon spiritual gifts as abilities, flashy or not, may have the similar, if unintended, effect of spawning pride rather than humility. In such a climate, Paul, if he were able to speak with us today, would probably respond by once again directing people back to the necessity of all the members serving in their ministry roles for the greater good. Paul's concern that we serve one another in humility (Rom. 12:3–8; Eph. 4:2; Phil. 2:1–11; Col. 3:12–15) will naturally find greater emphasis in an approach that highlights the act of serving rather than the ability to serve.

STRENGTH OR WEAKNESS?

Moreover, as has already been explored at length in chapter 18, one implication of the spiritual-ministries approach is a renewed understanding of the place of weakness as it relates to ministry. God usually empowers us to do whatever ministries he has called us to do, but he sometimes calls us to serve out of weakness, and always in an attitude of dependence. The conventional view of spiritual gifts as abilities emphasizes serving out of one's strengths. But Paul would emphasize that sometimes God chooses to glorify himself by showing his strength in our weakness as we serve in the ministries into which he has called us.[7]

DISCOVERING YOUR SPIRITUAL GIFTS?

The final implication to be mentioned here comes as a response to that which is so commonly encouraged by proponents of the conventional view—the quest to discover one's hidden spiritual talents. If the gifts actually are ministry roles rather than abilities, such a search is unnecessary and even unhelpful. This is not to say that we as Christians will immediately know what ministries God has given to us. It does, however, move us toward a perspective that has been common among Christians throughout history. This perspective is addressed at the beginning of the final chapter of this book, asking the question, Where do we go from here?

TWENTY-TWO

Knowing Where to Serve

WHERE DO WE go from here? What do we do now? If spiritual gifts are not abilities to discover, but rather are ministry roles, how can we as Christians know which ministry or ministries we should get involved in?

First, here's what you don't need to do. You don't need to take a spiritual gifts test or check off the boxes on a spiritual gifts inventory, trying to discover the special spiritual abilities you've been told are there for you to find.[1] Rather, you need to replace such a search with the simple question that Christians have been bringing to the Lord for the past two millennia: "Lord, what do you want me to do; where do you want me to serve?"

Doing so still may not, of course, entirely resolve your dilemma. You'll still likely find yourself asking what God wants you to do in ministry. This question will be discussed momentarily. But let it first be clearly stated—whether or not believers agree with the premise of this book, all believers must ask this question. Every follower of Christ who has entered the believing community through faith in Jesus Christ must ask in prayer how he or she can further the work of God by building up the body of Christ. Regarding the furthering of this work, the main difference between the conventional view and the spiritual-ministries view is this: those who hold to the conventional view have to ask two questions, whereas those who follow the spiritual-ministries view need to ask only one question.

Someone who holds to the spiritual-gifts-as-abilities view must ask, (1) Which ministry should I serve in? and (2) Which special ability do I have or not have? That person then must try somehow to correlate the answers. The person who follows the spiritual-ministries approach need ask only a single question—a question asked repeatedly throughout the history of Christianity: "Lord, where do you want me to serve?"

How do we find the answer to this question? We approach this question the same way that we pray through any decision, whether about marriage, vocation, or which ministries to be involved in. In other words, we find ourselves back at the more basic question of how Christians make decisions. Decision making itself is a subject about which numerous books have already been written. It would be counterproductive here to survey all the approaches to decision making that are current among Christians and to evaluate such approaches. But I don't want to leave the reader hanging on the issue of Christian decision making. So to help readers who have not yet worked through the biblical teaching on this subject, I will briefly describe my own understanding of the process, in the context of moving into ministries. The reader who wants to study more can refer to the books listed in the note.[2] It's important to recognize, however, that the premise of this book—that spiritual gifts are ministry assignments rather than special abilities—does not stand or fall upon one's view of decision making. The spiritual-ministries approach works well within a broad spectrum of approaches to decision making found among Christians today.

My own approach to decision making is to affirm the foundational role of wisdom without excluding the possibility that the Holy Spirit sometimes chooses to guide more directly the Christian's decision-making process. Thus, I believe that we should actively seek wisdom as the basis of our decision making, a search that is recommended repeatedly in the Bible (as in Prov. 2:1–5). In the context of ministries, a wise process would include the use of pros-and-cons lists and careful listening to mature counsel as we evaluate such issues as need, opportunity, past experiences, natural talents, and desire. The definition of what is wise, however, must not be based upon worldly wisdom—which would never view it a wise decision to be a missionary in a hostile country—but upon a biblical wisdom that teaches that we are on a mission to reach the world for Christ and strengthen his church, regardless of the sacrifice. Paul, for example, often made specific decisions of where to go next, not on the basis of personal comfort, but because he thought he could best fulfill his overarching mission to break down walls between Jews and Gentiles and take the gospel to areas yet untouched with the gospel (Rom. 15:20–24).

But sometimes we don't have enough wisdom for a decision, as James 1:5–8 indicates. In such cases we can ask God in faith for an increase of wisdom. Although such an increase of wisdom appears to be a supernatural work of God in our thought processes,[3] it is nevertheless an increase in wisdom. It is not necessarily a revelation of what to do. This increase of wisdom appears to be normative for situations in which we do not know what to do.

In addition, God at times puts something into our minds or hearts that seems beyond a simple exercise of wisdom (Neh. 2:12; 7:5; Acts 20:22). He doesn't always do this, but sometimes he does. On an even more explicit level, the Bible relates many examples of direct communication from God, whether through dreams, visits by angels, visions, prophetic words, and the like. Paul himself received his primary ministry assignment through direct revelation from God (Acts 9:15–16; 22:10, 21; 26:16–20; Gal. 1:11–12; Eph. 3:3). Although God may choose at times to guide us through direct messages, nowhere does the Bible teach that such messages are always available to all Christians for every decision we must make. At best, God only sometimes gives those messages, so we need to be prepared to decide without a direct communication from him.

Many Christians testify that God uses an inward peace or lack of peace to help confirm or give a check on a decision. They appeal to the general character quality of peace represented in verses like

Isaiah 26:3: "You will keep in perfect peace him whose mind is steadfast, because he trusts in you." The command in Colossians 3:15 to "let the peace of Christ rule in your hearts" seems to assume that sometimes believers do not let Christ's peace rule in their hearts. On the other side, sometimes God gives an inner check, as seems to have been the case a couple times with Paul in the book of Acts.[4] Again, the controlling word is *sometimes*, not *always*.

It is interesting that the paths of wisdom and guidance appear to merge in the mature Christian. A Spirit-filled, mature believer often cannot tell whether the process she or he is undergoing is directed more by wisdom or by guidance. The person who grows closer to the heart of God begins to think thoughts that, as Paul suggests in 1 Corinthians 2:11–15, are more in line with the Spirit of God.

In the end, Christians who are faithful in seeking biblical principles, searching out mature counsel, and submitting their requests to God, should not worry about whether they've missed doing what God wants them to do. These Christians would miss it only if God had made clear to them what he wanted and they had not done it. I maintain, however, that God in his sovereignty doesn't always communicate his plan, but often allows us to choose the wisest path or pray for an increase in wisdom. Thus, we should move forward with confidence, along with humility, as we pray about and consider which ministries the Lord would have us do.

Finally, we will often have greater insight on where to serve in the future as we minister in the present. It is in the midst of service that we often find opportunities and spiritual desire to take the next steps into whatever areas of ministry God may have for us.

SUMMARY OF THE PROCESS OF KNOWING WHERE TO SERVE

Seek for wisdom, defined God's way (that is, mission decision making).

> God will increase our wisdom when we ask in faith.
>
> Sometimes God puts thoughts into our minds.
>
> Sometimes God gives direct messages.
>
> Sometimes God confirms through peace or lack of peace.
>
> Wisdom and guidance seem to merge in the mature believer.
>
> Do not be worried that you might miss God's plan.[5]

As mentioned at the beginning of this chapter, a person's view of spiritual gifts does not stand or fall upon his or her understanding of the process of decision making. Those who more emphasize wisdom in decision making will in all likelihood find that the spiritual-ministries approach works well with their understanding of decision making. Equally, those who more emphasize guidance by the Holy Spirit will likely find the same.

Here, at the close of this book, I leave you with a blessing as you pursue the ministries that God has given you to build up his church. This blessing is actually Paul's blessing for you, drawn from his own prayers and blessings.[6]

May God make all grace abound to you, that always having all sufficiency in everything, you may have an abundance for every good deed.

May you be filled with the knowledge of his will in all spiritual wisdom and understanding, so that you may walk in a manner worthy of the Lord, to please him in all respects, bearing fruit in every good work and increasing in the knowledge of God.

May God count you worthy of your calling, and fulfill every desire for goodness and the work of faith with power.

May our Lord Jesus Christ himself and God our Father, who has loved us and given us eternal comfort and good hope by grace, comfort and strengthen your hearts in every good work and word.

A Description of Each Item in Paul's Four Ministry Lists
(Eph. 4:11; Rom. 12:6–8; 1 Cor. 12:8–10; 1 Cor. 12:28–30)

SPACE ALLOWS ONLY brief descriptions of each item in these lists. The goal of this appendix is to describe the ministry roles in light of the contexts in which they are found and in light of other biblical evidence, as opposed to present-day usage of words for these ministries. In some cases, only a small amount of evidence can be culled from the Scriptures.

APOSTLE (1 COR. 12:28–29; EPH. 4:11)

It is possible to identify four categories of people referred to as "apostles" in the New Testament, though certain New Testament characters belong in more than one category. (1) The first category was limited to the Twelve, who were appointed by Christ himself and set apart to share in his mission (Matt. 10:1ff.; Mark 3:13–19; Luke 8:1; 9:1; John 6:70; Acts 1:26; 6:2; 1 Cor. 15:5). (2) The second category was a larger group but was still limited to those who were eyewitnesses of Christ's post-resurrection experiences, including, but not limited to, the Twelve (1 Cor. 9:1; 15:5–9). Notable in this group (apart from the Twelve) were James the half brother of Christ

(1 Cor. 15:7; Gal. 1:19; 2:9), and Paul, to whom Christ made a special appearance (1 Cor. 9:1; 15:8–9).[1] (3) The third category included those who were not necessarily eyewitnesses of the resurrection (although they may have been), but were specially appointed as missionaries for a broader ministry. Included in this category were Paul (Acts 13:2–3; cf. Eph. 3:7–9), Barnabas (Acts 13:2–3; 14:4, 14), Silas (Acts 15:40; 1 Thess. 2:6), and perhaps others such as Timothy (cf. 1 Tim. 4:14; 2 Tim. 1:6) and Titus (2 Cor. 8:19), who were not specifically referred to as "apostles" in the New Testament. (4) Finally, there are New Testament references to those who were simply messengers or representatives of particular churches sent out on short-term ministry tasks (1 Cor. 8:16–24; Phil. 2:25; cf. Acts 15:22; 8:14; 11:22; 15:3, 33; 19:22; 1 Cor. 4:17; Eph. 6:22; Col. 4:8; 1 Thess. 3:2; 2 Tim. 4:12).

Categories 1 and 2 above could be described as formal. Categories 3 and 4 could be described as functional.[2] Although category 1 (the Twelve) and category 4 (short-term messengers) are almost certainly not what Paul had in mind in 1 Corinthians 12:28–29,[3] it is otherwise difficult to say which of the other two categories Paul was thinking about when he placed "apostle" at the top of his list in 1 Corinthians 12:28–29. Although there may be overlap in concept, it seems more likely that Paul's usage was functional rather than formal. His earlier discussion of his own apostleship in 1 Corinthians 9:1–5 seems to have been more functional (cf. "if to others I am not an apostle, at least I am to you" in v. 2), while his later mention of apostles in 1 Corinthians 15:5–9 seems to have been more formal, although even there a functional meaning is possible in verse 9. A functional meaning would fit the other items in the list of 1 Corinthians 12:28–29, which are themselves more functional. A list, after all, usually includes items that fit together under a single conception. Moreover, the main issues in 1 Corinthians concern the local church, although, of course, there is relevance to the worldwide church. Taken together, the preceding evidence points toward a more functional meaning, although it is almost impossible to believe that there was not some overlap with formal conceptions in Paul's mind.

If, in fact, Paul's usage was more functional than formal, the functional aspects might also be transferable to our contemporary context. Thus, just as missionaries are commissioned to take the gospel to other countries or pastors sometimes give spiritual oversight to more than a single church, so the work of apostle (in the functional sense) is probably still operative today. But there is no one alive who has seen the resurrected Lord, and thus apostles of the Peter and Paul type are not present in the church today. It is probably unwise to apply the term *apostle* to a present-day believer because of almost certain confusion between the original apostles and so-called present-day apostles. Other terms that describe the function (missionary, church-planter, etc.) would seem to be more appropriate in our present context.

PROPHET/PROPHECY (1 COR. 12:10, 28–29; EPH. 4:11; ROM. 12:6)

One of Paul's major concerns in 1 Corinthians 12–14 was to recommend prophecy over and against the unbridled tongues-speaking in vogue in Corinth. The prophecy under discussion appears to have been primarily the forth telling of messages from God, messages of a revelatory nature (1 Cor. 14:30).[4] That prophecy is primarily forth telling is a reasonable inference from the connection between prophecy and such responses as edification, conviction of sin, and learning in 1 Corinthians 14:5, 24, 31. Still, prophecy in the New Testament apparently also included, at least sometimes, foretelling (cf. Agabus's foretelling of a famine in Acts 11:28). Grudem has highlighted the way New Testament prophecies were received in the church—apparently with less authority than Old Testament prophecies—which argues that they never were intended to be viewed as infallible or on the level of Scripture.[5] Rather, prophecies were specific instructions for certain individuals or groups of believers and were not to be universalized.

Prophetic activity should be regulated by the explicit instructions in 1 Corinthians 14. The goal of prophetic activity is the edification, exhortation, and encouragement of the church (v. 3). Two or three prophets can speak in a meeting (v. 29a). Prophecies are not to be uncritically received; they are to be evaluated (v. 29b). If one is prophesying and a revelation comes to another, the first should sit down and allow the next one to speak (v. 30). To keep meetings orderly (vv. 31, 40), prophets should speak one at a time (v. 30), because a prophetic word is not outside of regulation—"the spirits of prophets are subject to prophets" (v. 32).

The emphasis in the context of 1 Corinthians 12–14 (and probably Rom. 12:6) is upon the function of prophesying (as 1 Cor. 14 demonstrates), although one who prophesied regularly would be viewed as being among those called "prophets."

Teacher/Teaching/Pastor-Teacher (1 Cor. 12:28, 29; Rom. 12:7; Eph. 4:11)

It appears that teaching in the early church could include a wide range of activities, from the teaching that all Christians regularly should give to one another (Rom. 15:14; 1 Cor. 14:26; Col. 3:16), to more regular ministry assignments of teaching (Rom. 12:7; 1 Cor. 12:28–29), which often, although probably not always, overlapped into what is usually referred to as the office of teacher (Eph. 4:11). In Ephesians 4:11, the pastors and teachers in the list are probably a reference to a single person, the pastor-teacher (or shepherd-teacher).[6] In Acts 20:28, Paul refers to the activity of overseers as that of "shepherding" the church. The overlap of teacher with such spiritual oversight continues in the Pastoral Letters, where overseers were expected to be able to teach (cf. 1 Tim. 3:2; Titus 1:9).[7] Although the Pastorals probably do not limit the teaching role to an official role (cf. 2 Tim. 2:2 and the "false teachers" of 1 Tim. 1:7 and 4:3, who very likely were not overseers), there is in these letters "a strong relationship of the function of teaching to the leaders."[8] In the ranking of 1 Corinthians 12:28, the God-appointed teachers follow only apostles and prophets in importance.

EVANGELIST (EPH. 4:11)

In only two places in the New Testament apart from Ephesians 4:11 (Acts 21:8; 2 Tim. 4:5) does the noun *evangelist* appear. Philip, who was "one of the seven" in Acts 6:3–6, is referred to as "Philip the evangelist" in Acts 21:8. Timothy, rather than being referred to as an evangelist, is told by Paul to "do the work of an evangelist." What is this work? The work is to "evangelize" or to "proclaim the good news," which is the meaning of the verb from which the designation *evangelist* is derived—a very common verb in the New Testament, both in the ministry of Jesus (Matt. 11:5; Luke 4:18, 44; 8:1; 16:16) and in the early church (Acts 8:4, 12; 16:10; Rom. 15:20; 1 Cor. 1:17; 9:16, 18; 15:1; Eph. 3:8).[9]

MIRACLES (1 COR. 12:10, 28–29)

Literally "powers," in the list of 1 Corinthians 12:7–10, these are found immediately after healings, and immediately before healings in the list of 1 Corinthians 12:28–30. The connection of miracles with healings would suggest that Paul is using this term to refer to a range of non-healing supernatural activities. New Testament examples would include the incident with Ananias and Sapphira (Acts 5:1–11), the blinding of Bar-Jesus/Elymas the magician (Acts 13:6–11), and the many occurrences of driving out demons. Paul himself said that Christ's work through him for the Gentiles was "by word and deed, in the power of signs and wonders, by the power of the Spirit" (Rom. 15:18–19; cf. 2 Cor. 12:12; Gal. 3:5; 1 Thess. 1:5).

HEALINGS (1 COR. 12:9, 28, 30)

Physical healings seem to have been a regular part of the experience of the early church, as the narratives of Acts and the inclusion of healings in these lists attest. The use of the plural *healings,* especially in the list of 1 Corinthians 12:28 and 30 (and perhaps the linking with the word *charismata* in each of 1 Cor. 12:9, 28, 30), probably indicates not a regular office of healer, but that each healing should be viewed as an individual grace for the need of the moment.[10] Paul himself often was involved in healing (Acts 19:11–12; 28:8), although he did not (could not?) heal Trophimus (2 Tim. 4:20) or Epaphroditus (Phil. 2:25–30), he advised a little wine (not healing) for Timothy's sick stomach (1 Tim. 5:23), and was himself sometimes sick (Gal. 4:13–14 and perhaps 2 Cor. 12:7–10). Still, ample evidence is found—from the inclusion of healings in this list, the frequent mention of healings in the New Testament, and teaching outside of Paul (cf. James 5:14–18)—that prayers for healing were to be uttered with the expectation that God could and often would heal.

Helps (1 Cor. 12:28), Serving (Rom. 12:8), Giving (Rom. 12:8), Mercy (Rom. 12:8)

It is unclear to what the "helps" or "helpful deeds"[11] of 1 Corinthians 12:28 specifically refer. Fee may be correct when he suggests overlap in practice with the general descriptions in Romans 12:8 of serving, giving, and mercy.[12] It has also been suggested that such activities are more closely associated with the types of ministries that deacons would have been expected to do,[13] although such functions certainly should not be limited to people appointed as deacons. In the case of all these roles, it is less likely that they are particular and identifiable and more likely that they are general descriptions of the kinds of activities that go on in Christian communities.

Leadership (Rom. 12:8) and Administrations (1 Cor. 12:28)

Inasmuch as leadership in Romans 12:8 appears with three general categories of ministry (serving, giving, and mercy), it probably should also be understood to be a general category of ministry, rather than a specific type of leadership. *Leadership* would encompass various specific roles in the church, including, but probably not limited to, the role of overseer/elder/shepherd. The word translated "administrations" (1 Cor. 12:28) occurs only here in the New Testament, but evidence from the Septuagint[14] would point toward a leadership or guidance role of some kind. It is impossible to be any more specific than this.

EXHORTATION/ENCOURAGEMENT (ROM. 12:8)

Since it appears that Paul's purpose in Romans 12 was not to delineate specific roles, but rather to describe the categories of service in the church (note the general nature of the list), it is not surprising that he selected a word that has a rather broad range of meaning. It can in various contexts mean (1) encouragement or exhortation, (2) appeal or request, (3) comfort or consolation.[15] Paul's emphasis is probably closer to either 1 or 3, although there seems to be no way to determine from the passage which is preferable. It may be that Paul purposely chose such a broad word to encompass many different community ministries that would fit under such a title.

WORD OF WISDOM AND WORD OF KNOWLEDGE (1 COR. 12:8)

The first clue—and there aren't many—to the nature of these two activities is their inclusion in a list that focuses upon the more miraculous ministries found among the "manifestation of the Spirit" (1 Cor. 12:7–11). The second clue is found in the parallel nature of the expression "word of . . . ," suggesting that "word of wisdom" and "word of knowledge" are related or similar ideas. The mention of wisdom that is being proclaimed reminds us of Paul's earlier discussion of how God's wisdom is actually the "foolish" proclamation of the gospel (1 Cor. 1:17–2:16).[16] Although Jesus does not use the exact expression, it is noteworthy that Jesus promised that he himself would give a supernatural message of wisdom to his disciples whenever they declared the gospel under hostile conditions (Luke 21:12–15; cf. Acts 6:10). This "message of wisdom" could be related to the idea of a spontaneous revelatory word with its central content being the message of the gospel. "Knowledge," like "wisdom," was a word in vogue in the Corinthian church,[17] and, for Paul, not always having a positive connotation (cf. 1 Cor. 8:1). But the connection of knowledge with revelation (1 Cor. 14:6), prophecy (1 Cor. 13:2, 8–9), and mysteries (1 Cor. 13:2) might suggest that the "word of knowledge" in 1 Corinthians 12:8 was a message of a revelatory type. Beyond these suggestions, it seems there is little that can be known about these supernatural activities, except that, as with all these ministry functions, Paul wanted them to build up the community of believers.[18]

FAITH (1 COR. 12:9)

The faith listed here is not saving faith (cf. Rom. 3:21–28; 5:1), or the regular reliance upon God required of every believer (cf. Heb. 11:1, 6), or "the faith" (as in "what we believe," 2 Cor. 13:5; Gal. 1:23). Appearing as it does in the list of 1 Corinthians 12:7–11 (cf. 2 Cor. 8:7), this faith is an observably supernatural one that is put into practice. This same kind of faith is mentioned in 1 Corinthians 13:2 as the kind of faith that can "remove mountains" (cf. Matt. 17:20), implying that the activity of faith is in view.[19]

DISTINGUISHING BETWEEN SPIRITS (1 COR. 12:10)

Also sometimes translated as "discernment of spirits," its meaning falls under two main possibilities. One possibility, arising from the context, is its being a specific reference to what Paul will soon discuss in 1 Corinthians 14:29—the judging of prophecies (cf. 1 Thess. 5:20–21).[20] The other possible meaning refers to a broader role in which people are called upon to identify whether a particular activity is motivated by the Holy Spirit or whether somehow demonic forces are involved. The latter would be similar, then, to 1 John 4:1, which instructs believers to "test the spirits," although even there it is often connected with prophecy—"for many false prophets have gone out into the world."[21]

Tongues (1 Cor. 12:10, 28, 30) and Interpretation of Tongues (1 Cor. 12:10, 30)

E. H. Plumptre pointed out differences between the tongues of Acts 2 and the tongues mentioned in 1 Corinthians 12:10, 28, 30 (and throughout 1 Cor. 14).[22] Of the differences he mentions, a few are noteworthy. In Acts (Acts 2:4), all spoke in tongues; at Corinth all did not (1 Cor. 12:30). In Acts (Acts 2:6), tongues were understood by some people and no interpreter was necessary, but at Corinth an interpreter was required (1 Cor. 14:23, 28). In Acts, strangers were positively astounded (Acts 2:7, 8); in Corinth, Paul warns that strangers would consider tongues-speakers to be insane (1 Cor. 14:23).

Both what occurred in Acts 2 and what was occurring in Corinth were labeled as "tongues." But it would be an oversimplification to identify them as the same phenomenon. Rather, Acts 2 describes a miracle of gigantic proportions—the disciples were speaking in various known languages (Acts 2:5–12) even though they themselves did not know these languages apart from a miraculous work of the Holy Spirit. In contrast, the tongues described in 1 Corinthians appears to have been an unknown language (cf. "for no one understands," 1 Cor. 14:2). Unless someone interpreted, neither the listeners ("how will it be known what is spoken?" 1 Cor. 14:9) nor the speakers ("for if I pray in a tongue, my spirit prays, but my mind is unfruitful," 1 Cor. 14:14) could understand what was being said. Some in Corinth may have thought of tongues as an angelic language (1 Cor. 13:1), although 1 Corinthians 13:1 may simply be flowery language.

The evidence in 1 Corinthians 14 indicates that the content of the tongues was praise to God.[23] David Huttar comments,

> Particularly important are verses 14–18. From these we know that speaking in tongues can be viewed as prayer (14–15), blessing [God] (16), and thanksgiving (16–18), and it is almost certain that we should add song, interpreting "singing in the Spirit" (15) as singing in tongues. It also seems likely that these various terms do not refer to different kinds of tongues, but are generally synonymous. At least this is so with reference to "blessing" and "thanksgiving," which are virtually equated in verse 16.[24]

If Huttar is, in fact, correct, presumably the content of the interpretation of tongues would also be praise rather than exhortation.

In 1 Corinthians 14, Paul regulates the community use of tongues, as well as the use of prophecy, and recommends prophecy over and against tongues. Because tongues are primarily for personal edification (v. 4), a tongue spoken in a meeting needs to be interpreted if it is to help build up the community (vv. 5, 27). Uninterpreted tongues function as judgment upon an unbeliever who comes into an assembly, since the unbeliever will be unable to understand the confusion that is around him or her (vv. 21–23). Paul compares this to the judgment of the Babylonian captivity, where the exiles were taken to a foreign land by people speaking a language they could not understand (v. 21 [also v. 11]; cf. Isa. 28:11–12; Deut. 28:49). For the sake of order, only two or three, if any, should speak in a given meeting (v. 27). They should speak one at a time, and, of course, the tongue should be interpreted (v. 27). If there is no one to interpret, the one speaking in a tongue should pray that he can interpret the tongue himself (v. 14), otherwise he should remain silent (v. 28). The point is that both the spirit and the mind need to be involved and that without an interpretation only the spirit is involved (vv.

15–19). Everything, including speaking in tongues, should be done for edification (v. 26).

Paul says not to forbid speaking in tongues (1 Cor. 14:39). This instruction, however, as with all of these teachings, seems to envision smaller meetings for worship—what we would normally call home groups. It is unlikely that when Paul wrote these specific instructions, he had in mind the sometimes hundreds or even thousands who meet together for worship in many churches today.

Interpretation of tongues should be understood as translating the meaning of the tongue rather than as some sort of separate revelation that is unconnected to the meaning of the tongue itself. This seems to be part of the import of the comparison with languages in 1 Corinthians 14:10–11 and the direct prayer by the tongue-speaker for an interpretation of what he has just prayed when there is not another interpreter (1 Cor. 14:13). As previously mentioned, the content of the interpretation should probably be praise, since the content of the tongue is probably praise.

As in the days of the Corinthian church, so today tongues has the potential of being one of the most divisive of all the items appearing in the list of the "manifestation of the Spirit." It should be remembered that greater in importance by far is love (1 Cor. 13:1, 8, 13; 14:1) and that unity is to be evidence of the Spirit's work (Eph. 4:3).

APPENDIX B

Romans 12:4–8

One Sentence or Two?

WHICH PUNCTUATION FOR the first line of the Christmas song "We Three Kings" is correct?[1]

> Option 1: "We three kings of Orient are bearing gifts. We traverse afar . . ."
> Option 2: "We three kings of Orient are. Bearing gifts we traverse afar . . ."

Should the first line of the song be read as saying "We three kings from the Orient *are bearing* gifts"? Or should it be read as "We *are* three kings from the Orient"?

A somewhat similar scenario is found in Romans 12:4–8. The most pressing syntactical issue related to Romans 12:4–8 is whether the passage should be read as one sentence or two sentences. Is the participle of verse 6 ("having") governed by the "we are" verb of verse 5 (as in option 1 of the Christmas carol), or should a grammatical break be posited, and the participle used to introduce the second sentence (as in option 2 of the carol)?

A variety of difficulties confront the reader who seeks to answer this question. One initial difficulty is that grammarians and commentators who choose to mention this issue usually comment on one or two (or none) of the seven or so pertinent issues in the passage, and then weigh in with their opinion of whether it should be read as one sentence or two. A number of difficult issues, however, arise in Romans 12:4–8. These must be held in suspension and weighed all at once in order to arrive at an adequate understanding of what Paul intends. The goal of this appendix is to consider each of these issues and to argue that, when all have been considered, a one-sentence reading is the most satisfying option.

The majority view is that the passage consists of two sentences rather than one.[2] The first sentence consists of verses 4–5; the second sentence is verses 6–8. There appear to be two main reasons that interpreters adopt the two-sentence approach. The primary reason is the presence of the postpositive δέ ("and") after the participle ἔχοντες ("having") at the beginning of verse 6. Since similar constructions elsewhere frequently introduce new sentences, it is proposed that a new sentence should begin here.

The second reason commonly used to argue that Paul introduces a new sentence in verse 6 is the nature of the list that follows. It is suggested that Paul is not only listing the distribution of ministry functions; his purpose is hortatory as well. Thus, in this view, Paul is not only listing the *charismata* that Christians are said to have; he is encouraging their use. Beyond these two most common reasons, it should also be noted that from a translational perspective, the two-sentence approach is the simplest. Attempts to translate verses 4–8 as one sentence often end up unwieldy and unsatisfactory from a stylistic perspective.

I contend for the minority view that the passage consists of one sentence rather than two.[3] Seven main issues, plus various minor issues embedded within each, point to the one-sentence reading. Clarifying these seven issues should help to resolve how Paul is employing the list found in verses 6–8 and thus answer the second issue raised by two-sentence proponents. After these seven considerations have been laid out, this current chapter returns to a consideration of the function of the postpositive δέ and finishes with an annotated diagram of the issues discussed in the biblical text.

First, it should be noted that there is no main verb anywhere in verses 6–8. The last main verb in the passage is the ἐσμέν ("we are") of verse 5. The lack of a main verb in verses 6–8 is a substantial point and should not be minimized, thus strongly suggesting a reading of these lines as one sentence if at all possible. Although ellipses are not unusual in Paul, the type of ellipsis suggested here by two-sentence proponents is unparalleled in the letters of Paul. The assumed void has to be filled either by the addition of an entire clause ("let us use them" [RSV]; "each of us is to exercise them accordingly" [NASB]), or by a hortatory expression preceding each prepositional phrase, "whether prophecy, *let us prophesy* according to the proportion of faith . . ." (KJV, ASV). In the absence of a main verb in verses 6–8, if an acceptable way exists to read verses 6–8 together with verses 4–5, that approach should be given preference.

Second, it is possible to read the participle ἔχοντες ("having") together with the ἐσμέν ("we are") of verse 5 and thus supply the needed main verb for verses 6–8. Note that Paul elsewhere uses ἐσμέν together with an anarthrous (without an article) participle (1 Cor. 15:19; 2 Cor. 2:17; Eph. 2:10).

Third, and perhaps the most important observation, is the function of διάφορος ("differing") in the sentence. It is not merely an adjective modifying χαρίσματα (*charismata*), although it at the very least functions as an adjective. Its position at the end of the participial clause and as the word immediately preceding the list that follows appears purposeful on Paul's part. Through his use of this adjective, he distributes the list that follows and differentiates the various areas of ministry and attitudes. So rather than reading this as "having different *charismata* according to the grace given to us" and then trying to supply a verb, the διάφορος should be allowed to distribute what follows: "having *charismata* according to the grace given to us that differ."[4] The capacity of this adjective to distribute the following items is almost as effective as if Paul had used its verbal counterpart διαφέρω ("to differ") (cf. 1 Cor. 15:41). Had Paul tried to use διαφέρω as a main verb (so διαφέρουσιν, "they differ"), he would, of course, have lost syntactical contact with verses 4–5. But it appears that Paul did not want to lose contact with verses 4–5, and his choice of διάφορος may again be the evidence. That is, διάφορος has another function in this sentence in addition to the two already mentioned, that of modifying χαρίσματα (*charismata*) and of distributing the items in the list; διάφορος establishes a conceptual link with Paul's earlier statement in verse 4 (same sentence)—τὰ δὲ μέλη πάντα οὐ τὴν αὐτὴν ἔχει πρᾶξιν ("and all the members do not have the same function")—and could almost be viewed as shorthand for that expression. Moreover, διάφορος conceptually ties into his earlier point in verse 3 (same passage, different sentence) about humility, the issue he used to start the passage. In other words, a way that humility in relationships is engendered is through the recognition of the differing roles each member plays. Paul's use of διάφορος at a crucial moment in this sentence draws the passage together into a conceptual unity—a unity that is lost if two sentences are posited instead of one.

Fourth, if one reads this passage as two sentences rather than one, there is nothing in the apodosis of the purported first sentence (v. 5) to correspond to the third idea introduced by the physical body analogy of verse 4. Paul compares the human body (v. 4) to the "one body in Christ" (vv. 5–8), introducing three elements in verse 4 that have correspondences in the rest of the sentence (vv. 5–8). Note that the third element introduced in verse 4 seems to be the most important one Paul intends to compare. The three elements are as follows: (1) The body is a unity (cf. v. 4, "in one body," with v. 5, "one body in Christ" and "one of another"); (2) there are various members of the body, not just one (cf. v. 4, "many members," with v. 5, "the many" and "members individually one of another"); (3) there are different functions among the members (cf. v. 4, "all the members do not have the same function" with vv. 6–8, which is a list of ministry functions that differ [v. 6] from member to member). But whereas the oneness and the many-ness ideas introduced in verse 4 each correspond to something in verse 5, the differing functions idea, which is emphasized in verse 4, does not appear until verses 6–8. If the sentence ends after verse 5 and another sentence starts at verse 6, as two-sentence proponents suggest, the differing functions idea corresponds to nothing in the sentence to which it supposedly belongs.

Fifth, it appears that in the two-sentence approach, often a view of spiritual gifts as special abilities is read into the passage, in some cases without the interpreter being aware that it is an issue. Thus, in this approach, one has a special Spirit-given ability that allows him or her to serve effectively, and this ability must be used.[5] A teacher has a special ability to teach; a leader, a special ability to lead. This assumption is inadvertently superimposed upon Romans 12:3–8, which suggests to the interpreter's mind a conceptual break between verse 5 and verse 6. In other words, one reason for the popularity of the two-sentence approach may be the assumption that Paul's subject in verses 6–8 is spiritual gifts (read "special abilities"), which is only loosely connected to his theme of humility toward one another found in verses 3–5. But the idea of special abilities is nowhere mentioned in this passage.[6] Rather, being members in one body, the members having different functions, and being members in relation to one another are the ideas explicitly stated in this passage. The main idea of the entire passage is humility toward one another; verses 6–8 emphasize this need by pointing out that all of us have differing functions, thus implying that we all need each other. Paul introduces the main subject he wants to talk about in verse 3 and follows it through to the end of verse 8.[7] That this passage has a thematic unity is further established by the similarities between διὰ τῆς χάριτος τῆς δοθείσης μοι ("through the grace given to me") in verse 3 and κατὰ τὴν χάριν τὴν δοθεῖσαν ἡμῖν ("according to the grace given to us") in verse 6 as well as between the ὡς ὁ θεὸς ἐμέρισεν μέτρον πίστεως ("as God has measured out a measure of faith") in verse 3 and κατὰ τὴν ἀναλογίαν τῆς πίστεως ("according to the proportion of faith") in verse 6.

Sixth, for the list found in verses 6b–8 it is structurally simpler to read the first half of each pair (the functions themselves and the persons in those functions) under χαρίσματα (*charismata*) and the second half of each pair (each prepositional phrase) under διάφορα ("differing").[8]

Seventh, there are two shifts in the list (vv. 6–8) that both one-sentence proponents and two-sentence proponents have to address. The first seems to be a move from functions to the persons doing the functions (in the first part of the pair), which includes a shift from the first-person plural to the third-person singular.[9]

The second shift seems to be from the sphere or implementation of the function to the attitude of the one doing the activity (in the second part of the pair). This shift is acceptable under the general framework of differing functions and the encouragement toward humility, but creates difficulties for the reader who suggests that Paul wants us to act in some unstated way. What does it mean, after all, to use one's service in serving? Harder still for two-sentence proponents is what to do when, thirteen words later, Paul shifts from functions to persons in functions. How can one *use* a person? Does the suggested insertion "let us use them" influence the entire list or just the first part of the list?

These seven considerations suggest a way to read Romans 12:4–8 as one sentence, taking into account the various syntactical and conceptual difficulties encountered. Returning now to the postpositive δέ ("and") at the beginning of verse 6, the presence of this word seems to be the main concern of two-sentence proponents. From the perspective of a one-sentence approach, the most plausible solution[10] is to read the δέ, not as signaling the beginning of a new sentence, but rather as a connective on a lower level that functions more or less in the same way as the δέ in the immediately preceding phrase (τὸ δὲ καθ' εἷς ἀλλήλων μέλη, "and individually members one of another").[11] Since such a function of δέ exists in the preceding phrase (v. 5), it at least opens up the possibility that δέ is similarly used in the participial clause under consideration (v. 6). This use would be similar to several places, both in Paul's writings and elsewhere, where δέ functions on a lower level and not as a signal that a new sentence has begun.[12]

When the seven considerations discussed above are weighed against the δέ consideration, the one-sentence reading emerges as the likely reading of Romans 12:4–8. Thus, the current discussion might best be recapped with the annotated diagram below of the sentence in English,[13] illustrating the issues raised in the preceding discussion.

AN ENGLISH-ANNOTATED DIAGRAM OF ROMANS 12:4–8 AS ONE SENTENCE

```
For
just as
(we)                    have            many members
                    in one body
and
all the members    do not have     the same function
so
the many  (we) are  one body
                        in Christ
                        and
        (we are)    members
                        individually one of another
                        and
        (we are)    having    1. charismata
                                according to the grace
                                        of God
                                        that was given
                                                to us
                                2. differing (from
                                        other members)
                            whether
        (we are    having)    1. prophecy
```

2. (differing from other members) according to the proportion of (our) faith

whether

(we are   having)   1. service

2. (differing from other members) in (our ministry of) serving

whether

3. the one who teaches[14]

2. (differing from other members) in (one's ministry of) teaching

whether

3. the one who encourages

2. (differing from other members) in (one's ministry of) encouragement

(whether)

3. the one who gives

2. (differing from other members) in (the attitude of one's) generosity[15]

(whether)

3. the one who rules

2. (differing from other members) in (the attitude of one's) diligence

(whether)
3. the one who shows
 mercy
   2. (differing from
      other members)
      in (the attitude of
      one's) cheerfulness.

How Bible Translations Influence Readers Toward the Conventional View

Brian Asbill and Kenneth Berding

THIS BOOK HAS challenged two assumptions about English translations of spiritual gifts passages: (1) that *charisma* (χάρισμα)[1] is a technical term; (2) that the so-called spiritual gifts should be primarily understood as abilities.[2] In the list passages,[3] however, as well as in other passages that have affinities to the list passages, many translations use *gift* in such a way that a technical meaning is implied. Since the English word *gift* can mean ability, and the influence of the conventional view is quite prominent, many of these translations render aspects of these passages in ways that predispose readers to think along the lines of the conventional view.[4] In addition, some translations even go so far as to insert an explicit concept of ability into many of these texts.

The goal of this appendix, then, is to highlight and explain briefly the various factors in English Bible translations that might influence readers toward the conventional view. We make occasional suggestions about whether the translators themselves were operating under the influence of the conventional view, but it is often difficult to make such determinations and is not the primary goal of this appendix.[5] Similarly, whereas many of the factors described below relate to nearly all the translations, some do not. Therefore, in order not to diminish or exaggerate the significance of this data, readers should be mindful of how many and which translations are affected in each case in order to determine how significant any particular factor may be. We have included a set of charts in this appendix that illustrates how deeply the "ability" renderings pervade English translations of the list passages.

THE USE OF *GIFT* WHERE A TECHNICAL MEANING IS IMPLIED

CONFUSION OVER THE WORD GIFT

One of the arguments against a technical force for *charisma*[6] is that Paul only uses it sixteen times in his letters, and in a variety of ways.[7] Of these uses, only six occur in and around the list passages.[8] In many English translations, however, the occurrences of *gift*—the word most typically used to translate *charisma* in the list passages—are much more frequent. Furthermore, *gift* is also used in the translation of the so-called spiritual gifts outside the list passages (for example, translating "prophecy" as "gift of prophecy"). Thus, the simple fact that *gift* is used so commonly in these translations will likely influence readers to regard this word as somehow carrying on its back the entire theology of the conventional view, a theology they are already predisposed to read into these passages.

Understanding is further complicated because, unlike *charisma*, the English word *gift* is commonly used with the meaning "ability." As discussed in chapter 14, the two meanings of *gift* in *Webster's Unabridged Dictionary* are first, "a special or notable capacity, talent, or endowment either inherent, acquired, or given by a deity" (in short, an ability); and second, "something that is voluntarily transferred by one person to another without compensation"[9] (like a birthday gift). Therefore, even if readers are unaware of the conventional view and the implied technical usage of *gift* discussed above, they are still at risk for inappropriately thinking that the word *gift* constitutes a legitimate basis for understanding the so-called spiritual gifts as abilities.

CLARIFICATIONS

That being said, it is hardly legitimate to count up every use of *gift* and then suppose that each appearance of gift that is not a simple gloss of some Greek word is inappropriate and demonstrates the influence of the conventional view upon a particular translation. Therefore, clarifications identifying potentially legitimate reasons for the use of *gift* in such cases will be addressed next.

Clarification 1: Given-ness language is prominent in the list passages. The word *give* (δίδωμι) appears frequently in the broader context of the list passages (seven times),[10] along with the language of distribution or apportionment,[11] as well as two other common words almost always translated "gift"[12] (not *charisma*). Even *charisma* itself, being understood as a concrete expression of grace, has a focus on a sovereign God who gives. Translations using the English word *gift* may, in fact, simply be reflecting Paul's emphasis in these passages that these are all given by a gracious God. (The issue of what is given is, of course, the subject of this book.) So we recognize that even if a certain translation were totally unaffected by the conventional view, it might be possible for additional appearances of *gift* to enter a translation simply as an attempt to represent God's giving activity.[13]

Clarification 2: In some cases the word gift *may legitimately be drawn from its usage in the immediate context.* In Ephesians 4:11, for example, even though *gift* is not literally reflected in the Greek, a number of translations use this word in the opening of the verse. Two reasons suggest, however, that this use of *gift* could be viewed as appropriate: (1) *gave,* which is used with *gift* in verses 7–8, appears again in verse 11; (2) many translations seem to draw the word *gift* directly from verses 7–8, particularly verse 8. It is likely that this repetition of *gift* may often be included simply for the sake of clarity in light of the parenthetical statement in verses 9–10. A few translations make this especially clear by putting *gift,* and sometimes its surrounding phrase, in quotations (GNB/TEV, NJB, PHILLIPS).[14]

Clarification 3: It is possible that charisma *occurs in a summary position in two of the list passages: Romans 12:6 and 1 Corinthians 12:31.* If this is, in fact, the case, and if one grants that "gift" might be an appropriate way to render *charisma* in these two instances, and if the word *gift* was used somewhere else in the passage for clarification even though there was no corresponding Greek word, this may not mean that the additional appearance of the word *gift* was employed under the influence of the conventional view. Still, even if we grant this, such usage should not be taken to imply that *charisma* is a technical term that carries the weight of "spiritual gift theology." Furthermore, if readers find frequent occurrences of *gift* in these texts, all of which seem to refer to the so-called spiritual gifts, they may still be prone to read these passages along conventional lines.

The issue of a correct reading of the word *gift* makes it clear that the nature of the items in these lists and what unites them need to be identified. Such an examination, it has been argued in this book, leads us to view these items as either ministry assignments or people in their ministry assignments (see esp. chaps. 9–12). If this interpretation is correct, and in light of the confusion created by the use of the word *gift,*[15] we believe that this should be reflected in the translations, especially those translations that are more dynamic (e.g. NLT).[16] Doing so will prevent readers from unnecessary misunderstandings.

GIFT IN 1 CORINTHIANS 12–14

Nevertheless, in surveying the translations, the number of times that *gift* occurs is often well beyond what would be expected, even in light of the issues mentioned above. Whereas *charisma* occurs only five times throughout 1 Corinthians 12–14,[17] *gift* occurs twice as frequently in many English translations of these chapters, and even more than that in the more free translations. Frequency of appearance is illustrated in the chart below.[18]

THE FREQUENCY OF GIFT IN 1 CORINTHIANS 12–14

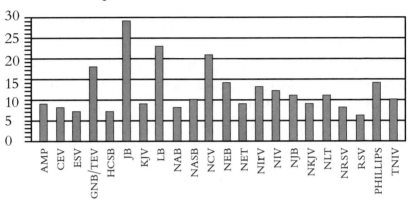

GIFT *OUTSIDE THE LIST PASSAGES*

While, as we have just noted, there may be some grounds for *gift* to be used at times in the list passages (evern though this might introduce confusion), there are a number of examples of *gift* being used with reference to ministries outside of the list passages where nothing in the context suggests such an insertion. It is difficult to know why translators would use the word *gift* in these situations unless they regarded it as a technical word that carries the theology of the conventional view. If readers were not already led to view *gift* as a technical term based on its usage in the list passages (esp. 1 Cor. 12–14), then these additional occurrences in other contexts will make resisting this interpretation even more difficult. In short, readers will see ministries uniformly referred to as "gifts," and thereby be inclined to view this word as a technical term representing the theology of spiritual gifts (as abilities).

1. Mark 16:17: In the longer ending to Mark, verse 17 introduces a list of signs that will accompany believers. The second of these signs is that "they will speak in/with new tongues" (γλώσσαις λαλήσουσιν καιναῖς). However, the JB and the NJB both translate this, "they will have the gift of tongues."

2. Acts 2:4: On the day of Pentecost, as the disciples were gathered together, the Holy Spirit came from heaven and filled them. Then it says that they "began to speak in other tongues as the Spirit gave them utterance" (ἤρξαντο λαλεῖν ἐτέραις γλώσσαις καθὼς τὸ πνεῦμα ἐδίδου ἀποφθέγγεσθαι αὐτοῖς). However, the JB says they "began to speak foreign languages as the Spirit gave them the gift of speech."[19]

3. Acts 21:9–10: In Acts 21:8, Paul and his companions arrive in Caesarea and go to the house of Philip the evangelist. Verse 9 notes that Philip had "four virgin daughters who prophesied" (θυγατέρες τέσσαρες παρθένοι προφητεύουσαι). However, the AMP, LB, NCV, NEB, NLT, and NRSV all speak of "the gift of prophecy" or of "prophesying" and the NAB reads, "gifted with prophecy."[20] Furthermore, Acts 21:10 speaks of "a prophet named Agabus" (προφήτης ὀνόματι Ἄγαβος) who came down from Judea. However, both the LB and the NLT translate this, "a man named Agabus, who also had the gift of prophecy."

4. 1 Thessalonians 5:20: Paul's first letter to the Thessalonians comes to a conclusion with a string of exhortations regarding Christian living, the last of which concerns prophecy. In verse 20, Paul writes, "Do not despise prophecies" (προφητείας μὴ ἐξουθενεῖτε). However, the AMP translates this, "Do not spurn the gifts and utterances of the prophets," and both the JB and NJB speak of "the gift of prophecy." Also, the NASB's footnoted reading is "do not despise prophetic *gifts*."

THE USE OF "SPIRITUAL GIFT"

Only once in Paul's letters does he use two words together that respectively could be rendered as "spiritual" and "gift" (χάρισμα . . . πνευματικὸν, Rom. 1:11).[21] However, as with *gift,* many translations use "spiritual gift" much more frequently. The more occurrences there are, the more likely readers will be influenced to understand it as a technical term. Even if some readers were able to avoid reading all of their "spiritual gift" theology into the term *gift,* even fewer will be able to avoid doing so when they see the actual phrase "spiritual gift."[22] In the charts that follow, occurrences of this phrase have been divided according to their underlying Greek words.

In some cases, *charisma* is translated "spiritual gift," implying that it is a technical term that carries the weight of "spiritual gift theology."[23]

TRANSLATIONS OF CHARISMA

Translations	1 Cor. 1:7	1 Cor. 12:4	1 Cor. 12:31	1 Tim. 4:14	2 Tim. 1:6
"spiritual gift(s)"	ESV, HCSB, LB, NAB, NET, NIV, NLT, NRSV, RSV	CEV, GNB/TEV, NAB, NLT, TNIV	NAB, PHILLIPS	GNB/TEV, JB, NASB,[24] NET, NJB, NLT, TNIV	NLT
"spiritual endowment"	AMP			NEB	
"gifts of the [Holy] Spirit"[25]	JB, NIrV				
"gift the Holy Spirit gave you"				NIrV	

Sometimes *pneumatikos[n]* (πνευματικός/ν) is translated "spiritual gift," even though it never elsewhere denotes "gift." As an adjective it usually means "spiritual" and as a plural noun can be a reference either to spiritual things or to spiritual persons.[26]

Translations of Pneumatikos[n]

Translations	1 Cor. 12:1	1 Cor. 14:1	1 Cor. 14:37
"spiritual gift(s)"	AMP, CEV, ESV, JB, KJV, NAB, NASB, NCV, NET, NIV, NKJV, NRSV, RSV	ESV, GNB/TEV, HCSB, JB, KJV, NAB, NASB, NCV, NET, NIV, NJB, NKJV, NRSV, RSV, TNIV	GNB/TEV
"spiritual endowment(s)"		AMP	AMP
"gifts of the [Holy] Spirit"	NEB, NIrV, NJB, TNIV	NEB, PHILLIPS	NIrV
"gifts [that come] from the Holy Spirit"	GNB/TEV	CEV	
"gifts the Holy Spirit gives"		NIrV	
"spiritually gifted" or "gifted by the Spirit"			NIV, TNIV

Sometimes *pneuma* (πνεῦμα) is translated "spiritual gift" although it almost always is elsewhere translated as "Spirit" (or occasionally "spirit"). But in these translations it is often rendered "spiritual gift" or something similar:

TRANSLATIONS OF PNEUMA

Translations	1 Cor. 14:12
"spiritual gift(s)"	CEV, [HCSB],[27] JB, KJV, NASB, NCV, NIV, NKJV, NRSV, PHILLIPS
"gifts of the Spirit"	GNB/TEV, NEB, NIrV, TNIV
"the Spirit's gifts"	[NET][28]
"special gifts from the Holy Spirit"	LB
"spiritual endowments" and "manifestations of the [Holy] Spirit"	AMP

In one example *phanerōsis* (φανέρωσις) is translated "spiritual gift," presumably under the assumption that "manifestation of the Spirit" is a synonym for "spiritual gift," and thus is allowed to carry the entire weight of "spiritual gift" theology.

TRANSLATION OF PHANERŌSIS

Translation	1 Cor. 12:7
"spiritual gift"	NLT

In a number of examples "spiritual gift" occurs with no clear basis. Only two examples are included here for illustration.

1. 1 Corinthians 4:8: After exhorting the Corinthians to stop passing judgment on one another, in verse 8, Paul picks up a sarcastic tone and "praises" them for their supposed superiority and maturity. He writes,

"Already you are filled. Already you have become rich. Without us you have become kings" (ἤδη κεκορεσμένοι ἐστέ, ἤδη ἐπλουτήσατε, χωρὶς ἡμῶν ἐβασιλεύσατε). However, in translating the second of these three phrases, the AMP says, "Already you have become rich [in spiritual gifts and graces]!"

2. Hebrews 6:2: Despite their immaturity identified in chapter 5, the readers of Hebrews are exhorted by the author to leave the elementary teachings of Christ and to go on to maturity (Heb. 6:1). Then it says, "not laying again a foundation" and lists six basic teachings. The fourth of these teachings is the "laying on of hands" (ἐπιθέσεώς τε χειρῶν, Heb. 6:2). However, the LB somehow manages to translate this phrase as "spiritual gifts."

THE USE OF "GIFT" AND "SPIRITUAL GIFT" IN THE SECTION HEADINGS

Although the primary concern here is the translation of the biblical text itself, a few comments on Bible section headings is merited. Where "Gift" and especially "Spiritual Gift" are used in the Bible section headings, readers are susceptible to the same misconceptions regarding this language that are indicated in the above two main sections of this appendix.

THE HIGH FREQUENCY OF "GIFT" AND "SPIRITUAL GIFT"

Not surprisingly most translations use "Spiritual Gift" in their section heading for the first half of 1 Corinthians 12.[29] Although this introduces a possibility for misconception, it may be viewed as somewhat understandable because of the emphasis on the Spirit and the five occurrences of *charisma*. However, as with the occurrences of *gift* in the text, throughout chapters 12–14 many translations continue to use "Gift" and "Spiritual Gift," particularly in the first half of chapter 14.[30] While the NEB uses the heading "Spiritual Gifts" for all of chapters 12–14, an even greater problem results when translations use "Spiritual Gift" in numerous headings throughout these chapters. Both the JB and the NJB, for example, use "Spiritual Gift" in four of their headings throughout these chapters.

OUTSIDE 1 CORINTHIANS 12–14

Concerns are also raised by the use of "Spiritual Gift" outside of 1 Corinthians 12–14. For Romans 12:3–8, the NKJV uses the heading, "Serve God with Spiritual Gifts." This, however, is not nearly so problematic as when such a heading is used in Ephesians 4:7–16: "Spiritual Gifts." But the gifts in Ephesians 4 are people in their ministries. The section title guides the reader toward an interpretation of spiritual gifts as abilities and away from the plain reading of the text, which is that God gives to the church people who are in equipping ministries to train the saints for the work of ministry.[31]

THE USE OF GIFTED AND UNGIFTED

CONFUSION OVER GIFTED LANGUAGE

Whereas *Webster's Dictionary* offers the idea of ability as one of two definitions for *gift*, that idea is involved in both definitions for the adjective *gifted*, thus, "1: endowed by nature or training with a gift: as *a:* having a special talent or other desirable quality . . . *b:* having superior intellectual capacity . . . 2: reflecting or revealing a special gift or talent."[32] Therefore, when *gifted* and *ungifted* appear in connection with the so-called spiritual gifts, readers will have an even greater tendency to read these as abilities. Sometimes adjectives such as *gifted, not gifted,* or *ungifted* are added into translations.

Gifted Language in *1 Corinthians 12–14*

Translations	1 Cor. 13:9	1 Cor. 14:16	1 Cor. 14:18	1 Cor. 14:23	1 Cor. 14:24	1 Cor. 14:37
[not] gifted	LB	AMP	NEB			NIV, TNIV
ungifted		NASB		AMP, NASB	NASB	

The Ungifted People in *1 Corinthians 14:16, 23, 24*

Since five of the nine occurrences of gifted language are related, a special note is merited. In 1 Corinthians 14, Paul emphasizes that it is vital for believers to understand one another in corporate worship. In verse 16, he tells them that if they praise God in the spirit (or Spirit), anyone in the position of the *idiōtēs* (ἰδιώτης) will not know what they are saying. Similarly, in verses 23 and 24, Paul uses *idiōtēs* to identify people who do not understand when the congregation speaks in tongues.

Although there are a number of complicated issues involved here, the most important is how *idiōtēs* (ἰδιώτης) is to be rendered. The NASB translates each of these occurrences as "ungifted" and the AMP uses "gifted" in verse 16 and "ungifted" in verse 23.[33] However, the entry in BDAG for *idiōtēs* (ἰδιώτης) in 1 Corinthians 14:23 simply reads, "one who is not knowledgeable about some particular group's experience."[34] Other translations translate this as "outsider" (ESV, NRSV, RSV), "those who do not understand" (NIV), "an inquirer" (TNIV),[35] or "uninitiated people" (JB, NJB). It is difficult to imagine that translators would translate *idiōtēs* using gifted language unless they were under the influence of the conventional view.

The Language of Using

Although the Greek language contains words that would normally be translated as "use" in English,[36] none of these occur in any of the passages under discussion. Many English versions of Romans 12:6, however, add the phrase "let us use them" (for example, ESV, NKJV, RSV; cf. NIV), or something similar.[37] (This issue has been discussed more fully in appendix B.) Note here that this insertion serves to separate the entity and the application, and thus tends to imply to a reader that the conventional separation of ability and ministry is present in the Greek text.

Similarly, many translations of 1 Peter 4:10 suggest a separation by rendering the participle of the verb *diakoneō* (διακονέω) (which is normally translated "serve" or "minister") as "employ" (for example, NASB, RSV) or "use" (NAB, ESV; cf. NIV). Nowhere else is *diakoneō* (διακονέω) rendered in such a way in the New Testament. The separation between the entity and the use of that entity tends to suggest to most readers a conventional reading, although such a reading is far from necessary.[38]

THE USE OF ABILITY LANGUAGE FOR THE SO-CALLED SPIRITUAL GIFTS

In referring to the so-called spiritual gifts, it is not uncommon for translations to use words such as *can, able, ability,* and *power.* Whereas many of the factors described above involve more subtle influences, the use of ability language is quite explicit. When ability language is used in this way, it is almost inevitable that an English reader will interpret the passage in categories that reflect the conventional view. Furthermore, when such language is used in conjunction with the word *gift,* readers will likely conclude that *gift* is being used in the sense of "ability."[39]

ABILITY LANGUAGE IN THE LISTS

Since four lists have played such a prominent role in this study, complete charts have been provided showing how they are translated in different versions. Even a quick perusal of these charts will demonstrate the pervasive influence of the conventional view on the way these lists have been translated, and thus on how people will tend to read them after they have been thus translated.

Ephesians 4:11 unquestionably has the least number of influences. This is not surprising because the gifts in this passage are the people in their ministries (for example, TNIV). So, at least in this passage, there should be far less confusion because if a people-in-their-ministries reading is understood, it is not possible to view these gifts as abilities. However, the LB and PHILLIPS do just that. Also, the fourfold repetition of *gift* in the NIrV might incline readers toward reading *gift* as a technical term for "spiritual gift theology."

In Romans 12:6–8 and 1 Corinthians 12:28–30, even more ability language and significant occurrences of *gift* can be seen. In Romans 12:6–8, note the occurrences of *use* and *exercise,* particularly in 6a.[40] In 1 Corinthians 12:28–30, take note of the even higher percentage of translations that use ability language.

The list in 1 Corinthians 12:8–10 is a little more complicated. While it clearly contains the largest amount of ability language, this is somewhat understandable because the items in this passage all require special enabling by the Spirit. Therefore, it is not wholly inappropriate to translate these items using such language. The danger, however, is that readers will understand these items exclusively in terms of ability.

On the charts, the following have been underlined: (1) any words or phrases that communicate the idea of ability or talent; (2) occurrences of "gift" that are not literally reflected in the Greek;[41] (3) words such as "use" and "exercise." Pay special attention to boxes that are shaded. Since "ability" language, more than any other, will tend to influence people to read along lines of the conventional view, boxes in which this occurs have been shaded.

1) *Ephesians 4:11*

Version	a	b	c	d	e
Greek	καὶ αὐτὸς ἔδωκεν	τοὺς μὲν ἀποστόλους,	τοὺς δὲ προφήτας,	τοὺς δὲ εὐαγγελιστάς,	τοὺς δὲ ποιμένας καὶ διδασκάλους,
AMP	And His gifts were [varied; He Himself appointed and gave men to us]	some to be apostles (special messengers),	some prophets (inspired preachers and expounders),	some evangelists (preachers of the Gospel, traveling missionaries),	some pastors (shepherds of His flock) and teachers.
CEV	Christ chose some of us to be	apostles,	prophets,	missionaries,	pastors, and teachers,
ESV	And he gave	the apostles,	the prophets,	the evangelists,	the pastors and teachers,
GNB/TEV	It was he who "gave gifts to people"; he appointed	some to be apostles,	others to be prophets,	others to be evangelists,	others to be pastors and teachers.

HCSB	And He personally gave	some to be apostles,	some prophets,	some evangelists,	some pastors and teachers,
JB	And to some, his gift was that they should be apostles;		to some, prophets;	to some, evangelists;	to some pastors and teachers;
KJV	And he gave	some, apostles;	and some, prophets;	and some, evangelists;	and some, pastors and teachers;
LB	Some of us have been given special ability as apostles;		to others he has given the gift of being able to preach well;	some have special ability in winning people to Christ, helping them to trust him as their Savior;	still others have a gift for caring for God's people as a shepherd does his sheep, leading and teaching them in the ways of God.
NAB	And he gave	some, apostles,	others as prophets,	others as evangelists,	others as pastors and teachers,
NASB	And He gave	some as apostles,	and some as prophets,	and some as evangelists,	and some as pastors and teachers,

NCV	And Christ gave gifts to people—	he made some to be apostles,	some to be prophets,	some to go and tell the Good News,	and some to have the work of caring for and teaching God's people.
NEB	And these were his gifts:	some to be apostles,	some prophets,	some evangelists,	some pastors and teachers,
NET	It was he who gave	some as apostles,	some as prophets,	some as evangelists,	and some as pastors and teachers,
NIrV	He is the One who gave some the gift to be apostles.		He gave some the gift to be prophets.	He gave some the gift of preaching the good news.	And he gave some the gift to be pastors and teachers.
NIV	It was he who gave	some to be apostles,	some to be prophets,	some to be evangelists,	and some to be pastors and teachers,
NJB	And to some, his 'gift' was that they should be apostles;		to some prophets;	to some, evangelists;	to some, pastors and teachers;
NKJV	And He Himself gave	some to be apostles,	some prophets,	some evangelists,	and some pastors and teachers,

NLT	Now these are the gifts Christ gave to the church:	the apostles,	the prophets,	the evangelists,	and the pastors and teachers.
NRSV	The gifts he gave were that	some would be apostles,	some prophets,	some evangelists,	some pastors and teachers,
RSV	And his gifts were that	some should be apostles,	some prophets,	some evangelists,	some pastors and teachers,
PHILLIPS	His "gifts to men" were varied.	Some he made his messengers,	some prophets,	some preachers of the Gospel;	to some he gave the power to guide and teach his people.
TNIV	So Christ himself gave	the apostles,	the prophets,	the evangelists,	the pastors and teachers,

2) ROMANS 12:6–8

Version	6a	6b	7a	7b	8a	8b	8c	8d
Greek	ἔχοντες δὲ χαρίσματα κατὰ τὴν χάριν τὴν δοθεῖσαν ἡμῖν διάφορα,	εἴτε προφητείαν κατὰ τὴν ἀναλογίαν τῆς πίστεως,	εἴτε διακονίαν ἐν τῇ διακονίᾳ,	εἴτε ὁ διδάσκων ἐν τῇ διδασκαλίᾳ,	εἴτε ὁ παρακαλῶν ἐν τῇ παρακλήσει	ὁ μεταδιδοὺς ἐν ἁπλότητι,	ὁ προϊστάμενος ἐν σπουδῇ,	ὁ ἐλεῶν ἐν ἱλαρότητι.
AMP	Having gifts (faculties, talents, qualities) that differ according to the grace given us, let us use them:	[He whose gift is] prophecy, [let him prophesy] according to the proportion of his faith;	[He whose gift is] practical service, let him give himself to serving;	he who teaches, to his teaching;	He who exhorts (encourages), to his exhortation;	he who contributes, let him do it in simplicity *and* liberality;	he who gives aid *and* superintends, with zeal *and* singleness of mind;	he who does acts of mercy, with genuine cheerfulness *and* joyful eagerness.
CEV	God has also given each of us different gifts to use.	If we can prophesy, we should do it according to the amount of faith we have.	If we can serve others, we should serve.	If we can teach, we should teach.	If we can encourage others, we should encourage them.	If we can give, we should be generous.	If we are leaders, we should do our best.	If we are good to others, we should do it cheerfully.

ESV	Having gifts that differ according to the grace given to us, let us use them:	if prophecy, in proportion to our faith;	if service, in our serving;	the one who teaches, in his teaching;	the one who exhorts, in his exhortation;	the one who contributes, in generosity;	the one who leads, with zeal;	the one who does acts of mercy, with cheerfulness.
GNB/TEV	So we are to use our different gifts in accordance with the grace that God has given us.	If our gift is to speak God's message, we should do it according to the faith that we have;	if it is to serve, we should serve;	if it is to teach, we should teach;	if it is to encourage others, we should do so.	Whoever shares with others should do it generously;	whoever has authority should work hard;	whoever shows kindness to others should do it cheerfully.
HCSB	According to the grace given to us, we have different gifts:	If prophecy, use it according to the standard of faith;	if service, in service;	if teaching, in teaching;	if exhorting, in exhortation;	giving, with generosity;	leading, with diligence;	showing mercy, with cheerfulness.

JB	Our gifts differ according to the grace given us.	If your gift is prophecy, then use it as your faith suggests;	if administration, then use it for administration;	if teaching, then use it for teaching.	Let the preachers deliver sermons,	the almsgivers give freely,	the officials be diligent,	and those who do works of mercy do them cheerfully.
KJV	Having then gifts differing according to the grace that is given to us,	whether prophecy, *let us prophesy* according to the proportion of faith;	Or ministry, *let us wait* on *our* ministering:	or he that teacheth, on teaching;	Or he that exhorteth, on exhortation:	he that giveth, *let him do it* with simplicity;	he that ruleth, with diligence;	he that sheweth mercy, with cheerfulness.
LB	God has given each of us the ability to do certain things well.	So if God has given you the ability to prophesy, then prophesy whenever you can—as often as your faith is strong enough to receive a message from God.	If your gift is that of serving others, serve them well.	If you are a teacher, do a good job of teaching.	If you are a preacher, see to it that your sermons are strong and helpful.	If God has given you money, be generous in helping others with it.	If God has given you administrative ability and put you in charge of the work of others, take the responsibility seriously.	Those who offer comfort to the sorrowing should do so with Christian cheer.

NAB	Since we have gifts that differ according to the grace given to us, let us exercise them:	if prophecy, in proportion to the faith;	if ministry, in ministering;	if one is a teacher, in teaching;	if one exhorts, in exhortation;	if one contributes, in generosity;	if one is over others, with diligence;	if one does acts of mercy, with cheerfulness.
NASB	Since we have gifts that differ according to the grace given to us, *each of us is to exercise them accordingly:*	if prophecy, according to the proportion of his faith;	if service, in his serving;	or he who teaches, in his teaching;	or he who exhorts, in his exhortation;	he who gives, with liberality;	he who leads, with diligence;	he who shows mercy, with cheerfulness.
NCV	We all have different gifts, each of which came because of the grace God gave us.	The person who has the gift of prophecy should use that gift in agreement with the faith.	Anyone who has the gift of serving should serve.	Anyone who has the gift of teaching should teach.	Whoever has the gift of encouraging others should encourage.	Whoever has the gift of giving to others should give freely.	Anyone who has the gift of being a leader should try hard when he leads.	Whoever has the gift of showing mercy to others should do so with joy.

NEB	The gifts we possess differ as they are allotted to us by God's grace, and must be exercised accordingly:	the gift of inspired utterance, for example, in proportion to man's faith;	or the gift of administration, in administration.	A teacher should employ his gift in teaching,	and one who has the gift of stirring speech should use it to stir his hearers.	If you give to charity, give with all your heart;	if you are a leader, exert yourself to lead;	if you are helping others in distress, do it cheerfully.
NET	And we have different gifts according to the grace given to us.	If the gift is prophecy, that individual must use it in proportion to his faith.	If it is service, he must serve;	if it is teaching, he must teach;	if it is exhortation, he must exhort;	if it is contributing, he must do so with sincerity;	if it is leadership, he must do so with diligence;	if it is showing mercy, he must do so with cheerfulness.
NIrV	We all have gifts. They differ in keeping with the grace that God has given each of us.	Do you have the gift of prophecy? Then use it in keeping with the faith you have.	Is it your gift to serve? Then serve.	Is it teaching? Then teach.	Is it telling others how they should live? Then tell them.	Is it giving to those who are in need? Then give freely.	Is it being a leader? Then work hard at it.	Is it showing mercy? Then do it cheerfully.

NIV	We have different gifts, according to the grace given us.	If a man's gift is <u>prophesy</u>-ing, let him use it in proportion to his faith.	If it is serving, let him serve;	if it is teaching, let him teach;	if it is encoura-ging, let him encourage;	if it is contributing to the needs of others, let him give generously;	if it is leadership, let him govern diligently;	if it is showing mercy, let him do it cheerfully.
NJB	Then since the gifts that we have differ according to the grace that was given to each of us:	if it is a <u>gift</u> of prophecy, we should prophesy as much as our faith tells us;	if it is a <u>gift</u> of practical service, let us devote ourselves to serving;	if it is teaching, to teaching;	if it is encouraging, to encouraging.	When you give, you should give generously from the heart;	if you are put in charge, you must be conscientious;	if you do works of mercy, let it be because you enjoy doing them.
NKJV	Having then gifts differing according to the grace that is given to us, *let us use them:*	if prophecy, *let us prophesy* in proportion to our faith;	or ministry, *let us use it* in *our* minister-ing;	he who teaches, in teaching;	he who exhorts, in exhortation;	he who gives, with liberality;	he who leads, with diligence;	he who shows mercy, with cheerfulness.
NLT	In his grace, God has given us different gifts for doing certain things well.	So if God has given you the ability to prophesy, speak out with as much faith as God has given you.	If your gift is serving others, serve them well.	If you are a teacher, teach well.	If your gift is to encourage others, be encouraging.	If it is giving, give generously.	If God has given you leadership ability, take the responsibility seriously.	And if you have a gift for showing kindness to others, do it gladly.

NRSV	We have gifts that differ according to the grace given to us:	prophecy, in proportion to faith;	ministry, in ministering;	the teacher, in teaching;	the exhorter, in exhortation;	the giver, in generosity;	the leader, in diligence;	the compassionate, in cheerfulness.
RSV	Having gifts that differ according to the grace given to us, let us use them:	if prophecy, in proportion to our faith;	if service, in our serving;	he who teaches, in his teaching;	he who exhorts, in his exhortation;	he who contributes, in liberality;	he who gives aid, with zeal;	he who does acts of mercy, with cheerfulness.
PHILLIPS	Through the grace of God we have different gifts.	If our gift is preaching, let us preach to the limit of our vision.	If it is serving others let us concentrate on our service;	if it is teaching let us give all we have to our teaching;	and if our gift be the stimulating of the faith of others let us set ourselves to it.	Let the man who is called to give, give freely;	let the man who wields authority think of his responsibility;	and let the man who feels sympathy for his fellows act cheerfully.
TNIV	We have different gifts, according to the grace given to each of us.	If your gift is prophesying, then prophesy in accordance with your faith;	if it is serving, then serve;	if it is teaching, then teach;	if it is to encourage, then give encouragement;	if it is giving, then give generously;	if it is to lead, do it diligently;	if it is to show mercy, do it cheerfully.

3) 1 CORINTHIANS 12:28–30

Version	28a	28b	28c	29	30
Greek	καὶ οὓς μὲν ἔθετο ὁ θεὸς ἐν τῇ ἐκκλησίᾳ	πρῶτον ἀποστόλους, δεύτερον προφήτας, τρίτον διδασκάλους,	ἔπειτα δυνάμεις, ἔπειτα χαρίσματα ἰαμάτων, ἀντιλήμψεις, κυβερνήσεις, γένη γλωσσῶν.	μὴ πάντες ἀπόστολοι; μὴ πάντες προφῆται; μὴ πάντες διδάσκαλοι; μὴ πάντες δυνάμεις;	μὴ πάντες χαρίσματα ἔχουσιν ἰαμάτων; μὴ πάντες γλώσσαις λαλοῦσιν; μὴ πάντες διερμηνεύουσιν;
AMP	So God has appointed some in the church [for His own use]:	first apostles (special messengers); second prophets (inspired preachers and expounders); third teachers;	then wonder-workers; then those with ability to heal the sick; helpers; administrators; [speakers in] different (unknown) tongues.	Are all apostles (special messengers)? Are all prophets (inspired interpreters of the will and purposes of God)? Are all teachers? Do all have the power of performing miracles?	Do all possess extraordinary powers of healing? Do all speak with tongues? Do all interpret?
CEV	First, God chose some people to be apostles and prophets and teachers for the church.		But he also chose some to work miracles or heal the sick or help others or be leaders or speak different kinds of languages.	Not everyone is an apostle. Not everyone is a prophet. Not everyone is a teacher. Not everyone can work miracles.	Not everyone can heal the sick. Not everyone can speak different kinds of languages. Not everyone can tell what these languages mean.

ESV	And God has appointed in the church	first apostles, second prophets, third teachers,	then miracles, then gifts of healing, helping, administrating, and various kinds of tongues.	Are all apostles? Are all prophets? Are all teachers? Do all work miracles?	Do all possess gifts of healing? Do all speak with tongues? Do all interpret?
GNB/TEV	In the church God has put all in place:	in the first place apostles, in the second place prophets, and in the third place teachers;	then those who perform miracles, followed by those who are given the power to heal or to help others or to direct them or to speak in strange tongues.	They are not all apostles or prophets or teachers. Not everyone has the power to work miracles	or to heal diseases or to speak in strange tongues or to explain what is said.
HCSB	And God has placed these in the church:	first apostles, second prophets, third teachers,	next, miracles, then gifts of healing, helping, managing, various kinds of languages.	Are all apostles? Are all prophets? Are all teachers? Do all do miracles?	Do all have gifts of healing? Do all speak in languages? Do all interpret?
JB	In the Church, God has given	the first place to apostles, the second to prophets, the third to teachers;	after them, miracles, and after them the gift of healing; good leaders, those with many languages.	Are all of them apostles, or all of them prophets, or all of them teachers? Do they all have the gift of miracles,	or all have the gift of healing? Do all speak strange languages, and all interpret them?

KJV	And God hath set some in the church,	first apostles, secondarily prophets, thirdly teachers,	after that miracles, then gifts of healings, helps, governments, diversities of tongues.	*Are* all apostles? *are* all prophets? *are* all teachers? *are* all workers of miracles?	Have all the gifts of healing? do all speak with tongues? do all interpret?
LB	Here is a list of some of the parts he has placed in his church, which is his body:	Apostles, Prophets—those who preach God's Word, Teachers,	Those who do miracles, Those who have the gift of healing, Those who <u>can</u> help others, Those who <u>can</u> get others to work together, Those who speak in languages they have never learned.	Is everyone an apostle? Of course not. Is everyone a preacher? No. Are all teachers? Does everyone have the <u>power</u> to do miracles?	<u>Can</u> everyone heal the sick? Of course not. Does God give all of us the <u>ability</u> to speak in languages we've never learned? <u>Can</u> just anyone understand and translate what those are saying who have that gift of foreign speech?
NAB	Some people God has designated in the church to be,	first, apostles; second, prophets; third, teachers;	then, mighty deeds; then, gifts of healing, assistance, administration, and varieties of tongues.	Are all apostles? Are all prophets? Are all teachers? Do all work mighty deeds?	Do all have gifts of healing? Do all speak in tongues? Do all interpret?

NASB	And God has appointed in the church,	first apostles, second prophets, third teachers,	then miracles, then gifts of healings, helps, administrations, *various* kinds of tongues.	All are not apostles, are they? All are not prophets, are they? All are not teachers, are they? All are not *workers of* miracles, are they?	All do not have gifts of healings, do they? All do not speak with tongues, do they? All do not interpret, do they?
NCV	In the church God has given a place	first to apostles, second to prophets, and third to teachers.	Then God has given a place to those who do miracles, those who have gifts of healing, those who can help others, those who are able to govern, and those who can speak in different languages.	Not all are apostles. Not all are prophets. Not all are teachers. Not all do miracles.	Not all have gifts of healing. Not all speak in different languages. Not all interpret those languages.
NEB	Within our community God has appointed,	in the first place apostles, in the second place prophets, thirdly teachers;	then miracle-workers, then those who have gifts of healing, or ability to help others or power to guide them, or the gift of ecstatic utterance of various kinds.	Are all apostles? all prophets? all teachers? Do all work miracles?	Have all gifts of healing? Do all speak in tongues of ecstasy? Can all interpret them?

NET	And God has placed in the church	first apostles, second prophets, third teachers,	then miracles, gifts of healing, helps, gifts of leadership, different kinds of tongues.	Not all are apostles, are they? Not all are prophets, are they? Not all are teachers, are they? Not all perform miracles, do they?	Not all have gifts of healing, do they? Not all speak in tongues, do they? Not all interpret, do they?
NIrV	First, God has appointed apostles in the church. Second, he has appointed prophets. Third, he has appointed teachers.		Then he has appointed people who do miracles and those who have gifts of healing. He also appointed those able to help others, those able to direct things, and those who can speak in different kinds of languages they had not known before.	Is everyone an apostle? Is everyone a prophet? Is everyone a teacher? Do all work miracles?	Do all have gifts of healing? Do all speak in languages they had not known before? Do all explain what is said in those languages?

NIV	And in the church God has appointed	first of all apostles, second prophets, third teachers,	then workers of miracles, also those having gifts of healing, those able to help others, those with gifts of administration, and those speaking in different kinds of tongues.	Are all apostles? Are all prophets? Are all teachers? Do all work miracles?	Do all have gifts of healing? Do all speak in tongues? Do all interpret?
NJB	And those whom God has appointed in the Church are,	first apostles, secondly prophets, thirdly teachers;	after them, miraculous powers, then gifts of healing, helpful acts, guidance, various kinds of tongues.	Are all of them apostles? Or all prophets? Or all teachers? Or all miracle-workers?	Do all have the gifts of healing? Do all of them speak in tongues and all interpret them?
NKJV	And God has appointed these in the church:	first apostles, second prophets, third teachers,	after that miracles, then gifts of healings, helps, administrations, varieties of tongues.	*Are all apostles? Are all prophets? Are all teachers? Are all workers of miracles?*	Do all have gifts of healings? Do all speak with tongues? Do all interpret?

NLT	Here are some of the parts God has appointed for the church:	first are apostles, second are prophets, third are teachers,	then those who do miracles, those who have the gift of healing, those who can help others, those who have the gift of leadership, those who speak in unknown languages.	Are we all apostles? Are we all prophets? Are we all teachers? Do we all have the power to do miracles?	Do we all have the gift of healing? Do we all have the ability to speak in unknown languages? Do we all have the ability to interpret unknown languages? Of course not!
NRSV	And God has appointed in the church	first apostles, second prophets, third teachers;	then deeds of power, then gifts of healing, forms of assistance, forms of leadership, various kinds of tongues.	Are all apostles? Are all prophets? Are all teachers? Do all work miracles?	Do all possess gifts of healing? Do all speak in tongues? Do all interpret?
RSV	And God has appointed in the church	first apostles, second prophets, third teachers,	then workers of miracles, then healers, helpers, administrators, speakers in various kinds of tongues.	Are all apostles? Are all prophets? Are all teachers? Do all work miracles?	Do all possess gifts of healing? Do all speak with tongues? Do all interpret?

PHILLIPS	And in his Church God has appointed	first some to be his messengers, secondly, some to be preachers of power, thirdly, teachers.	After them he has appointed workers of spiritual power, men with the gift of healing, helpers, organizers and those with the gift of speaking in "tongues."	As we look at the body of Christ do we find all are his messengers, all are preachers, or all are teachers? Do we find all wielders of spiritual power?	all able to heal, all able to speak with tongues, or all able to interpret the tongues? No, we find God's distribution of gifts is on the same principles of harmony that he has shown in the human body.
TNIV	And God has placed in the church	first of all apostles, second prophets, third teachers,	then miracles, then gifts of healing, of helping, of guidance, and of different kinds of tongues.	Are all apostles? Are all prophets? Are all teachers? Do all work miracles?	Do all have gifts of healing? Do all speak in tongues? Do all interpret?

4) *1 Corinthians 12:8–10*

Version	8a	8b	9a	9b
Greek	ᾧ μὲν γὰρ διὰ τοῦ πνεύματος δίδοται λόγος σοφίας,	ἄλλῳ δὲ λόγος γνώσεως κατὰ τὸ αὐτὸ πνεῦμα,	ἑτέρῳ πίστις ἐν τῷ αὐτῷ πνεύματι,	ἄλλῳ δὲ χαρίσματα ἰαμάτων ἐν τῷ ἑνὶ πνεύματι,
AMP	To one is given in *and* through the [Holy] Spirit [the power to speak] a message of wisdom,	and to another [the power to express] a word of knowledge *and* understanding according to the same [Holy] Spirit;	To another [wonder-working] faith by the same [Holy] Spirit,	to another the extraordinary powers of healing by the one Spirit;
CEV	Some of us can speak with wisdom,	while others can speak with knowledge, but these gifts come from the same Spirit.	To others the Spirit has given great faith	or the power to heal the sick
ESV	To one is given through the Spirit the utterance of wisdom,	and to another the utterance of knowledge according to the same Spirit,	to another faith by the same Spirit,	to another gifts of healing by the one Spirit,
GNB/TEV	The Spirit gives one person a message full of wisdom,	while to another person the same Spirit gives a message full of knowledge.	One and the same Spirit gives faith to one person,	while to another person he gives the power to heal.

10a	10b	10c	10d	10e
ἄλλῳ δὲ ἐνεργήματα δυνάμεων,	ἄλλῳ [δὲ] προφητεία,	ἄλλῳ [δὲ] διακρίσεις πνευμάτων,	ἑτέρῳ γένη γλωσσῶν,	ἄλλῳ δὲ ἑρμηνεία γλωσσῶν.
To another the working of miracles.	to another prophetic insight (the gift of interpreting the divine will and purpose);	to another the ability to discern *and* distinguish between [the utterances of true] spirits [and false ones],	to another various kinds of [unknown] tongues,	to another the ability to interpret [such] tongues.
or the power to work mighty miracles.	Some of us are prophets,	and some of us recognize when God's Spirit is present.	Others can speak different kinds of languages,	and still others can tell what these languages mean.
to another the working of miracles,	to another prophecy,	to another the ability to distinguish between spirits,	to another various kinds of tongues,	to another the interpretation of tongues.
The Spirit gives one person the power to work miracles;	to another, the gift of speaking God's message;	and to yet another, the ability to tell the difference between gifts that come from the Spirit and those that do not.	To one person he gives the ability to speak in strange tongues,	and to another he gives the ability to explain what is said.

Version	8a	8b	9a	9b
HCSB	to one is given a message of wisdom through the Spirit,	to another, a message of knowledge by the same Spirit,	to another, faith by the same Spirit,	to another, gifts of healing by the one Spirit,
JB	One may have the gift of preaching with wisdom given him by the Spirit;	another may have the gift of preaching instruction given him by the same Spirit;	and another the gift of faith given by the same Spirit;	another again the gift of healing, through this one Spirit;
KJV	For to one is given by the Spirit the word of wisdom;	to another the word of knowledge by the same Spirit;	To another faith by the same Spirit;	to another the gifts of healing by the same Spirit;
LB	To one person the Spirit gives the ability to give wise advice;	someone else may be especially good at studying and teaching, and this is his gift from the same Spirit.	He gives special faith to another,	and to someone else the power to heal the sick.
NAB	To one is given through the Spirit the expression of wisdom;	to another the expression of knowledge according to the same Spirit;	to another faith by the same Spirit;	to another gifts of healing by the one Spirit;

10a	10b	10c	10d	10e
to another, the performing of miracles,	to another, prophecy,	to another, distinguishing between spirits,	to another, different kinds of languages,	to another, interpretation of languages.
one, the power of miracles;	another, prophecy;	another the gift of recognizing spirits;	another the gift of tongues	and another the ability to interpret them.
To another the working of miracles;	to another prophecy;	to another discerning of spirits;	to another *divers* kinds of tongues;	to another the interpretation of tongues:
He gives power for doing miracles to some,	and to others power to prophesy and preach.	He gives someone else the power to know whether evil spirits are speaking through those who claim to be giving God's messages—or whether it is really the Spirit of God who is speaking.	Still another person is able to speak in languages he never learned;	and others, who do not know the language either, are given power to understand what he is saying.
to another mighty deeds;	to another prophecy;	to another discernment of spirits;	to another varieties of tongues;	to another interpretation of tongues.

Version	8a	8b	9a	9b
NASB	For to one is given the word of wisdom through the Spirit,	and to another the word of knowledge according to the same Spirit;	to another faith by the same Spirit,	and to another gifts of healing by the one Spirit,
NCV	The Spirit gives one person the ability to speak with wisdom,	and the same Spirit gives another the ability to speak with knowledge.	The same Spirit gives faith to one person.	And, to another, that one Spirit gives gifts of healing.
NEB	One man, through the Spirit, has the gift of wise speech,	while another, by the power of the same Spirit, can put the deepest knowledge into words.	Another, by the same Spirit, is granted faith;	another, by the one Spirit, gifts of healing,
NET	For one person is given through the Spirit the message of wisdom,	and another the message of knowledge according to the same Spirit,	to another faith by the same Spirit,	and to another gifts of healing by the one Spirit,
NIrV	To some people the Spirit gives the message of wisdom.	To others the same Spirit gives the message of knowledge.	To others the same Spirit gives faith.	To others that one Spirit gives gifts of healing.

10a	10b	10c	10d	10e
and to another the effecting of miracles,	and to another prophecy,	and to another the distinguishing of spirits,	to another *various* kinds of tongues,	and to another the interpretation of tongues.
The Spirit gives to another person the power to do miracles,	to another the ability to prophesy.	And he gives to another the ability to know the difference between good and evil spirits.	The Spirit gives one person the ability to speak in different kinds of languages	and to another the ability to interpret those languages.
and another miraculous powers;	another has the gift of prophecy,	and another ability to distinguish true spirits from false;	yet another has the gift of ecstatic utterance of different kinds,	and another the ability to interpret it.
to another performance of miracles,	to another prophecy,	and to another discernment of spirits,	to another different kinds of tongues,	and to another the interpretation of tongues.
To others he gives the power to do miracles.	To others he gives the ability to prophesy.	To others he gives the ability to tell the spirits apart.	To others he gives the ability to speak in different kinds of languages they had not known before.	And to still others he gives the ability to explain what was said in those languages.

Version	8a	8b	9a	9b
NIV	To one there is given through the Spirit the message of wisdom,	to another the message of knowledge by means of the same Spirit,	to another faith by the same Spirit,	to another gifts of healing by that one Spirit,
NJB	To one is given from the Spirit the gift of utterance expressing wisdom;	to another the gift of utterance expressing knowledge, in accordance with the same Spirit;	to another, faith from the same Spirit;	and to another, the gifts of healing, through this one Spirit;
NKJV	for to one is given the word of wisdom through the Spirit,	to another the word of knowledge through the same Spirit,	to another faith by the same Spirit,	to another gifts of healings by the same Spirit,
NLT	To one person the Spirit gives the ability to give wise advice;	to another the same Spirit gives a message of special knowledge.	The same Spirit gives great faith to another,	and to someone else the one Spirit gives the gift of healing.
NRSV	To one is given through the Spirit the utterance of wisdom,	and to another the utterance of knowledge according to the same Spirit,	to another faith by the same Spirit,	to another gifts of healing by the one Spirit,

	10a	10b	10c	10d	10e
	to another miraculous powers,	to another prophecy,	to another distinguishing between spirits,	to another speaking in different kinds of tongues,	and to still another the interpretation of tongues.
	to another, the working of miracles;	to another, prophecy;	to another, the power of distinguishing spirits;	to one, the gift of different tongues	and to another, the interpretation of tongues.
	to another the working of miracles,	to another prophecy,	to another discerning of spirits,	to another *different* kinds of tongues,	to another the interpretation of tongues.
	He gives one person the power to perform miracles,	and another the ability to prophesy.	He gives someone else the ability to discern whether a message is from the Spirit of God or from another spirit.	Still another person is given the ability to speak in unknown languages,	while another is given the ability to interpret what is being said.
	to another the working of miracles,	to another prophecy,	to another the discernment of spirits,	to another various kinds of tongues,	to another the interpretation of tongues.

Version	8a	8b	9a	9b
RSV	To one is given through the Spirit the utterance of wisdom,	and to another the utterance of knowledge according to the same Spirit,	to another faith by the same Spirit,	to another gifts of healing by the one Spirit,
PHILLIPS	One man's gift by the Spirit is to speak with wisdom,	another's to speak with knowledge.	The same Spirit gives to another man faith,	to another the ability to heal,
TNIV	To one there is given through the Spirit a message of wisdom,	to another a message of knowledge by means of the same Spirit,	to another faith by the same Spirit,	to another gifts of healing by that one Spirit,

10a	10b	10c	10d	10e
to another the working of miracles,	to another prophecy,	to another the ability to distinguish between spirits,	to another various kinds of tongues,	to another the interpretation of tongues.
to another the power to do great deeds.	The same Spirit gives to another man the gift of preaching the word of God,	to another the ability to discriminate in spiritual matters,	to another speech in different tongues	and to yet another the power to interpret the tongues.
to another miraculous powers,	to another prophecy,	to another distinguishing between spirits,	to another speaking in different kinds of tongues,	and to still another the interpretation of tongues.

Additional Ability Language in 1 Corinthians 12–14[42]

Translations	12:1	4	6	7	11	13:1	2	8	9	14:1	2	5	12	13	22	28	37
ability, abilities	NLT, LB	LB	GNB/TEV (2x)		AMP				NCV	NLT (2x), LB	NLT		NLT	NLT, NEB			LB
able, can, could			CEV	NLT		LB, GNB/TEV				LB, PHILLIPS	LB	JB, LB, NEB, NLT (2x)		PHILLIPS	LB	NLT, LB	
power, energy	AMP	AMP			LB		AMP, NJB, NRSV, RSV	LB				LB	NJB	AMP, NRSV, RSV			NJB, NRSV

CONCLUSION

In this appendix, various factors have been explored that influence readers to understand the so-called spiritual gifts in accordance with the conventional view of spiritual gifts as abilities. First, the numerous occurrences of *gift* in connection with the so-called spiritual gifts incline readers toward a technical understanding of the word in accordance with the conventional view. Seeing these gifts as abilities is further enforced by the fact that the English word *gift* can actually mean "ability." Second, when readers encounter occurrences of "spiritual gift," they will have an even harder time refraining from reading "spiritual gift theology" into these passages. Third, gifted language will also influence readers in this direction since the English word *gifted* involves the idea of ability in both of its definitions. Fourth, the insertion of the language of using implies the conventional view. Fifth, many translations use ability language in connection with the so-called spiritual gifts thereby explicitly conveying the conventional understanding.

Even if some readers of this book are still unsure of the position advocated herein, we hope that all share a concern that readers form their conclusions from the exegesis of Scripture. Therefore, the ways that translations influence readers toward the conventional view should be the concern of all.

Notes

Preface

1. First Peter 4:11 also mentions "whoever speaks" and "whoever serves" as general descriptions that seem to overlap this subject. But since a Pauline theme is under study, and because of the brevity of Peter's comments, 1 Peter 4:11 will not play much of a role in the discussion.

2. The idea to begin with a hypothetical seminar was suggested to me by a similar approach in chapters 2–4 of Garry Friesen with J. Robin Maxson, *Decision Making and the Will of God: A Biblical Alternative to the Traditional View* (Portland: Multnomah Press, 1980), 29–77.

Paul's Four Lists

1. The items have been listed using as near an English equivalent as is possible in the grammatical forms in which they are found. (For example, verbs and participles have not been changed to nouns.)

The List Passages Translated

1. This word has been left untranslated because it is one of the issues under contention in this book. See chapters 5–6 and appendix C.

Chapter 1: Understanding the Conventional View

1. Typical definitions follow here: "Extraordinary powers, distinguishing certain Christians and enabling them to serve the church of Christ, the reception of which is due to the power of divine grace operating in their souls by the Holy Spirit" (J. H. Thayer, *Greek-English Lexicon of the New Testament* [New York: American, 1889], 667); "Certain capacities, bestowed by God's grace and power, which fit people for specific and corresponding service" (John R. W. Stott, *Baptism and Fullness,* 2d ed. [Downers Grove, IL: InterVarsity Press, 1976], 87); "Any talent or ability which is

empowered by the Holy Spirit and able to be used in the ministry of the church" (Wayne Grudem, *The First Epistle of Peter*, Tyndale New Testament Commentaries [Grand Rapids: Eerdmans, 1988], 175); "Sovereignly and divinely bestowed abilities" (Gene Getz, *Building Up One Another* [Wheaton, IL: Victor Books, 1976], 12); "A particular spiritual talent, a gracious divine endowment . . . powers and gifts granted to Christians" (The Amplified Bible of 1 Peter 4:10 as cited by Don and Katie Fortune, *Discover Your God-Given Gifts* [Grand Rapids: Chosen, 1987], 14). *The Living Bible* represents this conventional understanding in its translation of 1 Corinthians 12:1a: "And now, brothers, I want to write about the special abilities the Holy Spirit gives to each of you." That such is, in fact, the standard view today is evident in the definition used by George Barna, the leading pollster of spiritual attitudes today, in a survey he did about Christians' understanding of spiritual gifts. For his survey, Barna defines spiritual gifts as "supernatural abilities given by God, through His Holy Spirit, to those who believe in Jesus Christ" (George Barna, *The Index of Leading Spiritual Indicators* [Dallas: Word, 1996], 24).

2. For example, C. Peter Wagner, *Your Spiritual Gifts Can Help Your Church Grow* (Ventura, CA: Regal, 1994). Note the Wagner-Modified Houts Questionnaire included in Wagner's book and published separately. Also, Kenneth Cain Kinghorn, *Discovering Your Spiritual Gifts* (Grand Rapids: Zondervan, 1984).

3. For example, Robert L. Thomas, *Understanding Spiritual Gifts: A Verse-by-Verse Study of 1 Corinthians 12–14*, rev. ed. (Grand Rapids: Kregel, 1999), 205–9. Also, Rick Warren, *The Purpose-Driven Life* (Grand Rapids: Zondervan, 2002), 250–52.

4. An exception to this is Gene Getz, who, although working within the conventional view, says that it is not necessary or even advisable to try to discover one's gifts. See Getz, *Building Up One Another*, 9–16; cf. idem, *Sharpening the Focus of the Church* (Chicago: Moody, 1974), 114, 117. So also Richard B. Gaffin, *Perspectives on Pentecost: Studies in New Testament Teaching on the Gifts of the Holy Spirit* (Phillipsburg, NJ: Presbyterian & Reformed, 1979), 53–54.

5. "A possibility that always needs reckoning with concerning spiritual gifts is that they may be genuinely in the believer, and yet be lying dormant and unmanifested." Donald Gee, *Concerning Spiritual Gifts* (Springfield, MO: Gospel Publishing House, 1928), 80.

6. One of many examples I could give is Ray Stedman's book, *Body Life* (Glendale, CA: Regal, 1972), chap. 5, 51–58. Stedman seems to have been instrumental in raising the level of interest in spiritual gifts in non-charismatic evangelical churches.

7. "The Year's Most Intriguing Findings, from Barna Research Studies" (December 17, 2001), at http://www.barna.org/cgibin/PagePressRelease.asp?PressReleaseID=103&Reference=B, cited in Benny C. Aker, "*Charismata*: Gifts, Enablement, or Ministries?" *Journal of Pentecostal Theology* 11 (2002): 54.

8. Gene Getz shares his own experience in this regard in *Building Up One Another,* 14–15: "For a number of years I diligently taught that Christians should try to discover their spiritual gifts in order to function in the body of Christ. But little by little, I began to notice some serious problems in the lives of those who sat under my teaching—and the teaching of others who took this approach. For one thing, many became confused. Some tried diligently and desperately to find their gifts—to "pigeonhole" what they thought was a spiritual gift given to them at conversion. But many Christians—including many mature believers—could not seem to isolate their gifts. I remember one pastor who became frustrated because his most mature members were unable to discover for sure what their gifts were." Theologian and former editor of *Christianity Today*, Kenneth Kantzer, apparently commented once that he never knew what his gift was. He just served where he saw the need. Cited by Robertson McQuilkin, *Life in the Spirit* (Nashville: Broadman & Holman, 2000), 209.

9. The term *charismatic* is being used in its colloquial sense to represent anyone who believes that the miraculous activities such as healings, tongues, and prophecy continue to be a regular part of church life today.

10. The term *non-charismatic* in this context refers to a person who believes that miraculous activities such as healings, tongues, and prophecy ceased at an early stage in the history of the church and are not normative for contemporary church life.

11. Referred to here is, of course, Bible translators who translated the word *charisma,* but only in Romans 12 and 1 Corinthians 12. Chapters 5–6 will show that *charisma* actually is used rather broadly in Paul's writings. Note that Ephesians 4 does not even use *charisma,* showing that the issue isn't about the word; the issue

is the general intent of the author, which is represented by the context. Henceforth in the notes of this book, although other Greek words will be both transliterated and given in their Greek form, the word *charisma* (χάρισμα) will be presented only in its transliterated form because of its frequent appearance in both the text of this book and in the endnotes. When Greek words are mentioned in the main text, they will be given only in their transliterated form so that readers who do not know Greek will not be distracted by the Greek characters.

12. The two uses of the word are represented by the following two definitions from *Webster's Third New International Dictionary of the English Language Unabridged,* ed. Philip Babcock Gove (Springfield, MA: G. & C. Merriam, 1961), 956. The first is "a special or notable capacity, talent, or endowment either inherent, acquired, or given by a deity." The second and broader definition is "something that is voluntarily transferred by one person to another without compensation."

13. This perception of "special ability" is sharpened by the fact that only one of these two definitions is found in other non-nominal forms. The verb *to gift* means "to endow with some power, quality, or attribute." The adjective *gifted* (which often appears in discussions of spiritual gifts) is defined as "1: endowed by nature or training with a gift: as *a:* having a special talent or other desirable quality . . . *b:* having superior intellectual capacity . . . 2: reflecting or revealing a special gift or talent." *Webster's,* 956.

14. See discussion in Kenneth Berding, "Confusing Word and Concept in 'Spiritual Gifts': Have We Forgotten James Barr's Exhortations?" *Journal of the Evangelical Theological Society* 43 (2000): 49–50. I am not, in fact, opposed to the language of gifting in Greek. The confusion is raised in English (and other languages that have similar ambiguity in their word for *gift*). But conceptual confusion about the word *gift* appears to be extensive among English speakers. There is probably no other adequate way of dealing with this problem than using words other than *gift* in the discussion.

CHAPTER 2: A BIBLICAL ALTERNATIVE

1. Romans 12:4, 5; 1 Corinthians 10:17; 12:12–17; Ephesians 1:23; 2:16; 3:6; 4:4, 12, 16; 5:23, 30; Colossians 1:18, 24; 2:19; 3:15.

2. The items in this list are distinguished by Paul in 1 Corinthians 12:8–10. We will look at this list in detail in chapter 12 (also at the end of chap. 14).

3. The term *miracle*, and its adjective *miraculous*, has been defined in a number of ways. Used here is the broadly inclusive definition suggested by Wayne Grudem, *Systematic Theology* (Grand Rapids: Zondervan, 1994), 355: "A miracle is a less common kind of God's activity in which he arouses people's awe and wonder and bears witness to himself."

4. As opposed to the general empowering of the Holy Spirit given to all believers. See discussion in chapters 17 and 18. The activities that can be described both as ministries and as abilities are those found in Paul's list of "manifestation of the Spirit" in 1 Corinthians 12:7–11. See discussion in chapter 12 (and at the end of chap. 14).

5. For example, Ephesians 3:7; Colossians 1:29; 2 Thessalonians 1:11–12; 2:16–17; 3:3–5; 2 Timothy 1:7–8. See the discussion in chapter 18.

6. The premise of this book does not stand or fall upon one's view of decision making. For a brief description of the author's understanding of decision making in the context of deciding where to minister, see chapter 22.

7. For example, Henry T. Blackaby and Claude V. King, *Experiencing God* (Nashville: Broadman & Holman, 1994), 72–73, 146–48. Also Rick Warren, *The Purpose-Driven Life* (Grand Rapids: Zondervan, 2002), 227–31.

8. Perhaps the Holy Spirit wants to ensure that the practical life of the church isn't seriously affected and so is working to see that this teaching is sown in some form.

9. Among the few exceptions, perhaps the most notable is Max Turner, *The Holy Spirit and Spiritual Gifts in the New Testament Church and Today,* rev. ed. (Peabody, MA: Hendrickson, 1996), 261–73. This does not mean that Turner supports the position espoused in this book, but simply that he does make a conscientious effort to address the issue.

10. 1 Corinthians 14:3, 12, 26; cf. Romans 15:2; Ephesians 4:19; 1 Thessalonians 5:11.

11. See discussion in chapter 14 (cf. chap. 11).

12. Note that, in Ephesians 4:11, this could be pastors and teachers— that is, two roles—rather than pastor-teachers—that is, one role—

or even that they overlap insofar as they are two distinguishable roles but that all pastors should also be teachers. See discussion by Harold W. Hoehner, *Ephesians: An Exegetical Commentary* (Grand Rapids: Baker, 2002), 543–45.

13. 1 Corinthians 14:5, 13, 19, 26–28. See discussion of tongues in chapter 12 and appendix A.

14. For example, 1 Corinthians 16:15; 2 Corinthians 4:1; 5:18; 9:12–13; Colossians 4:17; 2 Timothy 4:5.

15. For given-ness language, see Romans 12:3, 6; 1 Corinthians 12:7–8; Ephesians 4:7–8, 11; for the language of having, see 1 Corinthians 12:30; 13:2; 14:26; Romans 12:6. Refer to chapters 13 and 14 for further discussion.

16. Both events actually happened and the second was taken word for word from a letter my daughters wrote. Another example comes from an e-mail sent by my colleague, Ron Pierce, to all the faculty members in our department (December 2, 2005). His encouraging e-mail ended with the following exclamation: "Thank God for the gift of meaningful ministries."

17. See discussion in chapters 4–6 and 14. On the Greek side is one example from the ministry of Jesus. In Mark 10:37, James and John bring a request to Jesus, a request about which the other ten disciples were not very happy (v. 41). They say literally, "*Give* to us that we may sit on your right hand in your glory." They were not asking Jesus to give them a special ability; they were asking Jesus to give them a position—or a role, or a function.

CHAPTER 3: SO WHAT?

1. Some working within the conventional approach would say that they are separate—you have natural abilities and you have special Spirit-given abilities. Others would say that a spiritual gift is an intensification of a natural ability. Neither opinion finds a place, of course, in Paul's discussions because that was not what Paul was concerned about.

2. 2 Corinthians 5:18–20.

3. Note the terminology here is not exactly as Paul most often uses it, although the distinctions are biblical nonetheless. Most often when Paul talks about a calling, he is referring to the call of God into salvation. Examples include Romans 1:6–7; 8:28–30; 9:24; 1 Corinthians 1:2, 9, 24–26; 7:15–24; Galatians 1:6, 14; Ephesians

4:1–4; Colossians 3:15; 1 Thessalonians 2:12; 1 Timothy 6:12; 2 Timothy 1:9 (cf. 1 Peter 2:9; 5:10; 2 Peter 1:10; Jude 1; Rev. 17:14). But the calling to salvation is also a calling into the body of Christ, including the responsibilities to build up the body, which are thereby suggested by such a calling (Eph. 4:1–3). Furthermore, there are instances in which God calls into particular ministries, as in Romans 1:1 and 1 Corinthians 1:1, where Paul refers to his own ministry assignment as a calling (cf. Acts 13:2, where Barnabas and Saul are called to spread the gospel; Acts 16:10, where Paul is called to preach in Macedonia; also Heb. 5:4 for calling into the Old Testament priesthood).

4. See the discussion of ministry in the letters of Paul in chapters 15–16 of this book and a list of all the ministries mentioned by Paul in chapter 19 (cf. chap. 20 for a list of New Testament ministries outside of Paul's letters).

5. Philippians 2:25–30, note especially verses 25 and 30.

Part 2: Arguing the Case

1. George Eldon Ladd, *A Theology of the New Testament,* ed. Donald A. Hagner, rev. ed. (Grand Rapids: Eerdmans, 1993), 580.

2. Every effort has been made to keep the technical details and scholarly jargon to a minimum in the main text and thus allow all Christians, not just biblical scholars, linguists, and historians, to work through the arguments themselves.

3. Jason, Kristen, Dr. Michaels, and Pastor Cole will not actually be appearing by name in the rest of the book.

Chapter 4: On the Meaning of Words

1. Linguists and those familiar with the use of linguistic theory in biblical interpretation may find the lack of specific terms in the following three chapters somewhat frustrating—particularly in my employment of the words *mean* and *meaning.* But linguists, ironically, are notorious for failing to translate their findings into terms that regular thinking people can understand. Even books written to bridge the gap between linguistics and biblical studies require a person to get significant training in the biblical languages and a willingness to learn dozens of specialized terms from linguistic jargon for even partial understanding of what is being communicated. The approach in this book is to use terms

that regular thinking people understand and to convey the most important linguistic concepts through the use of these terms. Having said this, it is nonetheless extremely useful to integrate findings from general linguistics into biblical studies, and warrants further pursuit by those so motivated. For those interested in how linguistic theory aids in biblical interpretation, the following books will be helpful in bridging general linguistics and biblical interpretation: Moisés Silva, *Biblical Words and Their Meaning: An Introduction to Lexical Semantics,* rev. ed. (Grand Rapids: Zondervan, 1994); David Alan Black, *Linguistics for Students of New Testament Greek: A Survey of Basic Concepts and Applications,* 2d ed (Grand Rapids: Baker, 1988); Peter Cotterell and Max Turner, *Linguistics and Biblical Interpretation* (Downers Grove, IL: InterVarsity Press, 1989); Peter James Silzer and Thomas John Finley, *How Biblical Languages Work: A Student's Guide to Learning Hebrew and Greek* (Grand Rapids: Kregel, 2004). A quite readable watershed book for the understanding of biblical words is James Barr, *The Semantics of Biblical Language* (1961; reprint, Philadelphia: Trinity Press International, 1991).

2. Or formal–equivalent translation. This is a translation that often uses one English word to correspond to one word in the original language, often using the same English word for that same word in the original language whenever possible.

3. This is what is usually referred to in linguistics as the sense of a word.

4. This is what is usually referred to in linguistics as the referent of a word. Still, it should be noted that "sense" and "referent" are not two distinct categories as could be inferred by some discussions of the subject; there are fuzzy, overlapping boundaries between the two categories.

CHAPTER 5: GREEK WORDS DON'T SOLVE THE PROBLEM (PART 1)

1. A technical term is a word that is used as a label for a concept. The word in such a case refers to the same concept whenever it is used in a discussion where the concept is being discussed (unlike most words that have a range of possible uses). An example of a technical term from systematic theology is the word *soteriology.* It is a technical term that refers to the study of salvation in any theological discussion. It will be argued in this chapter and in the

chapter that follows that *charisma* is used in such a variety of ways by Paul that it should not be viewed as a technical term.

2. Much of this chapter and the following chapter received their initial formulation in Kenneth Berding, "Confusing Word and Concept in 'Spiritual Gifts': Have We Forgotten James Barr's Exhortations?" *Journal of the Evangelical Theological Society* (March 2000): 37–51.

3. The thought process, usually subconscious, likely begins with the idea that *charisma* is equivalent to spiritual gift and then proceeds to projecting the idea of special ability onto the word.

4. This is particularly true if someone is using a looser translation (further on the continuum of dynamic or functional equivalency). For example, NLT (1996) translates *charisma* in Romans 12:6 as "the ability to do certain things well." A reader of that translation will have trouble being sympathetic to the argument at hand since the translator has already infused this expression with (conventional) meaning. See appendix C for further examples of how many translations influence readers to interpret along the lines of the conventional view.

5. Once again, those familiar with linguistics will be thinking about sense and referent. In fact, Max Turner, *The Holy Spirit and Spiritual Gifts in the New Testament Church and Today,* rev. ed. (Peabody, MA: Hendrickson, 1998), 264, strongly asserts regarding the definition of *charisma,* "We must not confuse sense and reference." Although Turner's concerns help in perceiving two horizons of communication—the general area of usage (the general sense) and the specific usage (the referent or, in his book, the "reference")—it should be understood that both sense and referent are delineated by usage, and the borders between the two are less distinct than Turner implies. He admits as much in a parallel discussion of lexical senses and word usages using a different illustration: "There is obviously a grey area here. . . . The available evidence for making the decision is not exactly overwhelming. We simply have to take the caution: not all contextual senses and usages are actually lexical meanings." Peter Cotterell and Max Turner, *Linguistics and Biblical Interpretation* (Downers Grove, IL: InterVarsity Press, 1989), 140.

6. In the New Testament outside of Paul this word only appears in 1 Peter 4:10.

7. Romans 1:11; 5:15–16; 6:23; 11:29; 12:6; 1 Corinthians 1:7; 7:7; 12:4, 9, 28, 30–31; 2 Corinthians 1:11; 1 Timothy 4:14; 2 Timothy 1:6.

8. Richard B. Gaffin, *Perspectives on Pentecost: Studies in New Testament Teaching on the Gifts of the Holy Spirit* (Phillipsburg, NJ: Presbyterian & Reformed, 1979), 46, suggests that Paul in Romans 1:11 "most likely does not have in view one of the gifts listed in Romans 12 or 1 Corinthians 12, but the overall strengthening Paul desires his presence and ministry to be among the Roman Christians." Max Turner, *The Holy Spirit and Spiritual Gifts,* 265, suggests that "the gift in question is . . . most probably upbuilding spiritual teaching which he hopes *they* will perceive as God's gracious gift through him." C. E. B. Cranfield, *A Critical and Exegetical Commentary on the Epistle to the Romans,* ICC (Edinburgh: T & T Clark, 1979), 1:79, keeps it general: "It is probably better to take the word here in a more general sense as denoting a blessing or benefit to be bestowed on the Christians in Rome by God through Paul's presence. There is an intentional indefiniteness (τι . . . χάρισμα), due to the fact that he has not yet learned by personal encounter what blessing they particularly stand in need of."

9. *Charismata* (χαρίσματα) is the plural form of *charisma* (χάρισμα).

10. W. Bauer, F. W. Danker, W. F. Arndt, and F. W. Gingrich, *Greek-English Lexicon of the New Testament and Other Early Christian Literature,* 3d ed. (Chicago: University of Chicago, 2000), 1081. (Henceforth the common abbreviation BDAG will be used for all references to this lexicon.)

11. BDAG, 1081; John Koenig, *Charismata: God's Gifts for God's People* (Philadelphia: Westminster, 1978), 98; and C. K. Barrett, *A Commentary on the Second Epistle to the Corinthians* (Peabody, MA: Hendrickson, 1987), 67.

12. For example, George W. Knight, *The Pastoral Epistles: A Commentary on the Greek Text* (Grand Rapids: Eerdmans, 1992), 208. Walter L. Liefield, *1 and 2 Timothy, Titus,* The NIV Application Commentary (Grand Rapids: Zondervan, 1999) 167, states his opinion: "We may assume that this gift, like those in that chapter [1 Cor. 12] was an endowment by the Holy Spirit. We may also assume that it was a spiritual ability that one could fail to draw on." It appears that Liefield's entire case in 1 Timothy 4:14 rests upon the appearance of *charisma* in this verse.

13. Cf. Gordon D. Fee, *God's Empowering Presence: The Holy Spirit in the Letters of Paul* (Peabody, MA: Hendrickson, 1994), 772–73. Fee is emphatic that "in you" language must exclude reading these two passages as the carrying out of one's office. But the context of his remarks is in opposition to those who suggest a dichotomy between Spirit-leading in the first stage of the church and the setting up of offices at a later stage (a position represented by such authors as Käsemann, Conzelmann, and Dunn). I would agree that appointed leadership should not be pitted against charismatic guidance in the early church; both would have functioned from the beginning in harmony with one another. But I do not think it can be argued on the basis of the prepositional phrase here translated "in you." For the view that there is no antithesis, see Ronald Y. K. Fung, "Charismatic Versus Organized Ministry: An Examination of an Alleged Antithesis," *The Evangelical Quarterly* 52 (1980): 195–214; and idem, "Function or Office? A Survey of the New Testament Evidence," *Evangelical Review of Theology* 8 (1984): 16–39. As representative of those who drive a wedge between charisma and office, see Hans von Campenhausen, *Ecclesiastical Authority and Spiritual Power in the Church of the First Three Centuries* (Stanford, CA: Stanford University Press, 1969), 55–75; James D. G. Dunn, *Unity and Diversity in the New Testament: An Inquiry into the Character of Earliest Christianity* (Philadelphia: Westminster, 1977); and in the context of the discussion of canon, "Has the Canon a Continuing Function?" in *The Canon Debate,* ed. Lee Martin McDonald and James A. Sanders (Peabody, MA: Hendrickson, 2002), 558–79; and Ernst Käsemann, "Ministry and Community in the New Testament," in *Essays on New Testament Themes,* trans. W. J. Montague (Naperville, IL: Alec R. Allenson, 1964), 63–94.

14. To get a sense of the variety of ways that the prepositional phrase translated "in you" is used elsewhere in the Bible, included here are a few references that show that this expression is not always used in reference to residence in a place (although it is used that way sometimes). In Paul's letters, note Romans 9:17 and Galatians 3:8; outside of Paul in the New Testament, see Matthew 26:33; Mark 1:11; and John 17:21 for other ways "in you" language is used. Some sort of spatial translation (that is, "in you") may be proper in 2 Timothy 1:6 because of the link with the previous verse (v. 5),

which seems to suggest such a translation. But the other passages cited here are warning enough that a little preposition cannot be the basis of our overall interpretation of a passage, particularly when arguments in the immediate context suggest a different way to understand it.

15. D. A. Carson, *Showing the Spirit: A Theological Exposition of 1 Corinthians 12–14* (Grand Rapids: Baker, 1987), 20. Koenig agrees that "2 Timothy identifies the charisma of God not with a special talent," but contrarily suggests that the charisma in these two passages is "the Holy Spirit which is granted to every believer" (*Charismata*, 98). Many authors (especially those more ecclesiastically oriented), consider this to be simply a reference to ordination, for example, Hans Küng, *The Church*, trans. Ray and Rosaleen Ockenden (New York: Sheed & Ward, 1967), 180, 183–84, 406, 426.

16. "In the context the gift has to do with Timothy's work of leading and teaching the Christian community, with the example he is to set the believers in speech, in conduct, in love, in faith, and in purity, and with his direction of the divine worship of the community in terms of his public reading of the Sacred Scriptures, preaching, and instruction." Arthur Carl Piepkorn, "Charisma in the New Testament and the Apostolic Fathers," *Concordia Theological Monthly* 42 (1971): 371.

17. Against the idea that *charisma* refers to both marriage and singleness is James D. G. Dunn, *Jesus and the Spirit: A Study of the Religious and Charismatic Experience of Jesus and the First Christians as Reflected in the New Testament* (Philadelphia: Westminster, 1975), 206–7. But rather than taking the simplest reading of the text, that marriage along with singleness is called a *charisma*, Dunn's procedure seems to be to start with the assumption that the *charisma* is "the enabling to refrain from sexual relations within marriage, and to restrain the sexual appetite when unmarried" (ibid., 206) and then to move to find an explanation of why marriage is not a *charisma*. Thiselton's comment on the "this" and "that" expression is appropriate: "The fact that Paul recognizes differing gifts ὁ μὲν οὕτως, ὁ δέ οὕτως prohibits our referring χάρισμα exclusively to the gift of chastity, unless we try to interpret οὕτως to mean *to this degree* rather than its more customary sense of *in this manner* or *of* 'this kind' (adverbial form of οὕτως, *this-ly,* that is, *thus*)." Anthony Thiselton, *The First*

Epistle to the Corinthians, New International Greek Testament Commentary (Grand Rapids: Eerdmans, 2000), 513.

18. Ephesians 4 does not use the word. Paul doesn't need to. He is able to communicate what he wants without the use of *charisma.* In Ephesians 4:11, what he communicates is that God has "given" people in their ministries to the church to equip people in the church to do ministry. See the discussion in chapter 9.

19. In literature before or contemporaneous to Paul, *charisma* is found only twice in variants in the LXX, twice in Philo, a few times in secular Greek, and once in 1 Peter 4:10. The earliest patristic writings continue, like the New Testament, to use the word broadly, as various ways that God manifests his grace. But not very far into the patristic period, the word *charisma* seems to narrow more and more until it becomes a word used to describe miraculous activities. Piepkorn, "Charisma in the New Testament," 370, comments, "A further problem inheres in the stubborn historical fact that since the days of Tertullian Western theological language has used *charisma* and its vernacular derivatives in a sense that the biblical and early postbiblical usage of the vocable does not support. That is, it uses *charisma* as the generic term for the extraordinary and at times miraculous phenomena." See references in ibid., 372–75; Ronald A. N. Kydd, *Charismatic Gifts in the Early Church* (Peabody, MA: Hendrickson, 1984); Eusebius A. Stephanou, *The Charismata in the Early Church Fathers* (Brookline, MA: Holy Cross Orthodox, 1976); and M. Parmentier, "The Gifts of the Spirit in Early Christianity," in *The Impact of Scripture in Early Christianity,* ed. J. den Boeft and M. L. van Poll–van de Lisdonk (Leiden: Brill, 1999), 58–78.

20. Turner asserts that *charisma* (χάρισμα) is derived from *charizomai* (χαρίζομαι) and that any similarities to *charis* (χάρις) should be viewed as incidental. Max Turner, "Modern Linguistics and the New Testament," in *Hearing the New Testament: Strategies for Interpretation,* ed. Joel B. Green (Grand Rapids: Eerdmans, 1995), 156–65; also Max Turner, *The Holy Spirit and Spiritual Gifts,* 264, 266 n. 17. It is, of course, possible that *charisma* was formed from *charizomai* (although it is not demonstrated by Turner), but it really doesn't make any difference, unless it is asserted (as Turner, in fact, does in *The Holy Spirit and Spiritual Gifts,* 266) that apart from "the obvious assonance," there is no connection between them. But

in light of Paul's intense interest in concepts that are described through his use of the word *charis* (χάρις), and since he directly relates the two words in Romans 12:3–8 and 1 Corinthians 1:4–7 (cf. 1 Peter 4:10), it would seem that Turner's sharp distancing of these two words is misguided. This distinction also appears to affect Turner's understanding of the general sense of *charisma* as simply "gift" (that is, something given) and nothing more.

21. A. T. Robertson, *A Grammar of the Greek New Testament in the Light of Historical Research* (Nashville: Broadman Press, 1934), 151, 153; and F. Blass and A. Debrunner, *A Greek Grammar of the New Testament and Other Early Christian Literature,* trans. and rev. Robert W. Funk (Chicago: University of Chicago Press, 1961), 59. David L. Baker, "The Interpretation of 1 Corinthians 12–14," *The Evangelical Quarterly* 46 (1974): 225, comments, "Similarly the relationship of χάρις to χάρισμα is that of abstract to concrete."

22. This, I am suggesting, is the general sense of *charisma* in all the places that Paul uses it. Each immediate literary context is necessary in order to assert anything more specific. The discussion in this chapter is basically in line with Fee's assessment (except that I am uncertain whether *charisma* is actually formed from *charis* [χάρις]). Fee says, "The noun has been formed from *charis* ("grace"), referring to *a concrete expression of grace,* which is what it means in every instance in Paul." Gordon D. Fee, "Gifts of the Spirits," in *Dictionary of Paul and His Letters,* ed. Gerald F. Hawthorne and Ralph P. Martin (Downers Grove, IL: InterVarsity, 1993), 341. C. K. Barrett, *A Commentary on the Epistle to the Romans* (Peabody, MA: Hendrickson, 1957, 1987), 237, would agree, defining *charisma* in Romans 12:6 as "an actualization, a practical expression, of the grace (χάρις) of God under which the church stands" and in 5:15–16 as "act of grace" or "actualization of grace" (ibid., 113). So also Gaffin, *Perspectives on Pentecost,* 47, who says that the idea that links these various uses is "a manifestation of grace."

CHAPTER 6: GREEK WORDS DON'T SOLVE THE PROBLEM (PART 2)

1. You may wish to refer to the translation of 1 Corinthians 12 found at the beginning of the book or have a Bible open near you as you study (preferably a more literal [formal equivalent] translation such as the NASB, RSV, ESV, HCSB, or NRSV).

2. In actuality, the thought process in many people's minds may not simply be that *charismata* = special abilities. Rather, it is likely that most people under the influence of the conventional view would be thinking something like, *"charismata* means 'gifts,' which in the passage represents 'special abilities.'" But the moment such thinking is exposed, it must be admitted by all that the theology is not carried on the shoulders of the word, but that the theology must be determined by Paul's explicit statements and contextual clues found in the chapter itself. (This topic will be taken up at length in chaps. 11–12.) Nevertheless, sometimes *charisma* and special ability are simply equated by some authors, as with K. S. Hemphill, "The Pauline Concept of Charisma" (Ph.D. diss., University of Cambridge, 1976), 223, who, while otherwise claiming that *charisma* is not a technical term, comments on it as used in Romans 12:6 (and with reference to 1 Cor. 12—note his word *again*): "Paul again uses χάρισμα in a specialized sense to mean 'abilities for service' in the short pericope concerning community ministry in Romans 12:6."

3. David L. Baker, "The Interpretation of 1 Corinthians 12–14," *The Evangelical Quarterly* 46 (1974): 226.

4. It may be, of course, that Paul only used it because the Corinthians liked the word since they were using it in reference to their miraculous abilities and Paul felt obliged to use it himself. See discussion in text.

5. Although the words *distributions* (so BDAG, 229) or *apportionings* (so Anthony Thiselton, *The First Epistle to the Corinthians,* New International Greek Testament Commentary [Grand Rapids: Eerdmans, 2000], 928–29) are somewhat rough, they pick up an idea supported in the context (see its verbal form in v. 11) that is lost when this word is simply translated as "varieties." But these two ideas should not be pitted against each other, since the variety idea also seems necessary in light of the repeated contrast with what is the "same" in these verses. Unfortunately, I know of no easy way to translate this word into English so as to convey both ideas of distribution and variety.

6. Each of these three words is found in its genitive plural form in the actual verse, thus *charismatōn* (χαρίσματων), *diakoniōn* (διακονίων), and *energēmatōn* (ἐνεργήματων).

7. Certainly in Paul's mind, these three words could have overlapping
    applications. But it is unlikely that the three words should be
    viewed, on the one hand, as synonymous or that they should be
    viewed, on the other hand, as encompassing areas that are mutually
    exclusive of the activities suggested by the other two words. Note
    the comment in D. A. Carson, *Showing the Spirit: A Theological
    Exposition of 1 Corinthians 12–14* (Grand Rapids: Baker, 1987),
    34: "The parallelism does not of course make the words strictly
    synonymous, any more than Spirit, Lord, and God are strictly
    synonymous; but because none of the three terms can be associated
    with only certain spiritual gifts and not with others, it is clear that
    Paul uses the three terms to describe the full range of what might
    be called spiritual-gift phenomena." Similarly, Ronald Y. K.
    Fung, "Ministry, Community and Spiritual Gifts," *The Evangelical
    Quarterly* 56 (1984): 10n. 29, comments, "It is commonly agreed
    that the χαρίσματα, διακονίαι, and ἐνεργήματα of 1 Corinthians
    12:4–6 do not represent three different categories, but are simply
    references to the same category under different names, because
    viewed from different angles."
8. So, Thiselton, *First Epistle to the Corinthians,* 928, 931–32.
9. I am intrigued by another interpretation of this triad, although I
    think the suggestion less likely to be correct than what has been
    presented in text. Joop Smit suggests that Paul's employment of
    the three words *charismata* (χαρίσματα), *diakoniai* (διακονίαι),
    and *energēmata* (ἐνεργήματα) in verses 4–6 functions as an
    introduction to the structure of the rest of the chapter (in rhetorical
    terminology, vv. 4–6 would be the *partitio*). Smit summarizes his
    understanding of the relationship of these three words to the rest
    of the chapter: "The *partitio* (vv. 4–6) mentions two genera, the
    'charismata of the Spirit' and the 'services of the Lord,' both, in
    their turn, species of the genus 'workings of God,' who works
    out all things in all people. The first part (vv. 7–11) enumerates
    the species of the genus 'charismata of the Spirit.' At the same
    time it indicates that all these fall under the 'workings of God'
    (v. 11). The second part (vv. 12–26) visualizes the many species
    of the genus 'services of Christ' as limbs of a body. This part also
    clearly indicates that they too fall under the 'workings of God'
    (vv. 18, 24). The conclusion (vv. 27–30) brings the 'services of
    Christ' and the 'charismata of the Spirit' together as species in one

enumeration of the genus 'workings of God' (v. 28)." Joop Smit, "Argument and Genre of 1 Corinthians 12–14," in *Rhetoric and the New Testament: Essays from the 1992 Heidelberg Conference,* Journal for the Study of the New Testament: Supplement Series 90, ed. Stanley E. Porter and Thomas H. Olbricht (Sheffield: Sheffield Academic Press, 1993), 218–19. Such a suggestion has the effect of focusing Paul's use of the word *charismata* upon the manifestational items in verses 7–11 alone. One reason I am uncertain about this suggestion is the real possibility that Paul is using *charismata* as a summary term in 1 Corinthians 12:31 (and also in Rom. 12:6). Furthermore, I am a little less optimistic than many scholars about the extent of the influence of the rhetorical tradition on the way Paul structured his letters. Sharing my caution about the application of formal rhetorical categories to Paul's letters is Jannes Reiling, "The Magna Charta of Spiritual Gifts: A Re-reading of 1 Corinthians 12, 1–11," in *Festschrift Günter Wagner,* ed. Faculty of Baptist Theological Seminary (Bern: Peter Lang, 1994), 144, who comments: "In the last three decades . . . many scholars have turned to the books of the ancient rhetoricians and tried to investigate how the rules of persuasive rhetoric have been applied by Paul (and the other writers of the New Testament). Interesting though this may be, I do not think that this approach is in the end very fruitful. In the first place it is doubtful whether there was a rhetorical theory of letter writing in Paul's time and secondly the rhetorical nature of his letters cannot be determined by checking them against the theory-books but by comparing them to writings of the same nature. Rhetorical analysis is not a question of rules applied but of intention and structure discovered."

10. This would be the likely interpretation if it were taken as an indicative rather than as an imperative. The contrast of the next line—"And I show you a still more excellent way"—is stronger if it is taken as an indicative rather than as an imperative. So Ralph P. Martin, *The Spirit and the Congregation: Studies in 1 Corinthians 12–15* (Grand Rapids: Eerdmans, 1984), 34–35, 66, following Iber, Baker, and Chevallier.

11. Martin actually formulates it as a question: "You are seeking, then, the great[est] gifts, are you? . . . Well, I will [or I intend to] show you a still better way." But this has the same effect as what was stated in text (ibid., 35).

12. The strongest argument for this seems to be the conceptual overlap between the "earnestly desire" (*zēloute;* ζηλοῦτε) of 1 Corinthians 12:31 and what seems to be a similar use of the verb in 1 Corinthians 14:1 and 14:39. If 1 Corinthians 12:28 were indicative, as Ellis notes, "1 Corinthians 14:1 would be a meaningless opening for that chapter." E. Earle Ellis, *Pauline Theology: Ministry and Society* (Grand Rapids: Eerdmans, 1989), 48 n. 88. I agree with Ellis that this is the most likely reading, but I am not yet convinced that it must be read this way.

13. And possibly 1 Corinthians 12:4, although, as has already been noted, the variety of suggestions for the function of the word *charisma* in 1 Corinthians 12:4 makes such a suggestion tentative at best. I think it unlikely.

14. Alternately, Fee suggests that 1 Corinthians 12:31 belongs at the beginning of the argument of 1 Corinthians 14 (with 1 Cor. 13 as a parenthesis) instead of being aligned with the preceding context. Gordon D. Fee, *God's Empowering Presence: The Holy Spirit in the Letters of Paul* (Peabody, MA: Hendrickson, 1994), 195–97. This suggestion might be slightly more plausible than it presently stands if it could be demonstrated that Paul were simply inserting a pre-formed hymn at this point (as some have suggested). But this has not yet been demonstrated, at least to my satisfaction. The numerous connections between chapter 13 and chapters 12 and 14, combined with the evidence of meticulous care in the production of the poem, make it less likely that Paul suddenly decided to make this insertion. The poem is so special (demonstrating painstaking care) and at the same time so well integrated with the surrounding chapters that it seems unlikely that chapter 13 appeared on the scene after Paul had begun to move into the discussion he takes up in chapter 14.

15. In fact, I do not have any problem with gifting language in Greek; the hesitation comes as a result of ambiguity in English (and some other languages). See the discussion of the problem of gifting language in chapter 14.

16. *Pneumatika*, both as an adjective and as a noun, is as Ellis comments, "of Christian coinage," being used both by Paul and by those that Paul is addressing in Corinth. E. Earle Ellis, "Christ and Spirit in 1 Corinthians," in *Christ and Spirit in the New Testament: Studies*

in Honour of C. F. D. Moule, ed. Barnabas Lindars and Stephen S. Smalley (Cambridge: Cambridge University Press, 1973), 274.

17. First Corinthians 7:1 is the point in the letter where Paul begins to answer questions. Until that point in the letter, it seems he is addressing various problems that he has heard about in Corinth.

18. Other passages in 1 Corinthians fail to clear up the ambiguity related to *pneumatika*; 2:15; 3:1; and 14:37 show that this can be used in reference to "spiritual people," but 2:13 and 9:1 show that it could be a reference to "spiritual things." It has been far more common for interpreters and translations to view this as neuter and then to connect it to the discussion of spiritual gifts that follows. For the alternative, that this refers to "spiritual persons," see John D. Ekem, "'Spiritual Gifts' or 'Spiritual Persons'? 1 Corinthians 12:1A Revisited," *Neotestamentica* 38 (2004): 54–74. Also, John Painter, "Paul and the Πνευματικοί at Corinth," in *Paul and Paulinism: Essays in Honour of C. K. Barrett,* ed. M. D. Hooker and S. G. Wilson (London: SPCK, 1982), 237–50. Just below, in the main text, I suggest that this is the term the Corinthians liked to use as shorthand for the miraculous activities that had so captured their imaginations. Thus, it is probably wiser to translate 1 Corinthians 12:1 and 14:1 using the more general expression "spiritual things" rather than "spiritual gifts," particularly since the second imports nuances associated with talents that are part of the range of the English word *gift.* For further orientation on the difficulties of this word in the letters of Paul and in its broader linguistic environment, see John M. G. Barclay, "Πνευματικός in the Social Dialect of Pauline Christianity," in *The Holy Spirit and Christian Origins: Essays in Honor of James D. G. Dunn,* ed. Graham N. Stanton, Bruce W. Longenecker, and Stephen C. Barton (Grand Rapids: Eerdmans, 2004), 157–67.

19. It is more likely that this is a reference to "spiritual things," and in particular, to those things that the Corinthians would have labeled as "spiritual"; its appearance in 1 Corinthians 14:1, followed by the line "especially that you may prophesy," highlights the difficulty in viewing this as "spiritual persons." Because of the difficulty of reading *pneumatika* (πνευματικά) in 14:1 as "spiritual persons" and, in light of its contextual relationship to 12:1, we probably should read 12:1 also as a neuter and translate the verse, "Now concerning the spiritual things [implied: "that you are so interested in"] . . ." This is similar to the Latin rendering "*de*

spiritalibus . . ." *(Biblia Sacra Vulgata).* Noted in Ekem, "'Spiritual Gifts' or 'Spiritual Persons'?" 68.

20. Baker, "The Interpretation of 1 Corinthians 12–14," 228–30.

Chapter 7: Paul's Central Concern

1. Paul's impulse also is to move the discussion toward love, as 1 Corinthians 13 clearly shows (and bracketed by 1 Cor. 12:31b and 1 Cor. 14:1). Note also "Let love be without hypocrisy" (Rom. 12:9) as the first line after his list in Romans and "the building up of itself in love" in Ephesians 4:16.

2. Note other passages in Paul apart from those mentioned in the text where he uses the body metaphor in similar ways: 1 Corinthians 10:17; Ephesians 1:23; 2:16; 3:6; Colossians 1:18, 24; 2:19; 3:15. In Ephesians and Colossians, the metaphor differs slightly from 1 Corinthians 12 (and Rom. 12), in that Paul focuses more on Christ as head of the body.

3. Paul was actually drawing upon a metaphor that was not uncommon among writers in the time roughly contemporaneous with Paul, especially the Stoics. For an insightful study of the relationship of Paul's body imagery to the Stoics and others in the ancient world, see Michelle V. Lee, *Paul, the Stoics, and the Body of Christ: Being and Ethics in 1 Corinthians 12–14,* Society for New Testament Studies Monograph Series (Cambridge: Cambridge University Press, forthcoming).

4. Notice the similarity between 1 Corinthians 12:18 and 1 Corinthians 12:27, particularly the "God has placed/appointed" idea.

5. Ralph P. Martin, *The Spirit and the Congregation: Studies in 1 Corinthians 12–15* (Grand Rapids: Eerdmans, 1984), 30.

6. Ernest Best adds insight with the following comment: "We may notice that Paul contrasts hand and foot, eye and ear, members whose function only differs a little; men are usually jealous of those who are only a little superior to themselves rather than of those whose position seems unattainably far away." Ernest Best, *One Body in Christ: A Study in the Relationship of the Church to Christ in the Epistles of the Apostle Paul* (London: SPCK, 1955), 102.

7. A good resource for the discussion of Christian unity in the midst of diversity is Rex A. Koivisto, *One Lord, One Faith* (Wheaton, IL: Victor Books, 1993).

8. Notice the implicit trinitatianism in this passage represented by these statements (vv. 12, 27, "Christ"; v. 13, "Spirit"; vv. 18, 24, "God"). Cf. 1 Corinthians 12:4–6.

9. "When Paul speaks of weaker body parts (v. 22) he may be thinking of fingers or toes, or the less protected organs such as one's eyes. The 'less honorable' parts (v. 23a) may refer to internal organs, usually covered by clothing, since the verb for 'treat' can also mean 'clothe.' The 'unpresentable' parts (v. 23b) most naturally refer to genitalia and the excretory tracts." Craig Blomberg, *1 Corinthians,* The NIV Application Commentary (Grand Rapids: Zondervan, 1994), 246. For the view that verses 23–24 only refer to the body's genitalia (rather than internal organs), see Anthony Thiselton, *The First Epistle to the Corinthians,* New International Greek Testament Commentary (Grand Rapids: Eerdmans, 2000), 1008–10.

CHAPTER 8: HOW PAUL USES LISTS

1. It was necessary, of course (and not at all easy), to decide what should be meant by a list. The working definition upon which I settled, and which is fleshed out in this chapter is "a grouping of at least four items that in some way adhere to one another."

2. I decided that I would not count a triad of three items, such as "faith, hope, and love" as a list. Such triads are common in Paul and would be worth studying, but not in this context. Indeed, this decision is not arbitrary since the four lists we will be studying in the following chapters will each be at least four items long.

3. Quite a bit of subjectivity is involved, of course, in drawing up such a list of lists. It is far more intuitive than it is scientific. But no one who looks at these lists (and is working with a normal understanding of what most people think of when they use the English word *list*) will doubt that at least most of these passages could be described with the word *list,* even if a few of the examples are questionable.

4. A few examples of each type of list include virtue lists (1 Cor. 13:4–8; 2 Cor. 13:11; Gal. 5:22–23; Eph. 4:2–3; Phil. 2:1–4; 4:8; 1 Tim. 4:12; 6:11; 2 Tim. 2:22, 24–25; Titus 2:2–10; 3:1–2), vice lists (Rom. 13:13; 1 Cor. 5:11; 6:9–11; 2 Cor. 12:20; Gal. 5:19–21; Eph. 4:31; Col. 3:5, 8, 12–13; 2 Tim. 3:2–5; Titus 3:3), qualifications lists (1 Tim. 3:2–7, 8–12; 5:9–10; Titus 1:6–9), doxologies (Rom. 11:33–36; 1 Tim. 1:17; 6:15–16), and

confessional statements (1 Tim. 3:16). C. G. Kruse, "Virtues and Vices," in *Dictionary of Paul and His Letters,* ed. Gerald F. Hawthorne and Ralph Martin (Downers Grove, IL: InterVarsity Press, 1993), 963, offers an important warning on the interpretation of pre-formed virtue and vice lists: "If it is true that the lists of virtues and vices in the Pauline corpus are influenced to greater or lesser extent by similar lists in other literature, and if such lists have sometimes been incorporated with little adaptation to their context within his letters, then care will need to be taken not to over interpret such lists."

5. Romans 2:17–20 and Philippians 3:5–6 mix actions, attitudes, and things possessed. Colossians 3:12–13 is a mixed list beginning with heart attitudes and moving toward actions. The Pastorals contain a number of mixed lists, for example, 1 Timothy 1:9–10; 3:2–7, 8–12; 6:4–5; Titus 3:3.

6. We must, of course, leave the door open to the possibility that a given author might lose track of his conceptual framework as he is listing, but this happens rarely.

7. Ephesians 4:11 is a list of four items (or five if "pastors" and "teachers" are two rather than one role); Romans 12:6–8 is a list of seven items; 1 Corinthians 12:28–30 is a list of nine items (once "interpretation of tongues" is mentioned in v. 30); 1 Corinthians 12:8–10 has nine items.

8. Although everyone does not agree, I'm assuming that Ephesians was written some time during Paul's first Roman imprisonment. For a brief summary of this position (in connection with a discussion of Colossians), see Donald Guthrie, *New Testament Introduction* (Downers Grove, IL: InterVarsity Press, 1970), 515, 556–57.

9. There may be objections to this arrangement out of concerns that Paul himself is considered by some not to be the author of Ephesians. Since I believe that Paul himself authored the letter, that some doubt the authenticity of Ephesians is not reason enough to change the order, especially when there are good reasons for the current order of presentation. See the defense of Pauline authorship in Harold W. Hoehner, *Ephesians: An Exegetical Commentary* (Grand Rapids: Baker, 2002), 2–61.

10. Or five, if the last item, "pastors" and "teachers," are two roles (pastors and teachers) rather than the one (pastor-teachers).

11. At least as they relate to the particular concerns of this book.
12. This is a slight oversimplification since Romans and Ephesians are both situational as well. But with few exceptions biblical scholars agree that 1 Corinthians is far more situational than is either Ephesians or Romans. Kenneth S. Hemphill, *Spiritual Gifts: Empowering the New Testament Church* (Nashville: Broadman & Holman, 1988), 132, makes a similar set of observations about the differences between Romans and 1 Corinthians: "While there are a few modern scholars who suggest that Paul may have been aware of Corinthian-like gift problems in Rome, they are not very convincing. I would raise several general objections to such an assumption. (1) The letter as a whole betrays no misunderstanding like those in Corinth. You can simply contrast the tone of the two letters. (2) The brevity of the gift passage would be surprising if Paul were aware of this type of problem. (3) More surprising, however, would be the non-specific nature of the passage. The content is more in the form of general principles than corrective exhortation. The specific gifts mentioned certainly betray no such problems, and the ethical teaching in 12:9ff. is more general than 1 Corinthians 13."
13. Nor will we force-fit interpretations derived from Ephesians 4 and Romans 12 into 1 Corinthians 12. It is my sincere desire to represent each passage as it stands in its own literary and situational setting.

CHAPTER 9: THE LISTS IN CONTEXT (PART 1): EPHESIANS 4:11–12

1. See reason 3 in this chapter and the discussion of the "grace" + "given" connection in chapter 13.
2. The nature of "the gift of Christ" is not clear in this passage. Klyne Snodgrass, *Ephesians,* The NIV Application Commentary (Grand Rapids: Zondervan, 1996), 200, comments, "The identity of the gift is uncertain. It could be grace (as 3:7), the Holy Spirit (as 1 Cor. 12:7), or Christ himself."
3. Paul's use of Psalm 68:18 (68:19 in Hebrew MT; 67:19 in LXX) is difficult, particularly because Paul cites the verse using "*gave* gifts to men" whereas in the psalm it is "*received* gifts from among men." There have been many suggestions offered for how to deal with this. For orientation to this complex issue, see Richard A. Taylor, "The Use of Psalm 68:18 in Light of the Ancient Versions,"

Bibliotheca Sacra 148 (1991): 319–36; and Timothy G. Gombis, "Cosmic Lordship and Divine Gift-Giving: Psalm 68 in Ephesians 4:8," *Novum Testamentum* 47 (2005): 367–80. For a more detailed analysis of the primary literature, see W. Hall Harris III, *The Descent of Christ: Ephesians 4:7–11 and Traditional Hebrew Imagery* (Grand Rapids: Baker, 1996). Although somewhat tentative, the most likely solution to this problem is that Paul used "gave" instead of "received" because he was influenced by a traditional Jewish interpretation of the text of Psalm 68, which read "gave" instead of "received." Lying behind this traditional interpretation was a separate Hebrew text tradition, which read "gave" and was the source for the interpretive tradition from which Paul drew. There is no space to argue it here.

4. Andrew Lincoln lists the three main lines of interpretation of the descent motif in verses 9–10: "a descent into Hades, the descent of the preexistent Christ in his incarnation, and the descent of the exalted Christ in the Spirit." Andrew T. Lincoln, *Ephesians,* Word Biblical Commentary (Dallas: Word, 1990), 42:244. Lincoln has a succinct summary and evaluation of the issues on pp. 244–48. For references to primary literature and more extended discussion, refer to Harris, *The Descent of Christ.*

5. See reason 3 below in main text and chapter 13 as a whole for a discussion of the "grace" + "given" combination.

6. "Here the first gifts the exalted Christ gives to his body are a special group of persons who will in turn mobilize the other members of Christ's body for their ministries." Craig S. Keener, *Gift and Giver: The Holy Spirit for Today* (Grand Rapids: Baker, 2001), 110.

7. For the majority position that the apostles, prophets, evangelists, and pastor-teachers are the ones who train the saints but the saints do the work of the ministry, see Markus Barth, *Ephesians: Translation and Commentary on Chapters 4–6,* The Anchor Bible 34A (Garden City, NJ: Doubleday, 1974), 478–81; Ernest Best, *A Critical and Exegetical Commentary on Ephesians,* ICC (Edinburgh: T & T Clark, 1998), 395–99; and Harold W. Hoehner, *Ephesians: An Exegetical Commentary* (Grand Rapids: Baker, 2002), 547–51. This is also the position represented by almost all recent English translations. A detailed defense of the opposing view, that the apostles, prophets, etc., themselves (1) equip the saints, (2) do the work of the ministry, and (3) build up the body of Christ is Sydney

H. T. Page, "Whose Ministry? A Re-Appraisal of Ephesians 4:12," *Novum Testamentum* 47 (2005): 26–47.

8. To read this list as one of special abilities (or of persons possessing special abilities), that idea must be extrapolated from the mention of prophets (v. 11) or it must be contended that the "give" (vv. 7, 11) or "gift" (vv. 7–8) cognates refer to such a concept (for example, Bratcher and Nida's comment on v. 8 but with connection to v. 11: *"The phrase 'gave gifts to mankind' refers specifically to different kinds of endowments or abilities."* Robert G. Bratcher and Eugene A. Nida, *A Translator's Handbook on Paul's Letter to the Ephesians* [London: United Bible Societies, 1982], 101). But a prophet functions in a role—here of equipping—that is demonstrated by its connection with the other words in the list. And any appeal to the language of gifting as an automatic indicator of a special ability concept demonstrates a misunderstanding both of the immediate context and of Paul's general use of the language of gifting. Refer to chapters 4–6 of this volume on the meaning of words and to chapter 14 and appendix C on how broadly *give* is used in the letters of Paul and the influence of the English word *give* on the discussion.

9. Snodgrass, *Ephesians,* 200.

10. See appendix A for further discussion of these ministry assignments. Here the discussion will be limited to the question of whether these should be viewed as abilities or as ministry assignments.

11. Against much of critical scholarship, I hold the position that Paul himself was the author of the Pastoral Epistles (1 Timothy, 2 Timothy, and Titus). For this reason, I consider comparisons with the Pastorals to be fruitful. For a fairly detailed analysis of the case for the Pauline authorship of the Pastorals, as well as responses to those who think Paul did not write these letters, see the introduction to William D. Mounce, *Pastoral Epistles,* Word Biblical Commentary 46 (Nashville: Nelson, 2000), xlvi–cxxix. Since the argument from vocabulary and style seems to have been the most influential argument against Pauline authorship of the Pastorals, note E. Randolph Richards's comments on statistical analysis and analyzing style in chapter 9, "Analyzing Paul's Writing Style," in *Paul and First-Century Letter Writing: Secretaries, Composition, and Collection* (Downers Grove, IL: InterVarsity Press, 2004), 141–55. (Note also Richards's secondary sources for statistical analyses.)

I have recently entered the fray myself by arguing that Polycarp (ca. 120), who was perhaps the most important church leader of the early second century, considered Paul to be the author of the Pastoral Epistles. See Kenneth Berding, "Polycarp of Smyrna's View of the Authorship of 1 and 2 Timothy," *Vigiliae Christianae* 53 (1999): 349–60; and idem, *Polycarp and Paul: An Analysis of Their Literary and Theological Relationship in Light of Polycarp's Use of Biblical and Extra-Biblical Literature,* Supplements to Vigiliae Christianae 62 (Leiden: Brill, 2002), 142–55.

12. It is intriguing that Timothy is instructed to "do the work of an evangelist" in the verse following the warning that he would have to contend with false teachers (2 Tim. 4:3–5). Similarly, "evangelists" are listed among the "equippers" of Ephesians 4:11 just before warnings in 4:14 not to be deceived by false doctrine. Does the evangelist role, perhaps, include the preservation of the foundational doctrines, particularly those that are part of the evangelistic proclamation? This is an area needing further study. But if this were, in fact, the case, it might help to explain how evangelists are included in a list of equippers in Ephesians 4:11.

13. For the view that the "shepherds" and "teachers" in Ephesians 4:11 are two separate categories (albeit with overlapping roles), see Best, *Ephesians,* 391–93.

14. For the view that this is one role, see Barth, *Ephesians,* 438–39. The absence of the pronominal article and the *de* (δέ) before *didaskalous* (διδασκάλους) is the main reason for thinking that *poimenas* (ποιμένας) and *didaskalous* (διδασκάλους) should be somehow viewed together. For a version of this view that maintains some distinction but not a complete distinction (that is, "all pastors are to be teachers, though not all teachers are to be pastors"), see Daniel B. Wallace's evaluation of this Greek structure in "The Semantic Range of the Article-Noun-καί-Noun Plural Construction in the New Testament," *Grace Theological Journal* 4 (1983): 59–84.

15. It is probably proper to think in terms of the role of a pastor (literally, a shepherd) in New Testament times as synonymous with overseer and elder. Note particularly Acts 20:28: "among which the Holy Spirit has made you overseers, to shepherd the church of God"; and 1 Peter 5:1–2, "Therefore, I exhort the elders among you, as a co-elder . . . shepherd the flock of God which is among you, exercising oversight."

16. This is particularly evident when viewed against the backdrop of the overall argument of 1 Timothy, which has as a crucial component the correction of those who teach false doctrine (1 Tim. 1:3; 4:3; 6:4; 6:20; cf. 2 Tim. 4:3–4), those who want to be "teachers of the law" even though they don't know what they're talking about (1 Tim. 1:7), and those who are described as teaching "doctrines of demons" (1 Tim. 4:1).

17. For further discussion of Paul as a prophet, see David Hill, *New Testament Prophecy* (Atlanta: John Knox Press, 1979), 111–18.

18. Peter O'Brien, *The Letter to the Ephesians,* Pillar New Testament Commentary (Grand Rapids: Eerdmans, 1999), 304.

CHAPTER 10: THE LISTS IN CONTEXT (PART 2): ROMANS 12:6–8

1. Although Paul would not make the break absolute. The *gar* (γάρ) conjunction may still have some causal force, though it is probably weak.

2. "The difficult adverbial expression εἰς τὸ σωφρονεῖν in Rom 12:3 is best explained on the basis of the LXX as an adverb formed by literally rendering *lᵉ* with noun (Jer 4:30; 6:29); here Paul has made the infinitive into a noun (also on the LXX model) by prefixing the article." James Hope Moulten, *A Grammar of New Testament Greek,* vol. 4, *Style,* by Nigel Turner (Edinburgh: T & T Clark, 1976), 90.

3. See discussion of various possible meanings of this phrase in C. E. B. Cranfield, "Μέτρον πίστεως in Romans 12.3," *New Testament Studies* (1962): 345–51.

4. See reason 3 in this chapter and, especially, appendix B concerning the issue of whether this is one sentence or two.

5. "Humility is a major theme for Paul." David Lim, *Spiritual Gifts: A Fresh Look* (Springfield, MO: Gospel Publishing House, 1991), 225. Humility is a theme that somehow Paul works into each of his list passages (Rom. 12:16; 1 Cor. 12:25; 13:4; Eph. 4:2, 23).

6. To get an idea of how *praxis* (πρᾶξις) is similarly used in Greek literature, note the glosses in the first four categories in BDAG, 859–60: (1) acting, activity, function; (2) way of acting, course of action; (3) plan of action, undertaking; (4) act, action, deed. In the New Testament it is always used in one of these ways. Cf. Matthew 16:27; Luke 23:51; Acts 19:18; Romans 8:13; Colossians 3:9.

7. James D. G. Dunn, *Romans 9–16,* Word Biblical Commentary 38B (Waco, TX: Word, 1991), 724–25. I think Dunn has accurately observed what is going on in the sentences quoted, inasmuch as he has pointed out the importance of the word *function* for describing the list that follows. But Dunn seems to think more in terms of the spontaneity of the function; it is never an ongoing place of service. See especially his comments in James D. G. Dunn, *Jesus and the Spirit: A Study of the Religious and Charismatic Experience of Jesus and the First Christians as Reflected in the New Testament* (Philadelphia: Westminster, 1975), 254, 264.

8. Stott also comments that "teaching" and "encouragement" of Romans 12:7–8 are not solely Christian activities. "Now both instruction and encouragement are given by non-Christian people." John R. W. Stott, *Baptism and Fullness,* 2d ed. (Downers Grove, IL: InterVarsity Press, 1975), 93. Also on pp. 94–95: "Some gifts, far from being miraculous, appear to be quite ordinary, even prosaic. There is nothing miraculous about the gifts of teaching and encouraging, giving money and doing acts of mercy."

9. As discussed already in chapter 9, in the entirety of both lists, only one item, which is sometimes translated as "able to teach" (1 Tim. 3:2), is a contender that an ability is required for leadership. But, especially in light of the parallel passage, Titus 1:5–9, it is far more likely that Paul's reference is not to some inherent power that makes one a good communicator, but rather is, according to Titus 1:9, "holding fast the faithful word which is in accordance with the teaching, so that he will be able both to exhort in sound doctrine and to refute those who contradict."

10. English can be used to illustrate that many languages have many words that correspond both for a function and for a person in her or his function. Note that in this list, to keep the playing field level, I have purposely selected only functions that require a particular ability or skill.

LABEL FOR A FUNCTION	LABEL FOR A PERSON IN A FUNCTION
Coaching	Coach
Conducting	Conductor
Sewing	Seamstress
Counseling	Counselor

Mentoring	Mentor
Babysitting	Babysitter
Carpentry	Carpenter
Preaching	Preacher
Directing	Director
Engineering	Engineer
Teaching	Teacher
Building	Builder

This list took only a few moments and very little effort to compile. It could easily be extended much further. In contrast, so far I have been able to come up with only three illustrations in English of labels for abilities that correspond to persons using abilities, and these were difficult to locate.

LABEL FOR AN ABILITY	LABEL FOR A PERSON USING THE ABILITY
Musicianship	Musician
Craftsmanship	Craftsman
Psychic-sense	Psychic

11. Although many commentators observe that a shift takes place here in Romans 12:6–8 and in 1 Corinthians 12:28–30, that is quite a different thing from accounting for why the shift might have occurred. It seems difficult to account for this shift if one is reading these lists through conventional view lenses. I have suggested in the text that the function and the person in the function are conceptually so close that, for Paul, it wouldn't have felt like a shift. He could have viewed either the function or the person in the function as two ways of describing the same idea. But no such solution exists for a special abilities reading either of the list in Romans 12:6–8 or the one in 1 Corinthians 12:28–30.

12. See appendix B for Paul's employment of the word *differing* (*diaphoros;* διάφορος).

CHAPTER 11: THE LISTS IN CONTEXT (PART 3): 1 CORINTHIANS 12:28–30

1. This verb can also be translated as "placed." The items in the list, then, could be thought of as "placements," which suggests a concept virtually coextensive with what is usually meant by "appointments" or "assignments."

2. It is difficult to tell whether this should be viewed as a function or as a person in that function. I have translated it as a function. If it were in fact the person in the function, it would have to be translated as such, for example, "All are not workers of miracles, are they?"

3. See discussion in chapter 6.

4. As mentioned before, the term *miracle* (and its adjective *miraculous*) has been defined in a number of ways. I'm employing the broadly inclusive definition suggested by Wayne Grudem, *Systematic Theology* (Grand Rapids: Zondervan, 1994), 355: "A miracle is a less common kind of God's activity in which he arouses people's awe and wonder and bears witness to himself."

5. See the similar assessment that Paul is reacting to the Corinthians' overzealousness for the miraculous by K. S. Hemphill, "The Pauline Concept of Charisma" (Ph.D. diss., University of Cambridge, 1976), 52–65. On p. 63 n. 55, Hemphill comments, "The negative factor of the Corinthian pneumatic aberration must not be minimized. Much of Paul's thought in this area is developed over against the spirituals." See also his comments in Kenneth S. Hemphill, *Spiritual Gifts: Empowering the New Testament Church* (Nashville: Broadman & Holman, 1988), 61–63.

6. Verses 15 and/or 16 of 1 Corinthians 14 may be references to the Holy Spirit (for example, C. K. Barrett, *A Commentary on the Second Epistle to the Corinthians* [Peabody, MA: Hendrickson, 1987], 319–20, who says it is "the Holy Spirit as given to *me*"), although many interpreters consider these to be references to the human spirit (for example, F. W. Grosheide, *Commentary on the First Epistle to the Corinthians* [1953; reprint, Grand Rapids: Eerdmans, 1979], 325–26). Some sort of interplay between the Holy Spirit and the human spirit is suggested by Gordon D. Fee, *God's Empowering Presence: The Holy Spirit in the Letters of Paul* (Peabody, MA: Hendrickson, 1994), 229–32, cf. 123, 227, 254.

7. Anthony Thiselton, *The First Epistle to the Corinthians,* New International Greek Testament Commentary (Grand Rapids: Eerdmans, 2000), 918, says that "no less than twelve distinct explanations have been offered to try to account for the use of the phrase ἀνάθεμα Ἰησοῦς." See Thiselton's survey of approaches to interpreting verse 3 in ibid., 916–27.

8. So ibid., 928, 932–33.

9. See discussion in chapter 7.

10. Many commentators think that there is some sort of ranking, at least of the first three items in the list. So F. F. Bruce, *1 and 2 Corinthians,* New Century Bible (London: Marshall, Morgan & Scott, 1971; reprint, Grand Rapids: Eerdmans, 1980), 122–23. This does seem to be the most natural way to read this verse. Fee, in contrast, views these not as in any sort of ranking, per se, but as "*precedence* over the other in the founding and building up of the local assembly." Fee, *God's Empowering Presence,* 190.

11. Some translations translate this as "miracle-workers" but it seems more likely that the "miracles" is the first item of ministry activities themselves rather than the last item of persons doing the ministries.

12. See the discussion in chapter 6.

13. Anders Nygren, *Commentary on Romans* (Philadelphia: Fortress, 1949), 425, similarly observes the movement from these lists into a discussion of love in both Romans 12:9–21 and 1 Corinthians 13. He says about Romans 12, "One needs only to make 'love' the subject throughout 12:9–21 to see how close the contents of this section are to 1 Corinthians 13."

14. For other New Testament examples of *tithēmi* (τίθημι) being used in the sense of "to assign to some task or function," see John 15:16; Acts 13:47; 1 Timothy 2:7; 2 Timothy 1:11. So BDAG, 1004.

15. So, for example, Ernst Käsemann ("Ministry and Community in the New Testament," in *Essays on New Testament Themes,* trans. W. J. Montague [Naperville, IL: Alec R. Allenson, 1964], 81) makes the following comment: "But if all those endowed with charisma are *ipso facto* office-bearers, this seems to be as good as saying that really none of them are. Surely all trace of order is bound to disappear in a community run on these lines?" For similar views, see Hans von Campenhausen, *Ecclesiastical Authority and Spiritual Power in the Church of the First Three Centuries* (Stanford, CA: Stanford University Press, 1969), 55–75; James D. G. Dunn, *Unity and Diversity in the New Testament: An Inquiry into the Character of Earliest Christianity* (Philadelphia: Westminster, 1977); and in the context of the discussion of canon, idem, "Has the Canon a Continuing Function?" in *The Canon Debate,* ed. Lee Martin McDonald and James A. Sanders (Peabody, MA: Hendrickson, 2002), 558–79. Thiselton (*The First Epistle to the Corinthians,*

1020), in opposition to such ideas, comments on how certain structures and some form of leadership were necessary even at the earliest stage: "the development of the church in Acts 6:1–6 shows how all too readily an issue about whether funds were *fairly administered* arises from the very first . . . anyone familiar with the funding and management of even the smallest, most informal, most 'charismatic' group throws up questions about 'what was agreed' or how we go about 'implementing what was decided.'" For an excellent brief summary and critique of the wedge often driven between "charisma" and "office," see Herman Ridderbos, *Paul: An Outline of His Theology,* trans. John Richard deWitt (1975; reprint, Grand Rapids: Eerdmans, 1997), 438–40. Also Ronald Yam-Kwan Fung, "Charismatic versus Organized Ministry: An Examination of an Alleged Antithesis," *Evangelical Quarterly* 52 (1980): 195–214.

16.   The "all" has been added in the translation simply to designate that this is a second-person plural, not because there is anything in Greek to correspond to it.

17.   Leonhard Goppelt, *Apostolic and Post-Apostolic Times,* trans. Robert A. Guelich (New York: Harper, 1970), 183, observes: "When Paul enumerates the ministries or rather the charismata, he refers partly to designations of office and partly to functions." Although I think Goppelt has accurately identified the nature of this list, I would shy away from using the word *office,* not because leadership roles did not exist from the earliest times, but because they were not yet so developed or official as the English word *office* seems to suggest as a result of its use in ecclesiastical history.

18.   The list in Romans 12:6–8 is a little different in that Paul seems to be listing more general categories of ministry into which some of the more specific items in Paul's other lists could be grouped. First Corinthians 12:28–30 does include a few more general items, however.

19.   See the comments on these particular items in chapter 9 (on Eph. 4:11), especially the comments on "apostles," who were appointed to their roles, and not because they had some sort of "apostolic ability."

20.   John Knox, "The Ministry in the Primitive Church," in *The Ministry in Historical Perspective,* ed. H. R. Niebuhr and D. D. Williams (New York: Harper & Row, 1956), 10. So also Ralph P.

Martin, *The Spirit and the Congregation: Studies in 1 Corinthians 12–15* (Grand Rapids: Eerdmans, 1984), 33.

21. Gordon D. Fee, *The First Epistle to the Corinthians,* New International Commentary on the New Testament (Grand Rapids: Eerdmans, 1987), 622.

CHAPTER 12: THE LISTS IN CONTEXT (PART 4): 1 CORINTHIANS 12:8–10

1. Peter O'Brien, *The Letter to the Ephesians,* The Pillar New Testament Commentary (Grand Rapids: Eerdmans, 1999), 297. So also Leonhard Goppelt, *Apostolic and Post-Apostolic Times,* trans. Robert A. Guelich (New York: Harper, 1970), 183: "The Spirit gives different charismata (1 Cor. xii. 4 ff.) based on the historical needs of the Church. Such a charisma is not a supernatural power but the call of the Spirit to a service, a call which also enables one for a specific task."

2. "Paul does not present his own interpretation to his readers but takes their favourite words and utilizes them in his argument." Jannes Reiling, "The Magna Charta of Spiritual Gifts: A Re-reading of 1 Corinthians 12, 1–11," in *Festschrift Günter Wagner,* ed. Faculty of Baptist Theological Seminary (Bern: Peter Lang, 1994), 152.

3. I do not mean by "natural" that they are not God-given, simply that such abilities are shared both by people indwelt by the Holy Spirit and by those who are not. Every ability that any person has should be viewed as a divinely given gift. Calvin's development of the doctrine of common grace may be useful in this regard. Calvin suggests that we can regard particular abilities that are found in both regenerate and unregenerate people as still coming from God's grace (although this grace is certainly not saving grace). See John Calvin, *Institutes of the Christian Religion II,* sections 12–17, The Library of Christian Classics, ed. John T. McNeil, trans. Ford Lewis Battles (Philadelphia: Westminster, 1960), 20:270–76, for further discussion of common grace. Calvin says that "all of us have a certain aptitude" (ibid., 20:273). Furthermore, "with good reason we are compelled to confess that its beginning is inborn in human nature" (ibid.).

4. Notice also how this contrasts with Paul's other lists, though he no doubt understands those ministries to be assigned by the Spirit.

5. This could be more narrowly the judging of prophecies or more generally the identification of whether a particular activity is motivated by the Spirit of God or by a demonic spirit. See discussion in appendix A.

6. This is not to say that a more mundane activity could not be included under one of the categories of ministries found in this list. It is to say, however, that in this particular list, Paul focuses on manifestational aspects of these activities. Wanamaker comments, "We may perhaps think of the gifts of the Spirit that Paul enumerates in 1 Corinthians 12:8–10 as manifestations of what the apostle meant by 'power' [that is, as in 1 Thess. 1:5]. This power undoubtedly carried considerable ability to convince people of the truth of his preaching because its manifestations were interpreted as divine acts." Charles Wanamaker, *The Epistles to the Thessalonians: A Commentary on the Greek Text,* New International Greek Testament Commentary (Grand Rapids: Eerdmans, 1990), 79. For a contrary view, see Rudolf Bultmann, *Theology of the New Testament,* trans. Kendrick Grobel (New York: Charles Scribner's Sons, 1951), 1:154, who reads "word of wisdom" and "word of knowledge" as part and parcel of the "gift of teaching."

7. Notice that apart from prophecy, which is Paul's central concern along with tongues (cf. 1 Cor. 14), the following three items (in 1 Cor. 13:2) seem to parallel in the same order the first three items of the list in 1 Corinthians 12:8.

8. In addition, there clearly is an ability idea found in 1 Corinthians 12:2–3 in the passage leading up to this discussion ("no one is able to say 'Jesus is Lord' except by the Spirit"), and it is possible that "word of wisdom" and "word of knowledge" of verse 8 are somehow connected with verses 2–3, although that is not at all certain.

9. Someone would probably try to support this argument with the observation that "healings" is listed as "*charismata* of healings." But "*energēmata* (ἐνεργήματα) of powers" is also in the list, but no one tries to organize the entire list under "workings" even though, like *charismata,* it is one of the three headings Paul uses in verses 4–6.

10. See discussions in chapter 6.

11. "The ministerial purpose of gifts is especially plain in 1 Corinthians 12:4ff. In the most likely understanding of verses 4–6 with their triadic structure, 'gifts' (v. 4), 'ministries' (v. 5), and 'workings' (v.

6) do not refer to different entities but define each other so that the latter two serve to identify the nature of the former, and to make plain that the gifts listed in the following verses (vv. 8–10) are to function for service within the church." Richard B. Gaffin, *Perspectives on Pentecost: Studies in New Testament Teaching on the Gift of the Holy Spirit* (Phillipsburg, NJ: Presbyterian & Reformed, 1979), 49.

12. See chapters 7 and 11.

13. Gordon D. Fee, *The First Epistle to the Corinthians,* New International Commentary on the New Testament (Grand Rapids: Eerdmans, 1987), 601–2.

14. Anthony Thiselton, *The First Epistle to the Corinthians,* New International Greek Testament Commentary (Grand Rapids: Eerdmans, 2000), 995.

15. So, Colin Brown, ed., *The New International Dictionary of New Testament Theology* (Grand Rapids: Zondervan, 1986), 3:1147, 1151.

16. The five items are as follows: (1) "*charismata* of healings," identical in both lists; (2) "workings of miracles" in verse 10, but simply "miracles" in verse 28; (3) "prophecy" in verse 10, but "prophets" in verses 28–29; (4) "kinds of tongues," identical in verse 10 and verse 28 but also in verbal form in verse 30, "All do not speak with tongues, do they?"; (5) "interpretation of tongues" in verse 10, which is unparalleled in verse 28; the parallel is found in verse 30, "All do not interpret, do they?"

    The items that do not overlap are (first in 1 Cor. 12:8–10) (1) "word of wisdom," (2) "word of knowledge," (3) "faith," (4) "discernment of spirits," and (then in 1 Cor. 12:28–30) (5) "apostles," (6) "teachers," (7) "helps," (8) "administrations."

17. Some suggest, too, that these should be viewed in the category of ministries. This argument focuses upon the way Paul refers to "each one" in verse 7 and then again in verse 11. In other words, it is a suggestion based upon the kind of language that Paul uses in similar contexts.

    Although this little word (ἕκαστος) can be used in a variety of contexts, and Paul himself uses it in a variety of ways, he has a particular propensity toward using it in contexts that are ministry oriented. Four connections in particular suggest that his mention of "each one" in this passage perhaps should be viewed as suggesting a ministry orientation for this list.

The first connection is with Ephesians 4, in which verse 7 reads, "But to *each* one of us grace [that is, ministry—see chap. 9] was given" and in which verse 16 reads, "from whom the whole body, being fitted and held together by what every joint supplies, according to the proper working of *each* individual part, causes the growth of the body for the building up of itself in love." This is the first and last verse of the passage in which the list of Ephesians 4:11 is found, a context that plainly points to people in their ministry roles (see chap. 9).

The second connection is with 1 Corinthians 3:5–15. (Note that the next three connections are all found in 1 Corinthians itself.) In 1 Corinthians 3:5–15, Paul mentions "each one" four times in verses 5, 8, 10, and 13. That passage is all about the ministries of Paul, Apollos, and others who build upon the foundation that has been laid. The focus of the passage is defined with descriptions such as "servants" (v. 5), "planting" and "watering" (vv. 6–8), "labor" (v. 9), being "co-workers" (v. 9), laying a foundation and building upon it (vv. 10–15), and "each one's work" (vv. 13–15), all of which orient the reader toward ministry.

The third connection is with 1 Corinthians 7:17–24, where Paul mentions "each one" four times (twice in v. 17, and once each in vv. 20 and 24), and like Ephesians 4:7–16, this little expression is found in the first and last verses of the passage. In 1 Corinthians 7, "each one" is to remain in that condition in which he was called (vv. 17, 20, 24). In other words, the three times he mentions the key idea of this passage, and indeed of all of 1 Corinthians 7, it includes the little "each" idea. This passage is more general than 1 Corinthians 3 or Ephesians 4 inasmuch as it focuses on calling to salvation, but the idea of being called while in a particular life setting still orients one toward the place or activities that God assigns each person.

The fourth and final set of connections (and probably the most important) are found right within 1 Corinthians 12–14. The only other places in 1 Corinthians 12–14 (outside of 1 Cor. 12:7, 11) that Paul uses "each" are in 12:18 and 14:26. First Corinthians 12:18 says, "But now God has placed/appointed the members, *each* of them, in the body, just as he desired." As discussed in the previous chapter of this book, these words in this passage indicate that his discussion is about ministry placements or ministry roles (cf. 12:28). Moreover, in 1 Corinthians 14:26, Paul says, "What then, brothers? When you assemble, each one has a psalm, has a teaching, has a revelation, has a tongue, has an interpretation. Let all things be done for edification." This verse is about activities that are done during corporate worship that edify the corporate body. Finally, note similar uses of ἕκαστος in Romans 15:2; Ephesians 6:8; Galatians 6:4–5 (2x); and Philippians 2:4.

CHAPTER 13: "GRACE" THAT HAS BEEN "GIVEN"

1. More particularly, chapter 13 will look at every instance in Paul's letters in which *charis* (χάρις) works in tandem with a passive form of *didōmi* (δίδωμι). All instances are passive participles of *didōmi* (δίδωμι), except for Ephesians 3:8 and 4:7, which are clearly relevant to our discussion, but are aorist, passive, indicative.

2. John 1:17 is a possible exception, although there it is grace that is given in general and the participial form of *didōmi* (δίδωμι) is inferred because of the relationship with the previous clause.

3. I'm not suggesting that the word *grace* particularly means "ministry" in these passages, although in some of the passages it approaches such an application. Paul's use of the word *grace* in his writings is both rich and varied. He seems to operate within the understanding that everything that he had received, and indeed, that every believer in Christ has received, whether salvation or sanctification or calling to ministry, is a function of the grace of God. Thus, his broader understanding of grace for all of life informs his understanding that the ministries given to him and to all believers are subsumed under the exercise of God's grace in his and their lives. But in the passages observed in the chapter of this book, it is not just grace generally that he discusses, but grace that has been given. And for whatever reason, this particular expression is used in contexts where he is talking about particular ministry assignments and thus points toward those ministry assignments.

4. The language of apportionment or distribution in 1 Corinthians 12:4–6 (διαίρεσις) and 12:11 (διαιρέω) may also help to bring this passage into the discussion.

5. Probably the same idea is also represented in 1 Corinthians 15:10 ("But by the grace of God I am what I am, and his grace toward me was not empty, but I labored more than all of them; not I but the grace of God with me") and perhaps Romans 1:5 ("through whom we have received grace and apostleship to bring about the

obedience of faith among all the Gentiles for His name's sake"). But these will not be studied because they lack both the "grace" + "given" connection.

6. Cf. 1 Corinthians 15:57 and 2 Corinthians 8:16, where *charis* (χάρις) is used with the sense of thanks. Also Ephesians 4:29 and 2 Thessalonians 2:16. These are not included in the study of this chapter for lack of parallelism in form.

7. Actually, since this is in the dative case, it should be *charismati* (χαρίσματι). I have written it as *charisma* so as not to confuse those who do not read Greek.

8. Notice also the clear connection with 1 Corinthians 3:5, where *gave* is used similarly: "Who then is Apollos? And who is Paul? Servants through whom you believed, and to each as the Lord gave." What is it that the Lord gave? Paul and Apollos were given a place or position of service—in short, a ministry assignment.

9. Although some scholars think that chapters 8 and 9 of 2 Corinthians were two different letters put together at a later time, I view them as a unified argument. For a defense of the two-letter idea, see Hans Dieter Betz, *2 Corinthians 8 and 9: A Commentary on Two Administrative Letters of the Apostle Paul,* Hermeneia (Philadelphia: Fortress, 1985). Arguing against Betz is D. A. Carson, Douglas J. Moo, and Leon Morris, *An Introduction to the New Testament* (Grand Rapids: Zondervan, 1992), 275–77.

10. The New Living Translation renders *charis* (χάρις) in 2 Corinthians 8:6 as "ministry of giving" and the New International Version in 2 Corinthians 8:7 as "grace of giving." Cf. also translations of 8:19.

11. It also could almost be inferred from 8:7 that the ministry of generous giving, on the one hand, and faith, word, and knowledge, on the other hand, could all be described as works of grace.

12. The Greek word is *dōrea* (δωρεά).

13. Note also the similarity with Colossians 1:25.

14. See chapters 15 and 16.

Chapter 14: "But What About . . . ?"

1. Many of these objections are ones that I anticipate, rather than objections that have actually been raised, despite dozens of conversations and written interactions with others over the past few years.

2. This is a comprehensive list of every time Paul uses the verb *didōmi* (δίδωμι) in reference to what has been given by God, with the exception of all the times that the "grace" + "given" combination is found (since those have already been looked at in detail in chap. 13), and when *charismata* (Rom. 12:6) or *charisma* (1 Tim. 4:14) are said to have been given, since that is part of what is in question in this study.

3. Not *charisma*, rather *doma* (δόμα) in verse 8. It is undefined in the context. A study of Psalm 68:18 (MT 68:19; LXX 67:19)—a very difficult passage in its own right—is necessary to determine the meaning of this passage here. See Richard A. Taylor, "The Use of Psalm 68:18 in Light of the Ancient Versions," *Bibliotheca Sacra* 148 (1991): 319–36; Timothy G. Gombis, "Cosmic Lordship and Divine Gift-Giving: Psalm 68 in Ephesians 4:8," *Novum Testamentum* 47 (2005): 367–80; and W. Hall Harris III, *The Descent of Christ: Ephesians 4:7–11 and Traditional Hebrew Imagery* (Grand Rapids: Baker, 1996).

4. Note the language here of a person being given. Note that this shows that the language of persons who are given in Ephesians 4:11, although unusual in English, is not so unusual in Paul's Greek usage.

5. Possibly Ephesians 1:17 and 2 Timothy 1:7 could be taken to suggest a Spirit-given ability, although in both cases there is considerable debate about whether *pneuma* (πνεῦμα) should be understood as in some way referring to a person's spirit or to the Holy Spirit (or to something else). For Ephesians 1:17, see the discussion in Harold Hoehner, *Ephesians: An Exegetical Commentary* (Grand Rapids: Baker, 2002), 256–58. For 2 Timothy 1:7, see the opposing views of William D. Mounce, *Pastoral Epistles,* Word Biblical Commentary 46 (Nashville: Nelson, 2000), 477–78; Gordon D. Fee, *God's Empowering Presence: The Holy Spirit in the Letters of Paul* (Peabody, MA: Hendrickson, 1994), 786–89.

6. Entry for ἔχω in BDAG, 420–22.

7. A possible exception is Ephesians 4:28a, where Paul encourages one who steals to stop stealing and to start working "in order that he may have [something? the ability?—not stated in text] to share with one in need." But it looks more like this verse is about having food, clothing, and money to share rather than some abstract ability to share and so probably excludes it from the ability consideration.

There are instances in which "have" is used in contexts relating to *possessing* something, but not, that I can find in Paul's letters, in the sense of possessing an ability, capacity, or talent.

8. Archippus, in Colossians 4:17, is told to "pay attention to the ministry *which you have received* in the Lord, that you may fulfill it" (cf. Acts 20:24; 2 Tim. 4:5, "your ministry"). Colossians 4:17; Acts 20:24; and 2 Timothy 4:5 all point toward the idea that a ministry can be given and that it can be something that someone has (even though the Greek word ἔχω is not present in these verses.

9. It is still important when working within a supernatural worldview to be careful not to allow the word *natural* in "natural talents" to suggest to one's mind something that has *naturalistically* (apart from the superintendence of God) been passed through the gene pool.

10. John Calvin, *Institutes of the Christian Religion II,* The Library of Christian Classics, ed. John T. McNeil, trans. Ford Lewis Battles (Philadelphia: Westminster, 1960), 20:273. Refer to sections 12–17 of Battles for further discussion of common grace. See also Richard J. Mouw, *He Shines in All That's Fair: Culture and Common Grace* (Grand Rapids: Eerdmans, 2001), 31–51; and Abraham Kuyper, "Common Grace," in *Abraham Kuyper: A Centennial Reader,* ed. James D. Bratt (Grand Rapids: Eerdmans, 1998).

11. And in the case of 1 Corinthians 12:8–10, that those items should not be viewed primarily in the category of abilities (although that is a valid category for that list), but should primarily—like the other lists—be viewed in the category of activities that build up the body of Christ (that is, ministries).

12. Barclay M. Newman, *A Concise Greek-English Dictionary of the New Testament* (London: United Bible Societies, 1971), 178.

13. Ibid., 41.

14. "'Talent' in the figurative sense of mental endowment or natural ability is derived from this very parable [Matt. 25:14–30] and was first used this way in English circa 1430." Ben Chenoweth, "Identifying the Talents: Contextual Clues for the Interpretation of the Parable of the Talents (Matthew 25:14–30)," *Tyndale Bulletin* 56 (2005): 65, n. 13, citing *The Oxford English Dictionary,* 2d ed. (Oxford: Clarendon, 1989), 17:580.

15. The Greek word *dunamis* (δύναμις), which normally is used to mean "power" or "miracle," can sometimes point toward a

person's ability, as in Matthew 25:15 and 2 Corinthians 1:8 and 8:3 (although not a special God-given ability for a particular task, but a general capacity that a person has via common grace).

16. Ben Chenoweth, "Identifying the Talents," 61–72, presents a convincing argument that the referent for the talents in this parable is "knowledge of the mysteries of the kingdom of heaven." The referent is the key issue in understanding what Jesus is teaching in this parable.

17. *Webster's Third New International Dictionary of the English Language Unabridged,* ed. Philip Babcock Gove (Springfield, MA: G. & C. Merriam, 1961), 956.

18. This definition seems to have been primarily suggested by the relationship of *charisma* to other "gift" words (δωρεά and δώρημα) in Romans 5:15–17.

19. Once again, I do not have any trouble with the language of gifting in Greek because there is no parallel to the ambiguity found in English. My concern is entirely with English usage.

20. A representative comment that shows how people read the entire discussion through the lens of the first list in 1 Corinthians 12 is found in Jack W. MacGorman, *The Gifts of the Spirit* (Nashville: Broadman Press, 1974), 27: "The importance of this paragraph [that is, 1 Cor. 12:4–11] can scarcely be exaggerated. . . . Actually, the rest of the chapter is but an elaboration by analogy and reiteration of the basic insights offered here."

Similarly, Donald Gee, although rightly acknowledging that the second list in 1 Corinthians 12 (vv. 28–30) is a list of ministries, still feels compelled to read them as based upon Spirit-given abilities, which he derives from 1 Corinthians 12:8–10. "Thus we find Paul, in the early part of 1 Corinthians 12, with perfect consistency, stating the various gifts of the Spirit with which believers are endowed, and then, at the end of the chapter, naturally gliding into a statement of the resultant offices or ministries which come from them. God 'sets' in the body by the bestowal of various gifts for service, and the gift given indicates the particular work to be done." Donald Gee, *The Ministry-Gifts of Christ* (London: Assemblies of God Publishing House, 1930), 85.

An example of reading the list in Romans 12:6–8 through the lens of 1 Corinthians 12:8–10 is the following quotation from Craig S. Keener, *Gift and Giver: The Holy Spirit for Today* (Grand

Rapids: Baker, 2001), 104: "Teaching [in Rom. 12:7] is a special endowment of grace that is also, as 1 Corinthians 12:8–11 shows, a special empowerment of God's Spirit." Does 1 Corinthians 12:8–11 really lead to such an interpretation of the teaching of Romans 12:7?

Walter L. Liefield, *1 and 2 Timothy, Titus,* The NIV Application Commentary (Grand Rapids: Zondervan, 1999), 167, interprets 1 Timothy 4:14 through this same lens: "We may assume that this gift, like those in that chapter [1 Cor. 12] was an endowment by the Holy Spirit. We may also assume that it was a spiritual ability that one could fail to draw on." Liefield's entire case in 1 Timothy 4:14 appears to rest upon Paul's use of *charisma* in 1 Timothy 4:14 and what he has supposedly learned about it from 1 Corinthians 12.

21. Ellis comments on why he thinks the theme of love in 1 Corinthians 13 "is given greater emphasis here than in the other letters." He says, "The explanation appears to lie in the special needs of the church at Corinth and, especially, the aberrations of certain charismatics in that church." E. Earle Ellis, *Pauline Theology: Ministry and Society* (Grand Rapids: Eerdmans, 1989), 51.

22. Although more narrowly, Ephesians 4:11–12 is a list of people in those ministries; Romans 12:6–8 is a mixed list of ministry functions, people in those functions, and attitudes with which a person does those functions; 1 Corinthians 12:28–30 is a mix of people in their appointed ministries together with ministry appointments themselves; 1 Corinthians 12:8–10 is a list that can be described both under the conception of ministries and the ability to do those ministries. Refer to discussions in chapters 9–12 of this book.

23. Obviously, there has been no attempt in this analogy to make a one-to-one correspondence with any individual item in Paul's lists. But roughly, list 1, which is a list of activities that requires fast-ness, is supposed to represent 1 Corinthians 12:8–10; list 2, which is a list of persons in their activities followed by activities themselves—including a mix of activities that require fast-ness together with activities that do not require fast-ness—is supposed to represent 1 Corinthians 12:28–30; list 3, which is a list of persons in their activities followed by activities themselves, is intended to represent Romans 12:6–8; list 4, a list of persons in their activities, is supposed to represent Ephesians 4:11–12.

Chapter 15: Ministry and Service in the Letters of Paul

1. R. Eduard Schweizer, "Ministry in the Early Church," in *The Anchor Bible Dictionary* (New York: Doubleday, 1992), 4:836. This does not mean that all leadership roles are eliminated, but simply that Paul did not view the ministry of leaders as belonging to a category different from the ministries that each believer has received from God. Schweizer has accurately identified this distinction, although in his study of 1 Corinthians 12:28–30, he seems to downplay any possibility that there could be official nuances in any of the first three items in the list (apostles, prophets, teachers). Eduard Schweizer, *Church Order in the New Testament,* trans. Frank Clarke (Naperville, IL: Alec Allenson, 1961), 100. Although the list in 1 Corinthians 12:28–30 is more functional than formal, it seems that Schweizer has overstated the case and made the list merely functional.

2. Murray J. Harris, *The Second Epistle to the Corinthians: A Commentary on the Greek Text,* New International Greek Testament Commentary (Grand Rapids: Eerdmans, 2005), 437, says that the ἡμᾶς ("us") of 2 Corinthians 5:18 has been variously interpreted to refer to "(i) Paul alone, although not in an exclusive sense, (ii) Paul and his addressees, (iii) all believers, or (iv) all humanity." I think it more likely that the primary reference is to Paul, his co-workers, and other apostolic workers, although some principles that are modeled have further application.

3. Ridderbos comments in this regard about the words Paul uses when he talks about ministry: "The most striking thing is surely that these words have no sacral connotation and that, conversely, the words that are used in the LXX and in Hellenism for the sacral ministry in temple or sanctuary are not employed in Paul and in the New Testament generally for any service in the Christian church." Herman Ridderbos, *Paul: An Outline of His Theology,* trans. John Richard deWitt (1975; reprint, Grand Rapids: Eerdmans, 1997), 441. Ridderbos does mention (in n. 35 on the same page) the exception of Romans 15:16.

   Concerning this exception, Romans 15:16, Colin G. Kruse comments, "Paul also spoke of this ministry in priestly terms. He was 'a minister of Christ Jesus to the Gentiles, serving the gospel of Christ as a priest, so that the offering [consisting] of the Gentiles may be acceptable, sanctified by the Holy Spirit.' It was possibly in response to Jewish suspicions about the 'cleanness' of his Gentile converts that Paul was prompted to speak of his ministry in this way. He saw himself as a priest responsible for the offering of the Gentiles, and particularly for the purity of that offering." Colin G. Kruse, "Ministry," in *Dictionary of Paul and His Letters*, ed. Gerald F. Hawthorne and Ralph Martin (Downers Grove, IL: InterVarsity Press, 1993), 605. The Romans 15:16 reference, however, seems to be the only time Paul speaks of ministry in this way, though we might have expected him to tie into this theme.

Benny C. Aker, "*Charismata*: Gifts, Enablement, or Ministries," *Journal of Pentecostal Theology* 11 (2002): 63–65, suggests some perhaps fruitful connections through his use of anthropological temple imagery in Paul. Still, none of these references are explicit in the way one might have expected from Paul, who so often draws upon the Old Testament in his writings.

4. The same Greek word group (the διακον- group) underlies the words used in English for the two words *service* and *ministry* and their cognates.

CHAPTER 16: LEARNING BY EXAMPLE

1. Luke's record of Paul's defense before Agrippa includes the following reminiscence by Paul. He says that Jesus appeared and spoke to him on the Damascus road and said, "For this purpose I have appeared to you, *to appoint you a minister* and a witness" (Acts 26:16).

2. Note the parallel discussion in Colossians 1:25–29.

3. Speaking in tongues, which Paul says he did more than any of the Corinthians (1 Cor. 14:18), is also viewed as a ministry by Paul (see arguments in chap. 12 of this book). But since 1 Corinthians 14 also seems to suggest that there exists a non-ministry, private use of tongues, and since in context it appears that Paul may be referring to this when he mentions his own tongues-speaking, I have left it off of this list of ministries.

4. Paul follows this up by saying, "For this reason I have sent to you Timothy, who is my beloved and faithful child in the Lord, *and he will remind you of my ways which are in Christ,* just as I teach everywhere in every church" (1 Cor. 4:17), which also continues the general idea of modeling found in the previous verse.

5. The point of this paragraph is not to say that Paul himself was modeling each of these ministries in these particular instances, but rather that modeling in general extends to these types of areas, not just to attitudes. Obviously, even in Philippians, Paul himself is actually modeling the preaching and defense of the gospel and the reconciling of warring parties (Phil. 4:2–3—in his encouragement to Clement).

6. Paul goes on to say that the Thessalonians learned this lesson so well that their example became something for others to imitate (1 Thess. 1:7–8).

7. Paul elsewhere encourages the Thessalonians to "follow our example" and says that he and his co-workers "offer ourselves as a model for you, so that you would follow our example" (2 Thess. 3:7–9), although in that passage the discussion is focused on living a disciplined life and working for one's own keep.

8. See especially chapter 9 (reason 5) and chapter 13, (the study of Eph. 3:1–2, 7–8).

CHAPTER 17: THE HOLY SPIRIT IN THE LETTERS OF PAUL

1. In many ways, short comments often illustrate more what is core for an author even more than lengthy discussions do. See the similar comments about brevity in Peter Enns, *Inspiration and Incarnation: Evangelicals and the Problem of the Old Testament* (Grand Rapids: Baker, 2005), 142, 151. Although Enns's topic is apostolic exegesis of Old Testament passages and Second Temple interpretive influences, he recognizes that brief comments can often show how a particular thought in an author may be more deeply ingrained than lengthier discussions. Enns comments on p. 142, "Far from demonstrating their unimportance, the brevity and incidental nature of these interpretive comments demonstrate the degree to which these traditions were part of the common discourse about the Bible." Again, on p. 151, Enns remarks "that Paul can make such a brief, offhand comment about a moveable rock speaks to the existence, in some form, of a 'moveable well' tradition already in Paul's day, so much so that he can make such a truncated comment and expect to be understood."

2. Many aspects of the person and work of the Holy Spirit in the letters of Paul are briefly mentioned or ignored altogether in the concise summary in this chapter of this book. For further study, please refer to the most extensive theology of the Holy Spirit

in the letters of Paul that I am aware of, Gordon D. Fee, *God's Empowering Presence: The Holy Spirit in the Letters of Paul* (Peabody, MA: Hendrickson, 1994). The present chapter is based on a study of the Bible itself, without dependence upon any secondary literature, including Fee.

3. One of my greatest concerns in writing this book has been that someone might take these insights and use them in such a way that people's focus becomes entirely on the doing of activities without an appropriate recognition of the central role of the Holy Spirit in the life of the believer. Nothing could be further from Paul's intention and emphases, as I hope this chapter and the following will show.

4. In Galatians 5 the "deeds of the flesh" (vv. 19–21) are set in contrast to "the fruit of the Spirit" (vv. 22–23). The simple juxtaposing of "deeds/acts" of the flesh with "fruit" of the Spirit contrast things that a person can do (only evil) and the fact that any and all good is produced as a work of the Spirit, not as something we can produce on our own.

5. F. F. Bruce, *The Epistle to the Galatians*, New International Greek Testament Commentary (Grand Rapids: Eerdmans, 1982), 243, comments, "The antithesis between πνεῦμα and σάρξ can be brought out in written English if both Spirit and Flesh are spelt with initial capitals: 'the Flesh' is 'the power that opposes God' . . . and enslaves human beings (cf. Rom. 8:6ff.; 12f.)." This is a useful way of conceiving what Paul was getting at when Paul uses the term *flesh* (σάρξ) theologically. The "flesh" is the gravitational pull toward sin for all humans who are still in their earthly bodies. Thus, humans are weak (Rom. 6:19; 8:3; cf. Matt. 26:41), and are susceptible to temptation and the desire to participate in sin (Rom. 7:5; 13:14; Gal. 5:16–17; Eph. 2:3; Col. 2:23). The "flesh" is not a constituent part of a human (contra the "sinful nature" translation, eg. NIV). It is the frailty and susceptibility of all who are in bodies that have been affected by the fall and by past habits of sin. Paul longs for the day when his body will be transformed and he will no longer be tempted to sin (Rom. 7:24; 8:23; 2 Cor. 5:1–8; Phil. 1:22–24; 3:21).

6. The result of this strengthening by the Holy Spirit in Ephesians 3:16–19 includes the following: (1) the dwelling of Christ in the believer's heart through faith; (2) the rooting and grounding in love; (3) the comprehension and knowledge of the love of Christ;

(4) the filling up with all the fullness of God. Paul also prays in Colossians 1:9–12 that the Colossians would be "strengthened with all power, according to His glorious might" and ties it into (1) being filled with the knowledge of his will, (2) walking in a manner worthy of the Lord, (3) pleasing him, (4) bearing fruit in every good work, (5) increasing in the knowledge of God, (6) attaining of all steadfastness and patience, and (7) giving thanks.

In addition to these passages, other passages point toward empowering for sanctification that comes from God (although the Holy Spirit is not necessarily mentioned in the context); a few of those examples are listed here. Only God is able to make his servant stand (Rom. 14:4). God fills us with joy and peace in believing, and we abound in hope by the power of the Holy Spirit (Rom. 15:13). This same passage (Rom. 15:13–14) suggests that it is by the power of the Spirit that believers are "able also to admonish one another." God empowers us for perseverance and continuance in our faith (Rom. 16:25; 2 Tim. 1:12). We are given power to endure temptation and be able to escape it (1 Cor. 10:13). Suffering can be "according to the power of God" (2 Tim. 1:8). Second Timothy 3:5 implies that true godliness is accompanied by power. The Lord "will strengthen and protect you from the evil one" (2 Thess. 3:3). Evidence for empowering for ministry is dealt with in text in the following chapter.

7. "The promise of the Spirit" (Gal. 3:14) is probably a reference to the expectation that God would send the Holy Spirit, found in such Old Testament passages as Isaiah 44:3; Ezekiel 11:19–20; 36:26–27; and Joel 2:28–30.

8. There is also substantial evidence that Paul, while never developing this teaching directly, viewed the Holy Spirit as a member of a Trinity with the Father and the Son. See Romans 1:3–4; 8:9–11; 1 Corinthians 12:4–6; 2 Corinthians 3:17; 13:14; Galatians 4:6; Ephesians 4:3–4.

9. Romans 12:3, 6; 15:15; 1 Corinthians 1:4; 3:10; 2 Corinthians 8:1; Galatians 2:9; Ephesians 3:2, 7–8; 4:7; 2 Timothy 1:9.

10. In the list of "grace" + "given" passages cited in this sentence, the Holy Spirit is mentioned in the immediate contexts of Romans 15:15 (cf. 15:16, 19); 1 Corinthians 3:10 (cf. 3:16); Ephesians 3:2, 7–8 (cf. 3:5, 16); Ephesians 4:7 (cf. 4:3–4); 2 Timothy 1:9 (cf. 1:14); but not in Romans 12:3, 6 (unless "fervent in spirit" in 12:9

is read "fervent in the Spirit"); Romans 15:15; 1 Corinthians 1:4; 2 Corinthians 8:1; and Galatians 2:9.

CHAPTER 18: EMPOWERING AND WEAKNESS IN THE LETTERS OF PAUL

1. George W. Bush in his presidential acceptance speech, November 3, 2004.

2. "Some restrict χάρις here to earthly blessings or temporal benefits or material prosperity, but since the Macedonians' generosity of spirit is attributed to the operation of God's χάρις in their lives (8:1–4) and the use of πᾶσαν does not encourage any restriction of sense, it is preferable to regard χάρις as encompassing both material and spiritual blessings or benefits." Murray J. Harris, *The Second Epistle to the Corinthians: A Commentary on the Greek Text*, New International Greek Testament Commentary (Grand Rapids: Eerdmans, 2005), 637.

3. C. S. Lewis, *Prince Caspian: The Return to Narnia* (New York: Collier Books, 1970), 200. I am grateful to my colleague, Matthew Williams, for pointing out this citation.

4. "In every instance in Paul the term *adokimos* refers to those who will not pass the test, to those who do not belong to the people of God." Thomas R. Schreiner, *Paul, Apostle of God's Glory in Christ: A Pauline Theology* (Downers Grove, IL: InterVarsity Press, 2001), 286.

5. Paul adds one more suffering, the basket incident at Damascus, because it would probably have been (from a Near Eastern perspective) an incident that his detractors could have used to show how totally foolish he actually was (2 Cor. 11:32–33). He is carrying his "foolishness" demeanor to extreme lengths at this point.

6. Paul's "thorn in the flesh" has most often been interpreted as some sort of physical malady, although the idea that it referred to a person or persons who were opposed to Paul has proponents as well. For orientation and bibliography, a good starting point is Harris, *Second Epistle to the Corinthians,* 851–59 (note esp. his summaries on pp. 857 and 858–59).

7. "The final word in this connection stems from the experience of Paul. Extraordinarily gifted among Christians in the New Testament (Acts 19:11f.; 28:3–6, 8f.; 1 Cor. 9:1f.; 2 Cor. 12:1ff.), nevertheless only as he was brought face to face with his own

limitations and weakness, did he come to recognize the true secret of his usefulness in the church (2 Cor. 12:7ff.)." Richard B. Gaffin, *Perspectives on Pentecost: Studies in New Testament Teaching on the Gifts of the Holy Spirit* (Phillipsburg, NJ: Presbyterian & Reformed, 1979), 54.

8. "This is characteristic: God highlights the weakness of those whom he saves and uses, so that nothing will rival or obscure his glory (1 Cor. 1:27–29; 2 Cor. 4:7, see also 12:9)." J. I. Packer, *Keep in Step with the Spirit* (Old Tappan, NJ: Revell, 1984), 84.

9. Henry and Mel Blackaby, *What's So Spiritual About Your Gifts?* (Sisters, OR: Multnomah, 2004), 30.

CHAPTER 19: EARLY CHURCH MINISTRIES IN THE LETTERS OF PAUL

1. One way I defined the nature of this list was by asking whether it was an activity that could be pluralized. You cannot pluralize love; it is too general. But you can show hospitality over and over again.

2. This does not mean that every item on these lists is transferable into the present day. But I have attempted to list them all as a point of reference.

3. As Paul's apostleship was to the Gentiles, so the apostleship of Peter was to the Jews (Gal. 2:8).

4. For a recent discussion of hospitality, see Andrew Arterbury, *Entertaining Angels: Early Christian Hospitality in Its Mediterranean Setting* (Sheffield: Sheffield Phoenix, 2005).

5. See comments about martyrdom as a ministry in the notes to the list in the following chapter (chap. 20).

6. Notice how Paul introduces Romans 12 with the saying, "I encourage you . . ." in verse 1. How is Paul "encouraging" them? He is doing it through the writing of this great letter to the Romans. But this encouragement (a present tense of παρακαλέω) connects directly with the phrase found in verse 8, "whether the one who encourages [substantival participle of παρακαλέω] in encouragement [παράκλησις—a noun from the same root as the verb]." Apparently, Paul would consider letter-writing to be one example of the general category of "encouragement."

7. "So that the life of Jesus also may be manifested in our body" (2 Cor. 4:10); "my circumstances have turned out for the greater progress of the gospel" (Phil. 1:12).

8. ". . . and all for your upbuilding, beloved" (2 Cor. 12:19).
9. This "brother," says Paul, was *appointed* by the churches to travel with us" (2 Cor. 8:18–19).
10. Following is a list of all metaphors for ministry found in Paul's letters: feeding with milk (1 Cor. 3:1); planting (1 Cor. 3:6–8; 9:11); watering (1 Cor. 3:6–8); laying a foundation (1 Cor. 3:10); building on a foundation (1 Cor. 3:10); each person's work (1 Cor. 3:13–15); stewardship (1 Cor. 4:1; 9:17; Eph. 3:2; Titus 1:7); being a tutor in Christ (1 Cor. 4:15); being a father through the gospel (1 Cor. 4:15); serving as a soldier (1 Cor. 9:7); planting a vineyard (1 Cor. 9:7); tending a flock (1 Cor. 9:7); being a plowman (1 Cor. 9:10); being a thresher (1 Cor. 9:10); an open door for ministry (1 Cor. 16:9; 2 Cor. 2:12); servants of a new covenant (2 Cor. 3:6); ministry of the Spirit (contrasted with the ministry of death) (2 Cor. 3:8); ministry of reconciliation (2 Cor. 5:18–20); ambassadors for Christ (2 Cor. 5:20); ambassador in chains (Eph. 6:20); as poor, yet making many rich (2 Cor. 6:10); the sphere that God apportioned to us as a measure (2 Cor. 10:13); spending and being expended for your souls (like a parent for his child) (2 Cor. 12:15); rebuilding the church I once destroyed (Gal. 2:18); the proper working of each individual part (Eph. 4:16); partakers of grace with me (Phil. 1:7); serving in the furtherance of the gospel like a child serving his father (Phil. 2:22); gently caring like a nursing mother tenderly cares for her own (1 Thess. 2:7); imploring like a father would his own children (1 Thess. 2:11); having charge over you in the Lord (1 Thess. 5:12); taking care of the household of God (1 Tim. 3:5); being a good servant of Christ Jesus (1 Tim. 4:6); washing the saints' feet (1 Tim. 5:10); fighting the good fight of faith (1 Tim. 6:12; 2 Tim. 4:7); suffering hardship as a good soldier of Christ Jesus (2 Tim. 2:3–4); competing as an athlete (2 Tim. 2:5); working hard as a farmer (2 Tim. 2:6); a workman (2 Tim. 2:15); a vessel for honor . . . prepared for every good work (2 Tim. 2:21); slave of Christ (Rom. 1:1; 1 Cor. 7:22; 2 Cor. 4:5; Gal. 1:10; Eph. 6:6; Phil. 1:1; 2 Tim. 2:24; Titus 1:1).
11. Worked hard for you (Rom. 16:6); worked hard in the Lord (Rom. 16:12); your toil in the Lord (1 Cor. 15:58); doing the Lord's work (1 Cor. 16:10); the work and labor (1 Cor. 16:16); his own work (Gal. 6:4); workers with you for your joy (2 Cor. 1:24); the work of ministry (Eph. 4:12); fruitful labor (Phil. 1:22); work

of faith and labor of love (1 Thess. 1:3); diligently laboring among you (1 Thess. 5:12); good works (1 Tim. 2:10; 5:10); rich in good works (1 Tim. 6:18); services (2 Tim. 1:18); engage in good deeds (Titus 3:8); engage in good deeds to meet pressing needs (Titus 3:14). Thomas R. Schreiner, *Paul, Apostle of God's Glory in Christ: A Pauline Theology* (Downers Grove, IL: InterVarsity Press, 2001), 399, comments, "Many scholars maintain that the term [*kopiaō*, "to work"] denotes missionary service, and this is as good a guess as any, though certainty eludes us."

CHAPTER 20: EARLY CHURCH MINISTRIES OUTSIDE THE LETTERS OF PAUL

1. Furthermore, it may be that some (although probably not all) of the ministries of disciples and followers of Jesus that are found in the Gospels were included by the authors of the Gospels partially because they were ministries that were being done in the early church. Remember, the Gospels were written by members of the early church to members of the early church. Examples might include Jesus' disciples as "fishers of men" (Mark 1:17; cf. 1:20), and the women (Mary Magdalene, Joanna, Susanna, and others) who contributed to the financial support of Jesus (Luke 8:2–3). Jesus himself gives one list of ministries that includes feeding the hungry, giving water to the thirsty, inviting in a stranger, clothing the naked, visiting the sick, and visiting those in prison (Matt. 25:34–36, 37–39, 42–43, 44). Jesus himself suggested that his messianic credentials, in fulfillment of Isaiah 61:1–2, included, of course, preaching the gospel to the poor, proclaiming release to the captives and recovery of sight to the blind, setting free the oppressed, and proclaiming the favorable year of the Lord.

2. As mentioned elsewhere, I am not suggesting that each and every ministry listed here will necessarily be functioning in the same way and to the same extent as its first-century manifestation. But I have attempted to make as comprehensive a list as possible of early church ministries as a help in the discussion. Both cessationists and continuationists can use this list to evaluate questions of continuity or discontinuity between the first century and today. As mentioned before, the premise of this book does not stand or fall upon one's understanding of whether the miraculous ministries are in full function today.

3. That prayer should be included in this list is suggested by the connection of "prayer" and "the ministry of the word" in Acts 6:4, perhaps by the connection between "ministering to the Lord" and "fasting" in Acts 13:2, and by the comment by Luke that "the prisoners were listening to them" as Paul and Silas prayed in the Philippian jail (Acts 16:25).

4. That enduring persecution as a Christian can be considered a ministry is supported by the connection Luke makes between the persecution that broke out after the martyrdom of Stephen (Acts 8:1–3) and the preaching of the word that ensued (8:4).

5. That persecution and martyrdom perhaps should be included in this list of ministries is suggested in Acts 8:4, where it is learned that the persecution that started as a result of Stephen's martyrdom caused the word to be spread.

6. There is also at least one example of Paul being an encouragement to unbelievers (Acts 27:22, 25, 33–34).

7. Referred to as a "service" in Acts 12:25.

8. Delivering the contents of this letter seems clearly to be a ministry that built up the believers; note "they rejoiced because of its encouragement" (Acts 15:31).

9. Luke comments that "the prisoners were listening to them" as Paul and Silas sang in the Philippian jail (Acts 16:25), suggesting his awareness of the evangelistic ministry represented by such an action.

10. Acts 28:15 says that "when Paul saw" some of the brothers who had come from Rome, traveling as far as to the Market of Appius and Three Inns to meet Paul, "he thanked God and took courage." Clearly, their escorting Paul on his journey was a ministry to him.

11. John says that in supporting such people we become "co-workers with the truth" (3 John 8).

12. See chapter 19.

13. In the Gospels, Jesus does fairly regularly use metaphors or extended parables to represent ministry, but that is outside the range of the current study.

Chapter 21: What Difference Does It Make?

1. Max Turner, *The Holy Spirit and Spiritual Gifts in the New Testament Church and Today,* rev. ed. (Peabody, MA: Hendrickson, 1998),

276, comments, "But similarly, even concerning 'manifestation of the Spirit' in the assembly, Paul expects that a person might have the gift of more than one gift—if one may put it that way. He expects the one with tongues to pray for the gift to interpret his tongues (1 Cor. 14:13)."

2. See also Ephesians 4:16; 1 Corinthians 12:18; 14:26.

3. For example, Ernst Käsemann, "Ministry and Community in the New Testament," in *Essays on New Testament Themes,* trans. W. J. Montague (Naperville, IL: Alec R. Allenson, 1964), 63–94; Hans von Campenhausen, *Ecclesiastical Authority and Spiritual Power in the Church of the First Three Centuries* (Stanford, CA: Stanford University Press, 1969), 55–75; James D. G. Dunn, *Unity and Diversity in the New Testament: An Inquiry into the Character of Earliest Christianity* (Philadelphia: Westminster, 1977). For a response, see Ronald Y. K. Fung, "Charismatic Versus Organized Ministry: An Examination of an Alleged Antithesis," *The Evangelical Quarterly* 52 (1980): 195–214.

4. The only possible exception is the line "able to teach" in 1 Timothy 3:2. But the parallel passage, Titus 1:9, shows us what such an ability is: ". . . so that he may be able to give instruction in sound doctrine and also to rebuke those who contradict it." The focus is not on ability, as it is usually conceived, but is upon knowing sound doctrine and thus having the capacity to refute false doctrine.

5. According to C. Peter Wagner, *Your Spiritual Gifts Can Help Your Church Grow* (1979; reprint, Ventura, CA: Regal, 2005), 23–28, discovering your spiritual gifts (read: abilities) is the primary way you discover the will of God for your life. A more poignant example of trying to discover one's "spiritual gift" in daily life is represented in a magazine article where a seventeen-year-old girl and her father are interacting with the daughter's decision of whether to go to college or not. See Bill Smith and Bethany G. Smith, "The College Decision: A Father and Daughter Share Perspectives on How to Decide if Higher Education Is Right for Your Child," *Home School Enrichment* (July–August 2005): 36–38. In the father's own words, "After prayer that God would guide us, I turned to the white board hung on the wall for this special occasion. I began by listing what we have discovered over the years are Bethany's spiritual gifts—the ones that motivate her.

For her, they are mercy and service" (ibid., 36). In the daughter's words, "If your own special blend of personality and giftings seem to be sending you in the direction of a lawyer, scientist . . . then college . . . is a wonderful tool for the job. However, if, like me, you happen to be made of humanitarian worker, missionary . . . ingredients, then, no matter how you try, college . . . cannot turn you into a very good lawyer" (ibid., 38).

6. This does not mean that the way God has equipped someone should be neglected when considering what area(s) of ministry in which to serve. Being so equipped is one aspect that God uses to guide someone. Refer to chapter 14 on talents (also chap. 18 on empowering and weakness).

7. Henry and Mel Blackaby, *What's So Spiritual About Your Gifts?* (Sisters, OR: Multnomah, 2004), 25, comment, "When it comes to serving God, we tend to evaluate what we're good at and what we like to do, then serve according to our ability. We figure out what talents we have, then offer them to God, assuming that these are our spiritual gifts. This, in fact, is what others usually encourage us to do—to recognize where we're proficient and what we like to do, then serve according to our ability, all the while asking God to bless our efforts. We never consider serving outside the areas of our strength, and can't imagine God asking us to do that which we don't like to do."

CHAPTER 22: KNOWING WHERE TO SERVE

1. Recently, I did a simple Internet search using the keywords "spiritual gifts." The first two dozen hits were mostly sites that offered spiritual gifts tests that could be taken by people who wanted to discover their special spiritual abilities.

2. The following books will be a good starting point for anyone who wants to interact with various approaches to decision making, but within the boundaries of those who have a high view of Scripture. The books here will be listed beginning with those that allow a greater role to subjective guidance from the Spirit and will end with those that mostly or entirely exclude "guidance" in this sense: Jack Deere, *Surprised by the Voice of God: How God Speaks Today Through Prophecies, Dreams, and Visions* (Grand Rapids: Zondervan, 1996); Dallas Willard, *Hearing God: Developing a Conversational Relationship with God* (Downers Grove, IL: InterVarsity Press,

1984); Bill Thrasher, *Living the Life God Has Planned: A Guide to Knowing God's Will* (Chicago: Moody, 2001); Bruce Waltke, *Finding the Will of God: A Pagan Notion?* (Gresham, OR: Vision House, 1995); Gary T. Meadors, *Decision Making God's Way: A New Model for Knowing God's Will* (Grand Rapids: Baker, 2003); Garry Friesen with J. Robin Maxson, *Decision Making and the Will of God: A Biblical Alternative to the Traditional View* (Portland: Multnomah, 1980).

3. This seems to be the implication of the line in verse 5, "and it will be *given* to him" (and in v. 7 the more general statement that the one who doubts when he asks for wisdom, "ought not to expect that he will *receive* anything from the Lord").

4. See Acts 16:7; 27:9–10, 21. Acts 16:6 says that they had been "forbidden by the Holy Spirit" whereas 16:7 says that "the Spirit of Jesus did not permit them." The change in language implies a difference in means—perhaps a prophetic word or dream in the first instance and an inward check or circumstance change in the second. The language of Acts 27:9–10 and 21 contrasts with the mention of a word from an angelic visitor in 27:23–26. The first appears to have been an inward check and the second a divine revelation.

5. Don't be worried that you might miss God's plan unless (as mentioned in the main text) God has communicated that he has something specific for you to do in a particular instance.

6. This blessing is drawn from 2 Corinthians 9:8; Colossians 1:9–10; 2 Thessalonians 1:11–12; 2:16–17.

Appendix A: A Description of Each Item in Paul's Four Ministry Lists

1. There is no way to know whether Barnabas or Silas was included among this group of five hundred who saw Christ after his resurrection, although both or either could have been (especially Barnabas, who first appears among the primitive church shortly after Pentecost—Acts 4:36–37).

2. Although categories 1 and 2 are not merely formal, they, of course, also have functional aspects. The question is whether their role is primarily envisioned as a formal/authoritative role, or whether it is primarily envisioned as a functional role, meeting particular needs at particular times.

3. Against category 1, Paul then would not be among the group. Against category 4, this would not account for its placement at the top of the list.

4. "A prophecy was certainly not a sermon by twentieth-century standards. It was a spontaneous utterance prompted by the Spirit (cf. vv. 29ff.) and based on a sudden and uncontrived revelation from God (v. 30)." Ben Witherington III, *Conflict and Community in Corinth: A Socio-Rhetorical Commentary on 1 and 2 Corinthians* (Grand Rapids: Eerdmans, 1995), 280.

5. For fuller discussion, refer to Wayne Grudem, *The Gift of Prophecy in the New Testament and Today* (Westchester, IL: Crossway Books, 1988). If you don't want to read the entire book, Grudem also summarizes his arguments in *Systematic Theology* (Grand Rapids: Zondervan, 1994), 1049–61. Three of Grudem's arguments stand out to me: (1) In 1 Corinthians 14, they were to test the prophets and (apparently) not stone them if their prophecies proved to be wrong; (2) Agabus appears to have generally given an accurate prophecy in Acts 21:10–11 but got some of the details wrong (Acts 21:27–36); (3) Paul apparently did not feel compelled to obey the urgings of those who "by the Spirit" told him not to go up to Jerusalem (Acts 21:4). In so doing, he apparently did not see himself as disobeying the word of God. For an opposing opinion see Richard B. Gaffin Jr., *Perspectives on Pentecost: Studies in New Testament Teaching on the Gifts of the Holy Spirit* (Phillipsburg, NJ: Presbyterian & Reformed, 1979), 58–72.

6. Markus Barth, *Ephesians: Translation and Commentary on Chapters 4–6,* Anchor Bible 34A (Garden City: Doubleday, 1974), 438–39. The absence of the pronominal article and the *de* (δέ) before *didaskalos* (διδάσκαλος) is the main reason for thinking that *poimēn* (ποιμήν) and *didaskalos* (διδάσκαλος) should be viewed together. Thus "teaching shepherd" or "shepherding teacher" or the more common "pastor-teacher" are the best designations in Ephesians 4:11. For the view that the "shepherds" and "teachers" in Ephesians 4:11 are two separate categories (albeit with overlapping roles), see Ernest Best, *A Critical and Exegetical Commentary on Ephesians,* ICC (Edinburgh: T & T Clark, 1998), 391–93.

7. See earlier comments on "able to teach" in chapter 9. The "able to teach" expression in 1 Timothy 3:2 is about knowledge of doctrine, and thus the ability to correct false doctrine, as its parallel in Titus 1:9 shows.

8. Robert L. Saucy, "Women's Prohibition to Teach Men: An Investigation into its Meaning and Contemporary Application," *Journal of the Evangelical Theological Society* 37 (1994): 89.

9. Cf. Eusebius, *Ecclesiastical History* 3.37, who seems to view the "office of evangelist" as proclaiming Christ "to those who had not yet heard the faith," particularly in "foreign parts." It is also possible that the role of evangelist included the preservation of true foundational doctrines. This could be the reason that "evangelists" are found among the "equippers" of Ephesians 4:11 just before Paul warns them not to be deceived by false doctrine (4:14) and is listed in 2 Timothy 4 just after Paul emphasizes the preservation of doctrine (vv. 3–4).

10. Gordon D. Fee, *The First Epistle to the Corinthians* (Grand Rapids: Eerdmans, 1987), 594.

11. BDAG, 89.

12. Fee, *First Epistle to the Corinthians,* 621.

13. John Knox, "The Ministry in the Primitive Church," in *The Ministry in Historical Perspective,* ed. H. R. Niebuhr and D. D. Williams (New York: Harper & Row, 1956), 10. Also, Ralph P. Martin, *The Spirit and the Congregation: Studies in 1 Corinthians 12–15* (Grand Rapids: Eerdmans, 1984), 33.

14. Cf. especially the Septuagint (or LXX) of Proverbs 11:14; and 24:6. The Septuagint is the Greek translation of the Hebrew Bible, translated in Egypt before the time of Christ. Comparisons with the Septuagint are sometimes helpful in determining the meaning of a word, particularly when there are few examples in the New Testament, as in this case.

15. BDAG, 766.

16. First Corinthians 1:17–2:16 (note esp. 2:4, 13; cf. 1:17, 18; 2:1) has very similar terminology to the "word of wisdom" in 1 Corinthians 12:8, although there Paul is contrasting wisdom (that is, the preaching of the cross) with the Corinthians' supposed wise words.

17. James D. G. Dunn, *Jesus and the Spirit: A Study of the Religious and Charismatic Experience of Jesus and the First Christians as Reflected in the New Testament* (Philadelphia: Westminster, 1975), 217. Dunn's entire discussion of knowledge and wisdom on pp. 217–22 is helpful.

18. Jannes Reiling may be correct in his claims that the reason we struggle to identify "word of wisdom" and "word of knowledge"

is that these were the Corinthians' words and *their* interest, not Paul's. "Once the rhetoric nature of Paul's arguing is perceived and the persuasive function of verse 8 is recognized it is clear why no convincing solution is found. The Corinthians had their own ideas about them and Paul does not care to correct them." Jannes Reiling, "The Magna Charta of Spiritual Gifts: A Re-reading of 1 Corinthians 12, 1–11," in *Festschrift Günter Wagner,* ed. Faculty of Baptist Theological Seminary (Bern: Peter Lang, 1994), 152.

19. George Müller is often mentioned as a person who exercised this kind of faith in receiving repeated answers to prayer for the thousands of orphans whom he kept clothed and fed year after year. See George Müller, *Answers to Prayer: From George Müller's Narratives,* comp. A. E. C. Brooks (Chicago: Moody, 1987).

20. Fee, *First Epistle to the Corinthians,* 596–97.

21. A possible reason for connecting the teachings of these two passages (1 Cor. 12; 1 John 4) is that both are concerned with the confession of Jesus in the immediate context (1 Cor 12:3; 1 John 4:2–3).

22. E. H. Plumptre, cited in J. Oswald Sanders, *The Holy Spirit and His Gifts* (Grand Rapids: Zondervan, 1940), 125.

23. The tongues of Acts 2:4, 11; 10:46; and 19:6 appear to be primarily or solely praise, although the evidence there is not overwhelming. Note especially 2:11, "we hear them in our own tongues *speaking of the mighty deeds of God*"; and 10:46, "For they were hearing them speaking with tongues *and exalting God.*" David Huttar, "An Important Test," unpublished paper, Nyack College, 1992.

24. David Huttar, "An Important Test."

Appendix B: Romans 12:4–8

1. A version of this chapter was forthcoming as an article in *New Testament Studies* when this book went to press. This appendix is entirely dedicated to Greek grammar, but for those without Greek training, English glosses of the first appearance of a Greek word or sentence have been included in the main text of the appendix (but not in the endnotes) to allow readers who do not know Greek to think through the arguments themselves.

2. See the following comments by proponents of the two-sentence approach. H. A. W. Meyer, *The Epistle to the Romans,* trans. John C. Moore (1884; reprint, New York: Funk & Wagnalls, 1889), 471–72; Henry Alford, *The Greek Testament,* rev. Everett F.

Harrison (1958; reprint, Chicago: Moody, 1968), 441–42; C. E. B. Cranfield, *A Critical and Exegetical Commentary on the Epistle to the Romans,* ICC (Edinburgh: T & T Clark, 1979), 2:618; William Sanday and Arthur C. Headlam, *A Critical and Exegetical Commentary on the Epistle to the Romans,* 5th ed., ICC (Edinburgh: T & T Clark, 1902), 356, who nevertheless refers to it as a "harsh ellipse"; John Murray, *The Epistle to the Romans,* 1 vol. ed., New International Commentary on the New Testament (Grand Rapids: Eerdmans, 1971), 120–21; Friedrich Adolph Philipi, *Commentary on St. Paul's Epistle to the Romans* (Edinburgh: T & T Clark, 1879), 261–63; and Douglas J. Moo, *The Epistle to the Romans,* New International Commentary on the New Testament (Grand Rapids: Eerdmans, 1996), 763–64.

3. Examples of other one-sentence proponents (the minority position) include James Denney, "St. Paul's Epistle to the Romans," in *The Expositor's Greek Testament* (1904; reprint, Grand Rapids: Eerdmans, 1961), 2:689–90; James D. G. Dunn, *Romans 9–16,* Word Biblical Commentary 38B (Waco, TX: Word, 1988), 725; James Hope Moulton, *A Grammar of New Testament Greek,* vol. 1, Prolegomena (Edinburgh: T & T Clark, 1906), 183–84; Berhard Weiss, *Der Brief an die Römer* (Göttingen: Vandenhoek und Ruprecht, 1899), 514–19; W. M. L. deWette, *Briefes an die Römer* (Leipzig: Weidmannsche, 1841), 170–72; and Johann Peter Lange, *The Epistle of Paul to the Romans* (New York: Funk & Wagnalls, 1889), 384. An entirely different approach is suggested by William Williams, *An Exposition of Paul to the Romans* (Cincinnati: Jennings and Pye, 1902), 359, who claims that Paul's "incoherent, and almost jerky" form represents merely brief notes that Paul intended to be filled out later in full sentences by his amanuensis, Tertius. This suggestion cannot be verified.

4. This passage is full of distributing expressions, arguing that distribution and comparison is Paul's main issue rather than some sort of unstated hortatory impulse. Indicators of distribution in this passage include (1) the χάρις in verse 3 τῆς δοθείσης and in verse 6 τὴν δοθεῖσαν; (2) ἑκάστῳ in verse 3, (3) ὡς ὁ θεὸς ἐμέρισεν μέτρον πίστεως in verse 3 (note that μερίζω is specifically a word of distribution), (4) τὰ δὲ μέλη πάντα οὐ τὴν αὐτήν ἔχει πρᾶξιν in verse 4, (5) τὸ δὲ καθ' εἷς ἀλλήλων μέλη in verse 5 (that is, distributed by God to each other—cf. Eph. 4:11), (6) διάφορα in

verse 6, (7) the use of εἴτε before various items in the list in verses 6–8a. Also, note that although the NRSV translates verses 4–8 as two sentences, the translation indicates that it is in agreement with the idea of διάφορος, distributing the list that follows: "We have gifts that differ according to the grace given to us: prophecy, in proportion to faith; ministry, in ministering; the teacher, in teaching; the exhorter, in exhortation; the giver, in generosity; the leader, in diligence; the compassionate, in cheerfulness."

5. Rather, I understand the ἔχοντες ... χαρίσματα to mean "participating in a particular function of ministry." Cf. Moulton, *Grammar of New Testament Greek*, 1:183, "The durative sense of ἔχω, *hold* and so *exercise,* must be once more remembered." Χαρίσματα should be read in light of πρᾶξιν (v. 4), which is preceded also by ἔχω.

6. Nor will an appeal to the word χάρισμα justify a two-sentence argument. See Kenneth Berding, "Confusing Word and Concept in 'Spiritual Gifts': Have We Forgotten James Barr's Exhortations?" *Journal of the Evangelical Theological Society* 43 (2000): 37–46 and chapters 4–6 in this book. Note that in this very passage, the objects of each of the three appearances of ἔχω are "members," "function," and *"charismata,"* the third of which should be read in light of "members" and "functions," not as special abilities. Refer to chapter 10 for further discussion of this passage.

7. Moreover, "by/according to the grace given to me/us" is an expression used eleven times in Paul's letters (twice here). In each case that he uses this expression the reader finds Paul reflecting upon specific ministry functions in the immediate context, whether his own or those of others. This is another clue that this passage is about ministry functions, not about special abilities.

8. For clarity, refer to the annotated diagram at the end of the appendix.

9. The fact that, elsewhere, Paul sometimes moves between functions and persons in their functions (1 Cor. 12:28–30) helps explain how he can easily move from functions in this passage (prophecy/ service) to members in these functions. The difference between a function and the person doing the function seems to be a somewhat fluid concept for Paul. Note also that this shift could have easily been suggested simply because Paul says "whether service" (that

is, the name of the function) to "in his serving" (the activity of serving).

10. Alternately, it might be possible to understand a correlative μέν to be implied in the first clause of verse 4 and then again in the first clause of verse 5. The reason the μέν would not be written into the text (apart from its commonly being dropped out in Hellenistic literature) is because it would be stylistically rough and potentially confusing to put a μέν together with the καθάπερ in verse 4 and similarly to put a μέν together with the οὕτως in verse 5. Thus, in this understanding, Paul would be writing as though he were using a μέν at the beginning of verse 5 and correlating with what follows, using not one δέ but rather two (cf. Matt. 25:15). It may be significant that in texts with parallel ideas, there is a preponderance of the use of μέν and δέ comparisons, with the μέν either explicitly stated (1 Cor. 12:12; also 12:8–10 and Eph. 4:11 followed by more than one δέ) or implied (1 Cor. 12:4–6, 20). Whether or not this correlative idea is correct, or whether Paul is employing δέ as a simple connective (as suggested in text), there are plausible ways to read the δέ in verse 6 in continuity with the previous sentence rather than as signaling the start of a new sentence.

11. Refer to the annotated diagram at the end of the appendix.

12. Two of many examples would be the second δέ in Romans 2:8 or the second and third δέ in Romans 6:22, which simply connects the phrases. Stanley Porter calls the simple connective "another significant usage" and notes that it is "often neglected in analysis." Stanley E. Porter, *Idioms of the Greek New Testament,* 2d ed. (Sheffield: Sheffield Academic, 1994), 208. As interpreters work with this passage, they should remain aware of the broad range of ways this particular particle is used (cf. BDAG, 213).

13. In this case English makes the issues clearer than Greek, thus the use of English rather than Greek in the diagram.

14. Note a change from functions to the people ministering in those functions. Also, note that Paul at the same time shifts from addressing the issue in the first-person plural to addressing it in the third-person singular.

15. Here it seems that the focus switches subtly from the area of ministry to the attitude or way in which the ministry is carried out. This shift in focus could be because of the conceptual link between the issue of humility that Paul introduces in verse 3.

Appendix C: How Bible Translations Influence Readers Toward the Conventional View

1. Henceforth in this appendix, as in the rest of the book, *charisma* will simply be written in its transliterated form without the Greek letters beside it in parentheses. Otherwise, since this appendix is about translation, the Greek itself will be included.

2. Kenneth Berding, "Confusing Word and Concept in 'Spiritual Gifts': Have We Forgotten James Barr's Exhortations?" *Journal of the Evangelical Theological Society* (March 2000): 37–51, introduces some of the issues highlighted in this appendix.

3. The "lists" are as follows: Romans 12:6–8; 1 Corinthians 12:8–10, 28–30; and Ephesians 4:11–12. The list passages are to be understood as including the lists and their immediate contexts: Ephesians 4:1–16; Romans 12:1–8; and 1 Corinthians 12:1–31.

4. The translations used in this appendix and their abbreviations are as follows: The Amplified Bible (AMP), Contemporary English Version (CEV), English Standard Version (ESV), Good News Bible/ Today's English Version (GNB/TEV), Holman Christian Standard Bible (HCSB), The Jerusalem Bible (JB), King James Version (KJV), The Living Bible (LB), New American Bible (NAB), New American Standard Bible (NASB), New Century Version (NCV), The New English Bible (NEB), New English Translation (NET), New International Reader's Version (NIrV), New International Version (NIV), The New Jerusalem Bible (NJB), New King James Version (NKJV), New Living Translation (NLT), New Revised Standard Version (NRSV), The New Testament in Modern English (PHILLIPS), Revised Standard Version (RSV), and Today's New International Version (TNIV). This list is not intended to be exhaustive, but rather aimed to include a majority of the translations in use today. The NASB (1971) was referred to, but no significant variations from the NASB (1995) were found. The Message (MSG) was also used, but because most of its renderings appeared to be compatible with or partial to the view presented here, it was left out as well.

5. Of the factors described below, the insertion of the concept of ability in connection with the so-called spiritual gifts is probably the strongest generally applicable indicator that a translation is, in fact, under the influence of the conventional view. Factors such as the use of "gift," and more important, "spiritual gift," when they appear prominently in the translation are probably also good

indicators. For example, the JB uses "gift" twenty-nine times in 1 Corinthians 12–14 where *charisma* only occurs five times and the LB contains some rather perplexing uses of "spiritual gift" (for example, Heb. 6:2). Nevertheless, particularly when these latter two factors are seen in lesser degrees, it becomes much more difficult to know whether or not such an influence has taken place.

6. Throughout this discussion, it should be kept in mind that the two Greek words translated as "gift" in Ephesians 4:7–8 are δωρεά (v. 7) and δόμα (v. 8), not χάρισμα. Because "gift" is used, however, English readers are still under many of the same influences to understand these as abilities.

7. Romans 1:11; 5:15–16; 6:23; 11:29; 12:6; 1 Corinthians 1:7; 7:7; 12:4, 9, 28, 30–31; 2 Corinthians 1:11; 1 Timothy 4:14; 2 Timothy 1:6. See chapters 6 and 7.

8. Romans 12:6; 1 Corinthians 12:4, 9, 28, 30, 31.

9. *Webster's Third New International Dictionary of the English Language Unabridged,* ed. Philip Babcock Gove (Springfield, MA: G. & C. Merriam, 1961), 956.

10. Romans 12:3, 6; 1 Corinthians 12:7–8; Ephesians 4:7–8, 11. All three occurrences of χάρις in the list passages are used in conjunction with δίδωμι: Romans 12:3, 6; Ephesians 4:7. For further discussion of this "grace-given" pattern, see chapter 13.

11. First Corinthians 12:4–6, 11. The word διαιρέσεις in verses 4–6 is often translated as "varieties" but may actually carry more the idea of apportionments or distributions. This is partly supported by the use of the corresponding verb διαιρέω in verse 11, which, as a participle is usually translated as "distributing" in that verse.

12. Ephesians 4:7, δωρεά; and Ephesians 4:8, δόμα.

13. This does not mean that we recommend such a translation, simply that we are recognizing that additional appearances of "gift" in such instances are not necessarily out of hand.

14. For example, PHILLIPS reads, "His 'gifts to men' were varied."

15. See chapter 12 about English usage of "gift."

16. Possible translations for *charismata* in 1 Corinthians 12:4, 31 or Romans 12:6 might include, "ministries of grace," "works of grace," or maybe "gifts of ministry," although the use of the English word "gifts," as has been observed, could still introduce confusion.

17. All five occurrences are actually in chapter 12.

18. A number of these more free translations would have had even more occurrences of "gift," but sometimes in places where many other translations use "gift," the free translations go even further by using ability language. In 1 Corinthians 12:1, for example, while most translations have the phrase "spiritual gift," the LB and the NLT both say "special abilities."

19. It is also not surprising that the footnote for this verse makes reference to "the gift of *glossolalia*."

20. Also, at the end of the verse, the NET has the following footnote: "This is best taken as a parenthetical note by the author. Luke again noted women who were gifted in the early church."

21. As was discussed in chapter 5, this passage, inasmuch as it is directed toward the church as a whole, is almost impossible to read along the lines of the conventional view.

22. In the examples that follow in the main text, phrases similar to "spiritual gift" are noted (for example, "gifts of the Spirit"); however, these do not generally carry as much weight.

23. See chapters 5–6.

24. It is interesting that "spiritual" is not in italics according to the NASB's common practice of italicizing words that are not literally reflected in the Greek.

25. In these charts, some similar phrases have been grouped together and the words not occurring in all versions have been placed in brackets.

26. See the second half of chapter 6.

27. The main text reads, "matters of the spirit," but one of the footnoted readings is "spiritual gifts."

28. The main text reads, "manifestations of the Spirit," but the footnote says, "*Grk* 'eager for spirits,' the plural is probably a shorthand for the Spirit's gifts, especially in this context, tongues."

29. For example, CEV, ESV, HCSB, JB, MSG, NASB, NET, NIV, NJB, NKJV, NLT, NRSV, PHILLIPS, TNIV. Sometimes translations use a similar heading such as "gifts from the Holy Spirit" (NCV) or "gifts of the Holy Spirit" (NIrV).

30. "Spiritual gift": JB, NCV, NJB, NKJV; "gift": HCSB, NASB, NIrV, NIV, NLT, NRSV, PHILLIPS.

31. See chapter 9.

32. *Webster's Dictionary*, 956.

33. The translation "gifted" in the NASB in verse 16 has the following footnote: "i.e., unversed in spiritual gifts." Also, a number of versions give a similar translation using the word "gift." For example, the NET reads "someone without the gift" and the footnoted reading in the ESV and RSV is "him that is without gifts."

34. BDAG, 468.

35. The TNIV has the following footnote for "an inquirer" in verse 16: "The Greek word for *inquirer* is a technical term for someone not fully initiated into a religion; also in verses 23 and 24."

36. Note especially, χράομαι, which Paul uses elsewhere in different contexts.

37. NASB, similarly, adds the clause, "each of us is to exercise them accordingly."

38. Should one object that it is unusual to talk about ministering a ministry (which might, in line with the premise of this book, be a way to understand this sentence) it can only be replied that it is standard Greek to communicate in such a way. Greeks "fear a fear," "fight a fight," "sin a sin," "rejoice a joy," "judge a judgment." This is not too different from the English "think a thought," although it is much more common in Greek than in English. Since this book is dedicated to Pauline theology, the interpretation of this passage will not be further argued here.

39. Sometimes translations even *require* readers to understand "gift" as "ability." For example, 1 Corinthians 13:1 in the LB reads, "the gift of being able to speak in other languages."

40. See chapter 10 and appendix B.

41. Again, it is by no means implied that all of these non-literal translations have particular significance; the underlining is done for the sake of consistency between charts.

42. For some examples of ability language in the other list passages, see Romans 12:3 (AMP, PHILLIPS); Ephesians 4:7 (LB; cf. Eph. 3:7); and Ephesians 4:12 (LB). Some very significant occurrences of "ability" language also appear outside the list passages, particularly in the LB. See, for example, 1 Timothy 4:14–15 (LB); 2 Timothy 1:14 (LB); and 1 Peter 4:10–11 (AMP, LB, PHILLIPS).

Scripture Index

Page numbers in **bold** indicate a more extensive treatment of a passage.

Subject Index

and trying to discover your spiritual
gifts, 27, 35, 272n. 4, 273n. 8
Corinthian church
complaints against Paul from, 168–69
Paul's response to complaints from,
169
self-centered interest in miraculous
activities of, 77, 103–4, 120,
140–41, 300n. 5

decision making, 200–205
evangelical literature on, 324–25n. 2
and finding a ministry, 35, 201–4,
325n. 5
and growing in wisdom as a
supernatural process, 202,
325n. 3
guidance through biblical wisdom in,
201–2
guidance through divine guidance/
revelation in, 202–3, 325n. 4
as separate from the spiritual-
ministries approach, 201, 275n. 6
diairesis, 333n. 11
diaphoros, 219–20, 330n. 4
didaktikos
as the knowledge of doctrine that is
adequate to refute false teaching,
90–91, 297n. 16
didōmi
with charis (see "grace" and "given")
and persons, 309n. 4 (see also Eph.
4:11–12 [list])
possibly used with reference to special
abilities, 135, 309n. 5
and what has been given by God,
134–35, 309n. 2
distinguishing between spirits
and connecting 1 Corinthians 12:10
and 1 John 4:1, 214, 328n. 21
general description of, 303–4n. 5,
213–14
"distributions"
meaning of, 285n. 5
dunamis in Matthew 25:15, 138,
310–11n. 15

echō
as not used by Paul together with the
idea of possessing a special ability,
136, 309–10n. 7
Paul's various uses of, 135–36
in Romans 12:6, 219, 330n. 5
empowering from the Spirit. See Holy
Spirit
energēmata
as "activities" or "workings," 120
with charisma, 304n. 9
with charismata and diakoniai, 66,
116–17, 286n. 7, 286–87n. 9,
304–5n. 11
Ephesians
Pauline authorship of, 292n. 9
structure of, 85
Ephesians 4:1–16
descent motif in, 86, 294n. 4
Ephesians 3:1–13's ministry
assignment focus as a basis for
understanding, 91–92
the "gift of Christ" in, 293n. 2
"give" and "gift" in, 86, 295n. 8
"grace" and "given" in, 87–88, 123
key message of, 85, 87
logic and flow of thought of, 85–87
ministry-oriented terms in, 92
Paul's use of Psalm 68:18 in, 86,
293–94n. 3
purpose of and results from ministry
in, 87
special ability neither stated nor
implied in, 87
why the conventional view doesn't
work in, 87–92
Ephesians 4:11–12 (list), 85–92
chart of, 240–43
description of the items listed in,
88–91
people in their ministries rather than
abilities, as a list of, 86, 87–91,
294n. 6, 295n. 8
people in their ministries who are to
equip the body for ministry, as a
list of, 86, 294n. 6, 294n. 7
as similar to the list in 1 Corinthians
12:28–30, 109–10

Bible Version Permissions

Scripture quotations marked AMP are taken from the Amplified Bible, Copyright © 1954, 1958, 1962, 1964, 1965, 1987 by The Lockman Foundation. Used by permission. (www.Lockman.org)

Scripture quotations marked CEV are taken from the Contemporary English Version. Copyright © 1995 by American Bible Society. Used by permission.

Scripture quotations marked ESV are from the Holy Bible, English Standard Version, copyright © 2001 by Crossway Bibles, a division of Good News Publishers. Used by permission. All rights reserved.

Scripture quotations marked GNB/TEV are from *Today's English Version*. Copyright © 1966, 1971, 1976, 1992 by American Bible Society. Used by permission. All rights reserved.

Scripture quotations marked HCSB are from the Holman Christian Standard Bible®. Copyright © 1999, 2000, 2002, 2003 by Holman Bible Publishers. Used by permission.

Scripture quotations marked JB are from the Jerusalem Bible. Copyright © 1966, 1967, and 1968 by Darton, Longman and Todd Ltd., and Doubleday and Company, Inc. All rights reserved.

Scripture quotations marked KJV are from the King James Version.

Scripture quotations marked LB are from *The Living Bible*. Copyright © 1971 by Tyndale House Publishers, Wheaton, Illinois. Used by permission.

Scripture quotations marked MSG are from *The Message*. Copyright © 1993, 1994, 1995, 1996, 2000, 2001, 2002. Used by permission of NavPress Publishing Group. All rights reserved.